Excel Essentials

M.L. HUMPHREY

SELECT TITLES BY M.L. HUMPHREY

EXCEL ESSENTIALS
Excel for Beginners
Intermediate Excel
50 Useful Excel Functions
50 More Excel Functions

ACCESS ESSENTIALS
Access for Beginners
Intermediate Access

WORD ESSENTIALS
Word for Beginners
Intermediate Word

POWERPOINT ESSENTIALS
PowerPoint for Beginners
Intermediate PowerPoint

BUDGETING FOR BEGINNERS
Budgeting for Beginners
Excel for Budgeting

CONTENTS

AUTHOR'S NOTE:

Excel Essentials combines the content of four separate books: *Excel for Beginners, Intermediate Excel, 50 Useful Excel Functions,* and *50 More Excel Functions.*

Excel for Beginners and *Intermediate Excel* have been provided as they appeared when they were standalone titles.

Because the original versions of *50 Useful Excel Functions* and *50 More Excel Functions* had identical content at the beginning and end of each book, they have been edited and combined into one section of this book and retitled *100 Excel Functions.* However, the basic content of that section is the same as what was originally published as *50 Useful Excel Functions* and *50 More Excel Functions.*

Excel for Beginners
EXCEL ESSENTIALS BOOK 1

M.L. HUMPHREY

CONTENTS

INTRODUCTION

The purpose of this guide is to introduce you to the basics of using Microsoft Excel. I still remember when I was in college and helping a graduate student do research and he asked me to do something in Excel and I had no idea what to do and how frustrating that was to be limited by my lack of knowledge. I was later fortunate enough to work with a man who was absolutely brilliant with Excel who taught me lots of tips and tricks for using it and now I don't know what I'd do without it.

Excel is great. I use it both in my professional life and my personal life. It allows me to organize and track key information in a quick and easy manner and to automate a lot of the calculations I need. I have a budget worksheet that I look at at least every few days to track whether my bills have been paid and how much I need to keep in my bank account and just where I am overall financially. In my professional career I've used it in a number of ways, from analyzing a series of financial transactions to see if a customer was overcharged to performing a comparison of regulatory requirements across multiple jurisdictions. While it works best for numerical purposes, it is often a good choice for text-based analysis as well, especially if you want to be able to sort your results or filter out and isolate certain results.

If you want to learn Excel through the lens of managing your own money, the *Juggling Your Finances: Basic Excel Primer*, is probably a better choice. It walks you through how to do addition, subtraction, multiplication, and division using key questions you should be able to answer about your personal finances as the examples.

This book just focuses on the basics of using Excel without those kinds of specific examples. We'll cover how to navigate Excel, input data, format it, manipulate it through basic math formulas, filter it, sort it, and print your results.

This is not a comprehensive Excel guide. We are not going to cover more complex topics like conditional formatting and pivot tables. The goal of this guide is to give you a solid grounding in Excel that will let you get started using it. For day-to-day uses, this guide should cover 98% of what you need and I'll give you some tips on how to find the other 2 percent. (Or you can continue on with *Intermediate Excel* which covers more advanced topics like pivot tables, charts, conditional formatting, and IF functions.)

One note before we start: I'm working in Excel 2013, which will look familiar to users of Excel 2007 or later. If you're working in a version of Excel that's pre-2007, I'd recommend that you upgrade now rather than try to learn Excel in an older version. They're different enough that it's really like a completely different program.

If you do insist on using an older version of Excel, when I give you more than one method you can use (sometimes there are at least three ways to do the same thing in Excel), choose the option that tells you to right-click and open a dialogue box. Also, the Ctrl + [letter] options should be available in all versions of Excel. If that fails, use the help function to search for how the task can be completed in your version.

Alright then. Let's get started.

BASIC TERMINOLOGY

First things first, we need to establish some basic terminology so that you know what I'm talking about when I refer to a cell or a row or a column, etc.

Column

Excel uses columns and rows to display information. Columns run across the top of the worksheet and, unless you've done something funky with your settings, are identified using letters of the alphabet. As you can see below, they start with A on the far left side and march right on through the alphabet (A, B, C, D, E, etc.). If you scroll far enough to the right, you'll see that they continue on to a double alphabet (AA, AB, AC, etc.).

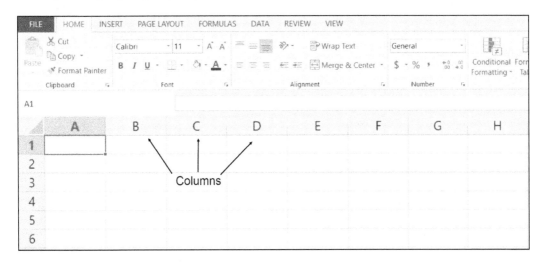

Row

Rows run down the side of the worksheet and are numbered starting at 1 and up to a very high number. You can hold down the ctrl key in a blank worksheet while hitting the down arrow to see just how many rows your version of Excel has. Mine has 65,536 rows per worksheet.

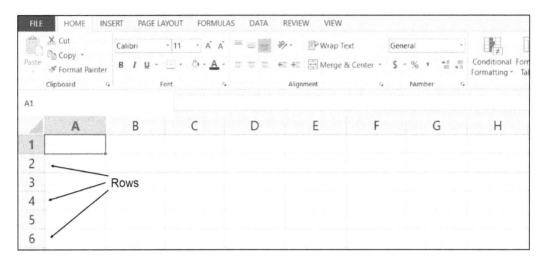

Cell

A cell is a combination of a column and row that is identified by the letter of the column it's in and the number of the row it's in. For example, Cell A1 is the cell in the first column and the first row of the worksheet. When you've clicked on a specific cell it will have a darker border around the edges like in the image below.

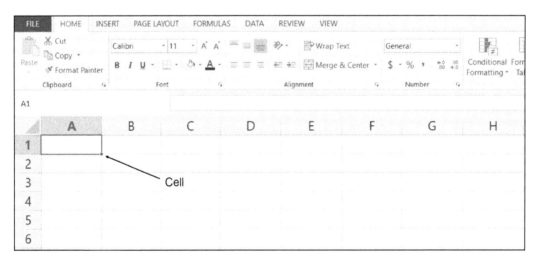

Click

If I tell you to click on something, that means to use your mouse (or trackpad) to move the arrow on the screen over to a specific location and left-click or right-click on the option. (See the next definition for the difference between left-click and right-click).

If you left-click, this selects the item. If you right-click, this generally creates a dropdown list of options to choose from. If I don't tell you which to do, left- or right-click, then left-click.

Left-click/Right-click

If you look at your mouse or your trackpad, you generally have two flat buttons to press. One is on the left side, one is on the right. If I say left-click that means to press down on the button on the left. If I say right-click that means press down on the button on the right. (If you're used to using Word or Excel you may already do this without even thinking about it. So, if that's the case then think of left-click as what you usually use to select text and right-click as what you use to see a menu of choices.)

Now, as I sadly learned when I had to upgrade computers and ended up with an HP Envy, not all track pads have the left- and right-hand buttons. In that case, you'll basically want to press on either the bottom left-hand side of the track pad or the bottom right-hand side of the trackpad. Since you're working blind it may take a little trial and error to get the option you want working. (Or is that just me?)

Spreadsheet

I'll try to avoid using this term, but if I do use it, I'll mean your entire Excel file. It's a little confusing because it can sometimes also be used to mean a specific worksheet, which is why I'll try to avoid it as much as possible.

Worksheet

A worksheet is basically a combination of rows and columns that you can enter data in. When you open an Excel file, it opens to worksheet one.

My version of Excel has one worksheet available by default when I open a new Excel file. (It's possible to add more as needed.) That worksheet is labeled Sheet 1 and the name is highlighted in white to show that it's in use.

Formula Bar

This is the long white bar at the top of the screen with the $f\chi$ symbol next to it. If you click in a cell and start typing, you'll see that what you type appears not only in that cell, but in the formula bar. When you input a formula into a cell and then hit enter, the value returned by the formula will be what displays in the cell, but the formula will appear in the formula bar when you have that cell highlighted.

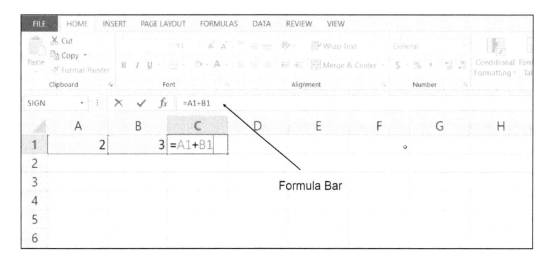

Tab

I refer to the menu choices at the top of the screen (File, Home, Insert, Page Layout, Formulas, Data, Review and View) as tabs. Note how they look like folder tabs from an old-time filing system when selected? That's why.

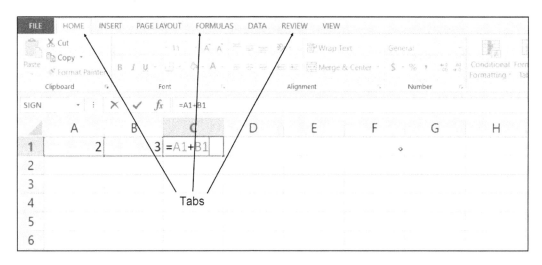

Each menu tab you select will show you different options. On my Home tab I can do things like copy/cut/paste, format cells, edit cells, and insert/delete cells, for example. (This is one place where things are very different for those using earlier versions of Excel and why if you're using an older version of Excel, I'd recommend upgrading now.)

Scroll Bar

On the right side and the bottom of the screen are two bars with arrows at the ends. If you left-click and hold on either bar you can move it back and forth between those arrows (or up and down for the one on the right side). This lets you see information that's off the page in your current view but part of the worksheet you're viewing.

You can also use the arrows at the ends of the scroll bar to do the same thing. Left-click on the arrow once to move it one line or column or left-click and hold to get it to move as far as it can go. If you want to cover more rows/columns at a time you can click into the blank space on either side of the scroll bar to move an entire screen at a time, assuming you have enough data entered for that.

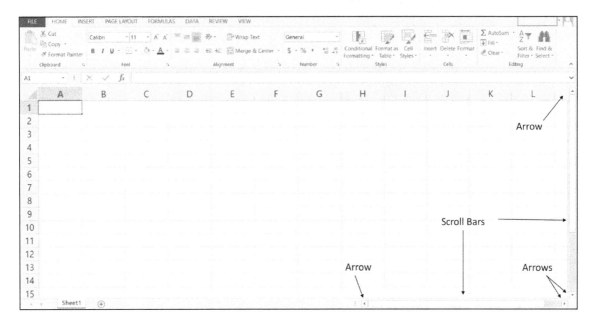

Using the arrows instead of clicking on the scroll bar lets you scroll all the way to the far end of the worksheet. Using the scroll bars only lets you move to the end of the information you've already entered.

Data

I use data and information interchangeably. Whatever information you put into a worksheet is your data.

Table

I may also refer to a table of data or data table on occasion. This is just a combination of rows and columns that contain information.

Select

If I tell you to "select" cells, that means to highlight them. If the cells are next to each other, you can just left-click on the first one and drag the cursor (move your mouse or finger on the trackpad) until all of the cells are highlighted. When this happens, they'll all be surrounded by a dark box like below.

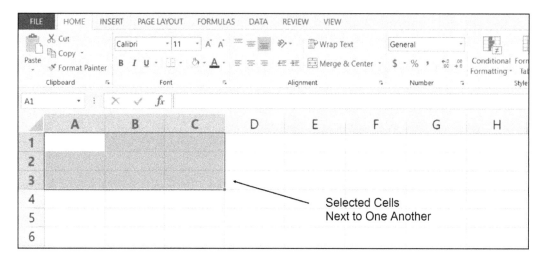

Selected Cells
Next to One Another

If the cells aren't next to each other, then what you do is left-click on the first cell, hold down the Ctrl key (bottom left of my keyboard), left-click on the next cell, hold down the Ctrl key, left-click on the next cell, etc. until you've selected all the cells you want. The cells you've already selected will be shaded in gray and the one you selected last will be surrounded by a dark border that is not as dark as the normal border you see when you just select one cell. In the image below cells A1, C1, A3, and C3 are selected.

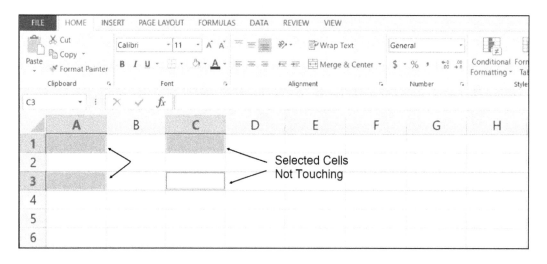

Selected Cells
Not Touching

Dropdown

I will occasionally refer to a dropdown or dropdown menu. This is generally a list of potential choices that you can select from. The existence of the list is indicated by an arrow next to the first available selection.

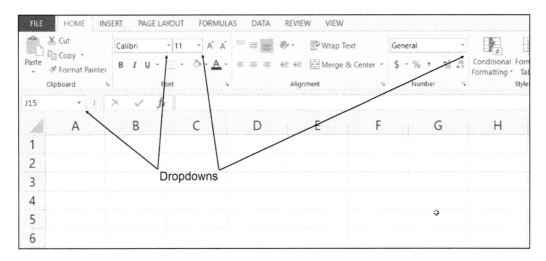

I will also sometimes refer to the list of options you see when you click on a dropdown arrow as the dropdown menu.

Dialogue Box

Dialogue boxes are pop-up boxes that contain a set of available options and appear when you need to provide additional information or make additional choices. For example, this is the Insert dialogue box that appears when you choose to insert a cell:

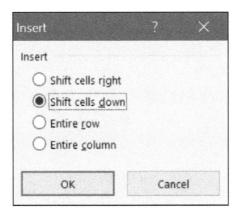

Cursor

If you didn't know this one already, it's what moves around when you move the mouse (or use the trackpad). In Excel it often looks like a three-dimensional squat cross or it will look like one of a couple of varieties of arrow. (Open Excel and move it to where the column and row labels are to see what I mean.) The different shapes the cursor takes represent different functions.

Arrow

If I say that you can "arrow" to something that just means to use the arrow keys to navigate from one cell to another. For example, if you enter information in A1 and hit enter, that moves your cursor down to cell A2. If instead you wanted to move to Cell B1, you could do so with the right arrow.

ABSOLUTE BASICS

It occurs to me that there are a few absolute basics to using Excel that we should cover before we get into things like formatting.

Opening an Excel File

To start a brand new Excel file, I simply click on Excel 2013 from my applications menu or the shortcut I have on my computer's taskbar, and it opens a new Excel file for me.

If you're opening an existing Excel file, you can either go to the folder where the file is saved and double-click on the file name, or you can (if Excel is already open) go to the File tab and choose Open from the left-hand menu.

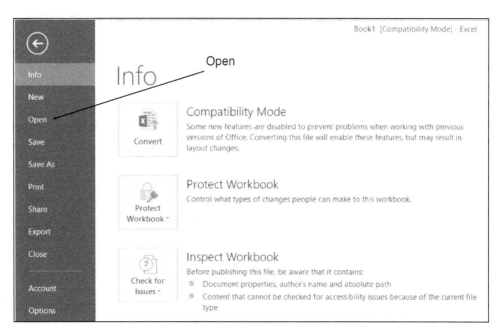

That will show you a list of Recent Workbooks. If it includes the one you're looking for, you can just click on it once and it will open.

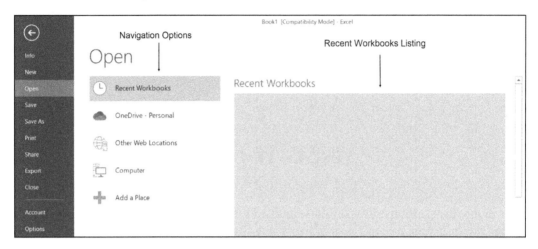

If you don't see the file you're looking for, you can click on the list of navigation options in between the left-hand menu and the list of Recent Workbooks and navigate to where the file is stored. When I click on Computer it gives me the current folder I'm in as well as five recent folders and an option to browse if the folder I want isn't one of the ones displayed.

Saving an Excel File

To save a file you can go to the File tab at the top of the screen and then choose Save or Save As from the menu options on the left side.

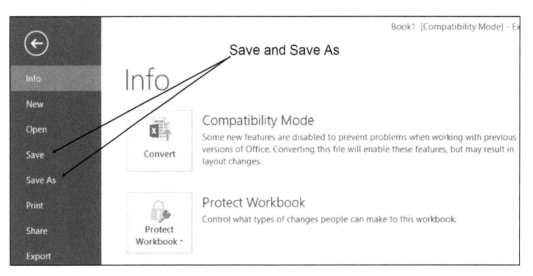

When you're dealing with a new Excel file, you really only have the Save As option. (When I click on Save it still takes me to Save As.) With Save As, Excel will ask you to choose which folder to save the file into. You can either choose from the list of recent folders on the right-hand side or navigate to the folder you want using the locations listing on the left of that list.

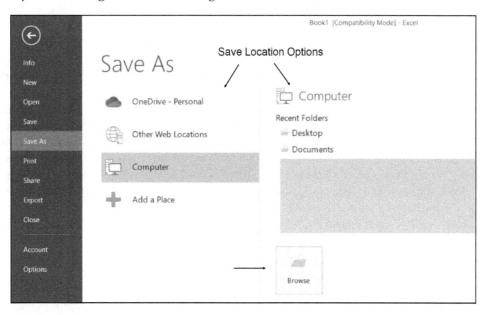

Once you choose a location, a dialogue box will appear where you can name the file.

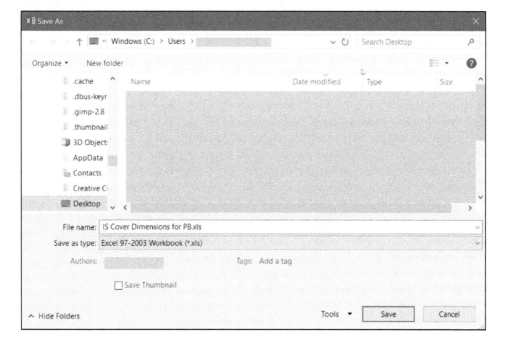

My save options default to an .xls file type. I don't know if this is standard or if I've set it up that way somewhere. If yours doesn't default to the .xls file type, I'd recommend using that file type as much as possible if you think you might share the file at any point. The newer versions of Excel actually are an .xlsx file type, but if you use that file type and want to share with someone who has a version of Excel that's pre-2007, they won't be able to open your file.

It's much easier to save down to an older version than have to convert up to a newer version. And I'm pretty sure if you're using this guide you won't be using any of the fancy options that are available in the newest versions of Excel that aren't available in older versions. If it turns out you are, Excel will generate a warning message about compatibility when you save the file as an .xls file, and you can decide not to save it to the older version at that time.

If you're saving a file you've already saved once before and you have no changes to its name, location, or type, you can go to File>Save and it will save it for you, keeping all of that information the same. You can also just type Ctrl and S at the same time (Ctrl+S) (Note: Even though I'm going to show these commands with a capital letter, you don't have to use the capitalized version of the letter.)

Or, and I think this is true of all Excel users, there should be a small computer disk image in the top left corner that you can click on. (You can customize that list and I have for my most-used functions, which is why I'm not 100% sure.)

If you're saving a file you've already saved once before but you want to save it to a new location, change its name, or change the file type (.xls to .xlsx, for example), use Save As.

Deleting an Excel File

You can't delete an Excel file from within Excel. You'll need to navigate to the folder where the file is stored and delete the file there without opening it. First, click on the file name. (Only enough to select it. Make sure you haven't double-clicked and highlighted the name which will then try to rename the file.) Next, choose Delete from the menu at the top of the screen, or right-click and choose Delete from the dropdown menu.

Renaming an Excel File

You might want to rename an Excel file at some point. You can Save As and choose a new name for the file, but that will mean you now have two versions of the file, one with the old name and one with the new name. Or you can navigate to where you've saved the file, click on it once to highlight the file, click on it a second time to highlight the name, and then type in the new name you want to use. If you do it that way, there will only be one version of the file, the one with the name you wanted.

If you do rename a file, know that you can't then access it from the Recent Workbooks listing under Open file. Even though it might be listed there, Excel won't be able to find it because it no longer has that name. (Same thing happens if you move a file from the location it was in when you were last working on it. I often run into this by moving a file into a new subfolder when I suddenly get inspired to organize my records.)

NAVIGATING EXCEL

The next thing we're going to discuss is basic navigation within Excel. These are all things you can do that don't involve inputting, formatting, or manipulating your data.

Basic Navigation Within A Worksheet

Excel will automatically open into cell A1 of Sheet 1 for a new Excel file. For an existing file it will open in the cell and worksheet where you were when you last saved the file. (This means it can also open with a set of cells already highlighted if that's what you were doing when you last saved the file.)

Within a worksheet, it's pretty basic to navigate.

You can click into any cell you can see in the worksheet with your mouse or trackpad. Just place your cursor over the cell and left-click.

From the cell where you currently are (which will be outlined with a dark border), you can use the up, down, left, and right arrow keys to move one cell in any of those directions.

You can also use the tab key to move one cell to the right and the shift and tab keys combined (shift + tab) to move one cell to the left.

To see other cells in the worksheet that aren't currently visible, you can use the scroll bars on the right-hand side or the bottom of the worksheet. The right-hand-side scroll bar will let you move up and down. The bottom scroll bar will let you move right or left. Just remember that the bars themselves will only let you move as far as you've entered data, you need to use the arrows at the ends of the scroll bars to move farther than that.

For worksheets with lots of data in them, click on the scroll bar and drag it to move quickly to the beginning or end of the data. To move one view's worth at a time, click in the blank space around the actual bar.

If you're using the scroll bars to navigate, remember that until you click into a new cell with your mouse or trackpad you will still be in the last cell where you clicked or made an edit. (You can test this by typing and you'll see that you're brought back to that last cell, wherever it is.)

Basic Navigation Between Worksheets

Between worksheets, you can either click on the name of the worksheet you want (at the bottom of the screen) or you can use Ctrl and Page Up (Ctrl + Page Up) to move one worksheet to the left and Ctrl and Page Down (Ctrl + Page Dn) to move one worksheet to the right.

F2

If you click in a cell and hit the F2 key, this will take you to the end of the contents of the cell. This can be very useful when you need to edit the contents of a cell or to work with a formula in that cell.

Insert a Cell in a Worksheet

(See the next section for how to insert an entire row or column.) Sometimes you just want to insert one cell in the worksheet. To do so, click on where you want to insert the cell, right-click, and select Insert.

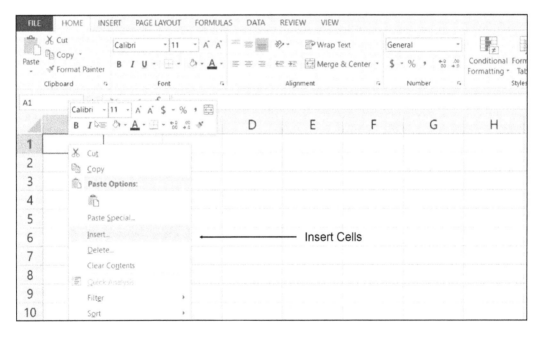

You'll be given four choices, Shift Cells Right, Shift Cells Down, Entire Row, and Entire Column.

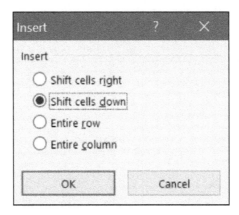

Shift Cells Right will insert your cell by moving every other cell in that row to the right. Shift Cells Down will insert your cell by moving every other cell in that column down. Entire row will insert an entire row instead of one cell. Entire column will insert an entire column instead of one cell.

Be sure that the option you choose makes sense given the other data you've already entered in the worksheet. Sometimes I find that I need to actually highlight a group of cells and insert cells for all of them to keep the rest of my cells aligned.

You can also highlight the cell(s) where you want to insert cell(s) and then go to the Cells section of the Home tab where it says Insert. Choose the insert option you want from there, the same way you would for inserting a worksheet.

Insert a Column or Row

Sometimes you'll enter information and then realize that you want to add an entire row or column right in the midst of the data you've already entered. If this happens, highlight the row or column where you want your new row or column to go, right-click, and select Insert. (By highlight, I mean click on either the letter of the column or the number of the row to select the entire column or row.) Your data will either shift one entire column to the right or one entire row downward, starting with the column or row you selected.

You can also just click in one cell and then choose Entire Row or Entire Column after right-clicking and choosing Insert.

Another option is to highlight the row or column and then go to the Cells section of the Home tab where it says Insert and choose the insert option you want from there.

Insert a New Worksheet

When you open a new Excel file, you'll have one worksheet you can use named Sheet 1. (In Excel 2007 I had three worksheets available when I opened a new file.)

If you need another worksheet, simply click on the + symbol in a circle at the end of your existing worksheets to add a new one. (In Excel 2007 the add a worksheet option looked like a mini worksheet with a yellow star in the corner.)

You can also go to the Home tab under the Cells section and left-click the arrow under Insert then select Insert Sheet from the dropdown menu.

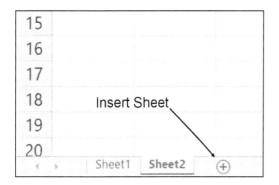 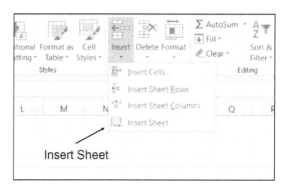

Delete a Cell in a Worksheet

Deleting a cell in a worksheet is a lot like inserting a cell. Right-click on the cell you want to delete and choose Delete from the dropdown menu. Next choose whether to shift cells up or left. (When you remove a cell everything will have to move to fill in the empty space it leaves.) Be sure that deleting that one cell doesn't change the layout of the rest of your data. As with inserting a cell, I sometimes find I need to delete more than one cell to keep things uniform in my presentation.

(Note that you can also delete an entire row or column this way as well.)

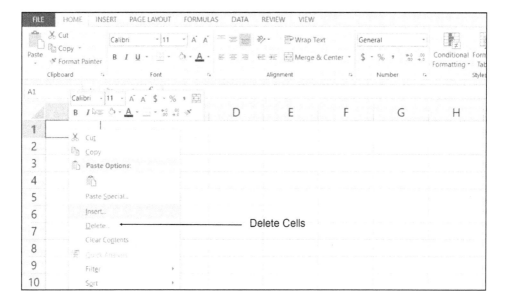

Another option is to highlight the cell(s) you want to delete, and then go to the Cells section of the Home tab where it says Delete and choose the delete option you want from there.

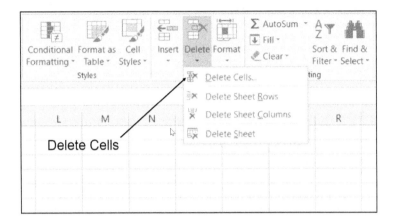

Delete Cells

Delete a Column or Row

Highlight the entire row or column you want to delete, right-click, and select Delete. It will automatically delete the row or column. You can also highlight the row or column and then go to the Cells section of the Home tab where it says Delete and choose the delete option you want from there. And, as with inserting a row or column, you can click into one cell, right-click, select Delete, and then choose Entire Row or Entire Column from the dialogue box.

Delete a Worksheet

Sometimes you'll add a worksheet and then realize you don't want it anymore. It's easy enough to delete. Just right-click on the name of the worksheet you want to delete and choose the Delete option from the dropdown menu.

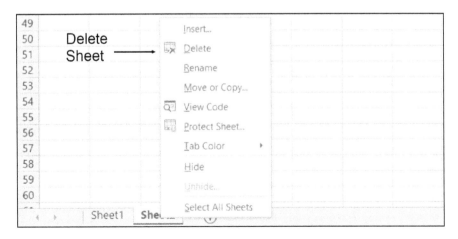

Delete Sheet

You can also go to the Cells section in the Home tab, left-click on the arrow under Delete, and choose Delete Sheet from the dropdown menu.

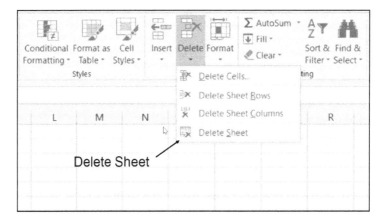

Delete Sheet

If there was any data in the worksheet you're trying to delete, it will give you a warning message to that effect. If you don't care, click Delete. If you didn't realize there was data and want to cancel the deletion, click Cancel.

Be sure you want to delete any worksheet you choose to delete, because you can't get it back later. This is one place where undo will not work.

Rename A Worksheet

The default name for worksheets in Excel are Sheet 1, Sheet 2, Sheet 3, etc. They're not useful for much of anything, and if you have information in more than one worksheet, you're going to want to rename them to something that lets you identify which worksheet is which.

If you double left-click on a worksheet name (on the tab at the bottom) it will highlight in gray and you can then delete the existing name and replace it with whatever you want.

You can also right-click on the tab name and choose Rename from the dropdown menu.

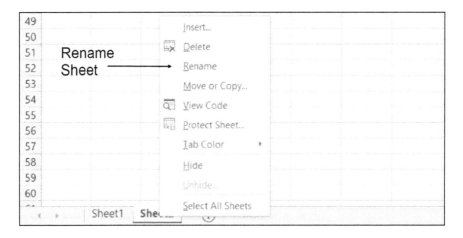

Rename Sheet

A worksheet name cannot be more than 31 characters long, be blank, contain the forward slash, the back slash, a question mark, a star, a colon, or brackets (/ \ ? * : [ ]), begin or end with an apostrophe, or be named History. Don't worry. In my version of Excel it just stops you from typing those characters or past the limit. (In earlier versions I believe it let you type the incorrect characters and then gave an error message and refused to accept the name.)

INPUTTING YOUR DATA

At its most basic, inputting your data is very simple. Click in the cell where you want to input information and type. But there are some tricks to it that you'll want to keep in mind.

First, let's take a step back and talk about one of the key strengths of a using Excel and that's the ability to sort or filter your data. For example, I self-publish books, and every month I get reports from the places where my books are published listing all of the sales of my books at those locations. But what if I only care about the sales of book A? How can I see those if I have a couple hundred rows of information in the report they've given me?

Well, if the site where I sold those books is nice and helpful and they understand data analysis, they've given me my sales listings in an Excel worksheet with one header row at the top and then one row for each sale or each book. If they've done that, then I can very easily filter my data on the title column and see just the entries related to title A. If they haven't, then I'm stuck deleting rows of information I don't need to get to the data I want.

Which is all a roundabout way of saying that you can input your data any way you want, but if you follow some key data principles you'll have a lot more flexibility in what you can do with your data once it's entered.

Those principles are:

1. Use the first row of your worksheet to label your data.

2. List all of your data in continuous rows after that first row without including any subtotals or subheadings or anything that isn't your data.

3. To the extent possible, format your data in such a way that it can be analyzed. (So rather than put in a free-text field, try to use a standardized list of values instead. See below. Column E, which uses a 1 to 5 point ranking scale, is better for analysis than Column D, which is a free text field where anyone can say anything.)

4. Standardize your values. Customer A should always be listed as Customer A. United States should always be United States not USA, U.S.A., or America.

5. Store your raw data in one location; analyze or correct it elsewhere.

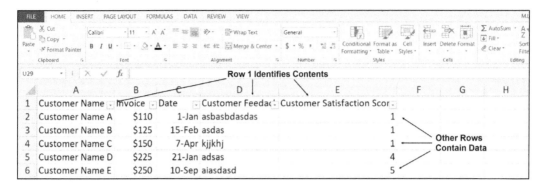

Now, I'm saying all of this, but some of the ways I use Excel don't conform to these principles. And that's fine. My budgeting worksheet is not meant to be filtered or sorted. It's a snapshot of information that summarizes my current financial position. But my worksheet that lists all vendor payments for the year? You bet it's formatted using this approach.

So before you enter any data into your Excel file, put some time into thinking about how you want to use that data. Is it just a visual snapshot? If so, don't worry about structuring it for sorting or filtering. Will it be hundreds of rows of values that you want to summarize or analyze? If so, then arrange it the way I listed above. You don't have to have row 1 be your column headings, but wherever you put those headings, keep everything below that point single rows of data that are all formatted and entered using the same definitions.

Okay. So what are some tricks to make entering your information easier?

Undo

If you enter the wrong information or perform the wrong action and want to easily undo it, hold down the Ctrl key and the Z key at the same time. (Ctrl + Z) You can do this multiple times if you want to undo multiple actions, although there are a few actions (such as deleting a worksheet) that cannot be undone.

Redo

If you mistakenly undo something and want it back, you can hold down the Ctrl key and the Y key at the same time to redo it. (Ctrl + Y)

Auto-Suggested Text

If you've already typed text into a cell, Excel will suggest that text to you in subsequent cells in the same column.

For example, if you are creating a list of all the books you own (something I once tried to do and gave up after about a hundred entries), and in cell A1 you type "science fiction", when you go to cell A2 and type an "s", Excel will automatically suggest to you "science fiction". If you don't want to use that suggestion, then keep typing. If you do, then hit enter.

Nice, huh? Instead of typing fifteen characters you were able to type one.

This only works when you have unique values for Excel to identify. If you have science fiction/fantasy and science fiction as entries in that column, it's not going to work. Excel waits until it can suggest one option, so you'd have to type science fiction/ before it made any suggestions.

Also, if there are empty cells between the entries you already completed and the one you're now completing and you have no other columns with completed data in them that bridge that gap, Excel won't make a suggestion.

Another time it doesn't work is if you have a very long list that you've completed and the matching entry is hundreds of rows away from the one you're now completing.

Excel also doesn't make suggestions for numbers. And if you have an entry that combines letters and numbers, it won't make a suggestion until you've typed at least one letter.

Despite all these apparent limitations, auto-suggested text can be very handy to use if you have to enter one of a limited number of choices over and over again and can't easily copy the information into your worksheet.

Copying the Contents and Formatting of One Cell To Another

This is very easy. Highlight the information you want to copy and hold down the Ctrl and C keys at the same time (Ctrl + C). Go to the cell where you want to put the information you copied and hit Enter.

If you want to copy to more than one location, instead of hitting Enter at the new cell, hold down the Ctrl and V keys at the same time (Ctrl + V). If you use Ctrl + V, you'll see that the original cell you copied from is still surrounded by a dotted line meaning that text is still available to be pasted into another cell.

You can also right-click and select Copy from the dropdown menu and then right-click Paste from the dropdown menu in the cell where you want the information. (In my version of Excel, right-click Paste is now represented by a clipboard with a plain white page under the Paste Options header.)

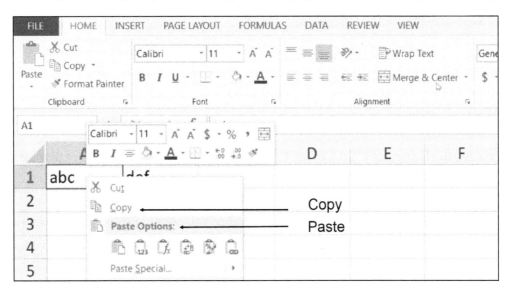

Once you're done pasting the values into new cells and want to do something else, just hit the Esc key. This will remove the dotted line from around the cell you were copying and ensure you don't accidentally paste it somewhere else. Typing in a new cell also works.

Moving the Contents of a Cell (Cutting)

To move the contents of a cell rather than copy it, you select the cell with the contents you want to move, type Ctrl and X at the same time (Ctrl + X), click on the new location, and hit Enter or type Ctrl + V. Unlike with copying, you can only move the contents of a cell to one new location.

Another option is to highlight the cell(s) you want to move, right-click, and choose Cut from the dropdown menu and then paste your cell contents in the new location.

Copying the contents of a cell (Ctrl + C) is different from cutting and moving the contents of a cell (Ctrl + X), because when you copy the contents of a cell they remain in their original location. When you move the contents, you are removing them from their original location to place them in their new location.

Copying Versus Moving When It Comes to Formulas

If you're dealing with text, copying (Ctrl + C) or cutting the text (Ctrl + X) doesn't really change anything. What ends up in that new cell will be the same regardless of the method you use.

But with formulas, that's not what happens.

With formulas, moving the contents of a cell (Ctrl + X) will keep the formula the exact same as it was. So if you're formula was =A2+B2 it will still be =A2+B2 in the new cell.

Copying the contents of a cell (Ctrl + C) will *change the formula* based upon the number of rows and columns you moved. The formula is copied relative to where it originated. If your original formula in cell A3 was =A2+B2 and you copied it to cell A4 (so moved one cell downward) the formula in cell A4 will be =A3+B3. All cell references in the formula will adjust one cell downward.

If you copy that same formula to cell B3 (so one cell to the right) the formula in B3 will be =B2+C2. All cell references in the formula will adjust one cell to the right.

If this doesn't make sense to you, just try it. Put some sample values in cells A2 and B2 and then experiment with Ctrl + C versus Ctrl + X.

Also, there is a way to prevent a formula from changing when you copy it using the $ sign to fix the cell reference. We'll talk about that next.

Copying Formulas To Other Cells While Keeping One Value Fixed

If you want to copy a formula while keeping the value of one or more of the cells fixed, you need to use the $ sign.

A $ sign in front of the letter portion of a cell location will keep the column the same but allow the row number to change. ($A1)

A $ sign in front of the number portion of a cell location will keep the row the same but allow the column to change. (A$1)

A $ sign in front of both will keep the referenced cell exactly the same. ($A$1)

This is discussed in more detail in the manipulating data section.

Paste Special

Sometimes you want to copy just the contents of a cell without keeping any of its formatting. Or you want to take a list of values in a column and put them into a single row instead.

That's where the Paste Special options come in handy.

First, know that you can only use Paste Special options if you've copied the contents of a cell (Ctrl + C). They don't work if you've cut the contents using Ctrl +X.

To Paste Special, instead of just typing Ctrl + V to paste what you copied into a new cell, right-click in the new cell and choose from the Paste Options section.

You should see in the dropdown menu something like this. What you see will be determined by what you've copied and how.

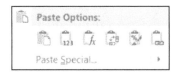

In my opinion, not all of these choices are useful. So I'm just going to highlight two of them for you.

Paste Values, which has the 123 on its clipboard, is useful for when you want the results of a formula, but don't want the formula anymore. I use this often.

It's also useful when you want the contents of a cell, but would prefer to use the formatting from the destination cell(s). For example, if you're copying from one Excel file to another.

Another way I use it is when I've run a set of calculations on my data, found my values, and now want to sort or do something else with my data and don't want to risk having the values change on me. I highlight the entire data set, copy, and then paste special-values right over the top of my existing data. (Just be sure to type Esc after you do this so that the change is fixed in place.)

The Paste Transpose option—the one with the little arrow arcing between two pairs of cells, fourth from the left above—is very useful if you have a row of data that you want to turn into columns of data or vice versa. Just highlight the data, copy, paste-transpose, and it will automatically paste a column of data as a row or a row of data as a column. Just be sure before you paste that there isn't any data already there that will be overwritten, because Excel won't warn you before it overwrites it.

There are more paste options available than just the six you can see above. Click on where it says Paste Special and you'll see another dropdown menu to the side with eight more options, and if you go to the bottom of that breakout menu and click on Paste Special again, it will bring up the Paste Special dialogue box:

Displaying The Contents Of A Cell As Text

Excel likes to change certain values to what it thinks you meant. So if you enter June 2015 into a cell, it will convert that entry to a date even if you intended it to be text.

It also assumes that any entry that starts with a minus sign (-), an equals sign (=), or a plus sign (+) is a formula.

To keep Excel from doing this, you can type a single quote mark (') before the contents of the cell. If you do that, Excel will treat whatever you enter after that as text and will keep the formatting type as General.

So if you want to have June 2015 display in a cell in your worksheet, you need to type 'June 2015.

If you want to have

- Item A

display in a cell, you need to type it as:

'- Item A

The single quote mark is not visible when you look at or print your worksheet. It is only visible in the formula bar when you've selected that cell.

Entering a Formula Into a Cell

The discussion just above about displaying the contents of a cell as text brings up another good point. If you want Excel to treat an entry as a formula then you need to enter the equals (=), plus (+), or negative sign (-) as your first character in the cell.

So, if you type

1+1

in a cell, that will just display as text in the cell. You'll see

1+1.

But if you type

+1+1

in a cell, Excel will treat that as a formula and calculate it. You'll see

2

in the cell and

=1+1

in the formula bar. Same with if you type

=1+1

It will calculate that as a formula, display 2 in the cell, and show =1+1 in the formula bar. If you type

-1+1

in a cell it will treat that as a formula adding negative 1 to 1 and will show that as 0 in the cell and display

=-1+1

in the formula bar. Best practice is to just use the equals sign to start every formula.

Including Line Breaks Within a Cell

I sometimes need to have multiple lines of text or numbers within a cell. So instead of a, b, c, I need

a

b

c

You can't just hit Enter, because if you do it'll take you to the next cell. Instead, hold down the Alt key at the same time you hit Enter. This will create a line break within the cell.

Deleting Data

If you enter information into a cell and later decide you want to delete it, you can click on that cell(s) and use the delete button on your computer's keyboard. This will remove whatever you entered in the cell without deleting the cell as well.

You can also double-click into the cell or use F2 to get to the end of the contents and then use your computer's backspace key to delete out the contents of the cell.

Deleting the contents of a cell will not remove its formatting. To delete the contents of a cell as well as its formatting, go to the Editing section of the Home tab, click on the dropdown next to the Clear option, and choose to Clear All.

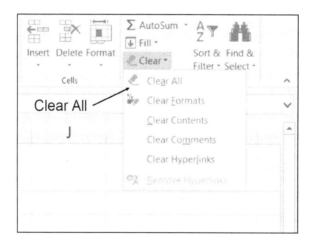

Find and Replace

Sometimes you have a big worksheet and you need to find a specific entry. An easy way to do this is to use the Find option. The easiest way to access it is to type Ctrl and F at the same time (Ctrl + F). This opens the Find dialogue box. Type what you're looking for into the "Find what" field and hit enter. The default is for find to look in formulas as well, so if you search for "f" and have a formula that references cell F11, it will hit on that as much as it will hit on the cell that actually contains the letter f in a word.

You can change this setting under Options.

The other way to access Find is through the Editing section of the Home tab. The Find & Select option has a dropdown menu that includes Find.

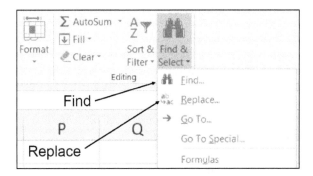

If you're looking for something in order to change it, you can use Replace instead. Type Ctrl and H (Ctrl + H) at the same time (or just Ctrl + F and then click over to the Replace tab), or you can access it through the Editing section of the Home tab.

When the Replace dialogue box opens, you'll see two lines, "Find what" and "Replace with." In the "Find what" line, type what you're looking for. In the "Replace with" line, type what to replace it with.

Be VERY careful using Replace. Say you want to replace "hat" with "chapeau" because you've suddenly become pretentious. If you don't think this through, you will end up replacing every usage of hat, even when it's in words like "that" or "chat". So you'll end up with "tchapeau" in the middle of a sentence instead of "that" because the hat portion of that was replaced with chapeau. (This probably happens in Word more than in Excel, but it's still something to be aware of.)

Replace is good for removing something like double spaces or converting formatting of a particular value, but otherwise you might want to use find and then manually correct each entry to avoid inadvertent errors.

Copying Patterns of Data

Sometimes you'll want to input data that repeats itself. Like, for example, the days of the week. Say you're putting together a worksheet that lists the date and what day of the week it is for an entire year. You could type out Monday, Tuesday, Wednesday, Thursday, Friday, Saturday, Sunday, and then copy and paste that 52 times. Or…

You could take advantage of the fact that Excel can recognize patterns. With this particular example, it looks like all it takes is typing in Monday. Do that and then go to the bottom right corner of the cell with Monday in it and position you cursor so that it looks like a small black cross. Left-click, hold that left-click down, and start to drag your cursor away from the cell. Excel should auto-complete the cells below or to the right of the Monday cell with the days of the week in order and repeating themselves in order for as long as you need it to.

If you're dealing with a pattern that isn't as standard as days of the week, sometimes it takes a few rows of data before Excel can identify the pattern. For example, if I type 1 into a cell and try to drag it, Excel just repeats the 1 over and over again. If I do 1 and then 2 and highlight both cells and start to drag from the bottom of the cell with the 2 in it, then it starts to number the next cells 3, 4, 5 etc.

You'll see the values Excel suggests for each cell as you drag the cursor through that cell, but those values won't actually appear in those cells until you're done highlighting all the cells you want to copy the pattern to and you let up on the left-click. (If that doesn't make sense, just try it a few times and you'll see what I mean.)

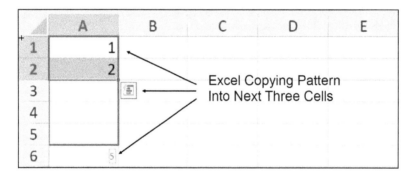

(You can combine Excel's ability to copy patterns with the AutoFill option by double-clicking in the bottom right-hand corner instead. This only works when your current column is next to a column that already has values in it for all of your rows. See the Manipulating Your Data section for more detail on AutoFill.)

Freeze Panes

If you have enough information in a worksheet for it to not be visible in one page, there's a chance you'll want to use freeze panes. What it does is freezes a row or rows and/or a column or columns at the top of your page so that even when you scroll down or to the right those rows or columns stay visible. So if you have 100 rows of information but always want to be able to see your header row, freeze panes will let you do that.

To freeze panes, go to the View tab and click on the arrow under Freeze Panes. It gives you three options: Freeze Panes, Freeze Top Row, and Freeze First Column. Those second two are pretty obvious, right? Choose "Freeze Top Row" and you'll always see Row 1 of your worksheet no matter how far down you scroll. Choose "Freeze First Column" and you'll always see Column A of your worksheet no matter how far to the right you scroll.

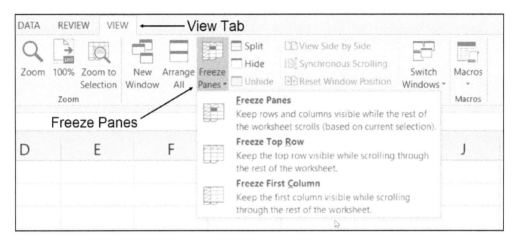

That first option, Freeze Panes, is more interesting. It will freeze as many rows or columns as you need to freeze. If I click on cell C4 (so down three rows and over two columns) and choose to Freeze Panes, it will keep the top three rows and the left two columns of my worksheet visible no matter how far I scroll in the document. So, for example, if you had customer name, city, and state in your first three columns and wanted to be able to see that information as you scrolled over to see other customer data, you could. Or say your worksheet has a couple of rows of text and then the real row labels begin in row 5, you can click in Cell A6, choose to freeze panes, and those top five rows will always stay visible.

Freeze panes is very handy when dealing with large amounts of data. Just be careful that you don't accidentally lose where you are. If you click into a frozen row or column and then arrow down or over, it will take you to the next row, not the data you're seeing on the screen. So if you were looking at row 10,522 and you had the top row frozen and click into row 1 for some reason and then arrow down it will take you to row 2. (It happens to be something I do often, so figured it was worth mentioning.)

To remove freeze panes, you can go back to the View tab and the Freeze Panes dropdown and you'll now see that that first option has become Unfreeze Panes. Just click on it and your document will go back to normal.

FORMATTING

If you're going to spend any amount of time working in Excel then you need to learn how to format cells, because inevitably your column won't be as wide as you want it to be or you'll want to have a cell with red-colored text or to use bolding or italics or something that isn't Excel's default.

That's what this section is for. It's an alphabetical listing of different things you might want to do. You can either format one cell at a time by highlighting that specific cell, or you can format multiple cells at once by highlighting all of them and then choosing your formatting option.

What you'll see below is that there are basically two main ways to format cells. You can use the Home tab and click on the option you want from there, or you can right-click and select the Format Cells option from the dropdown menu. For basic formatting, the Home tab will be the best choice. For less common formatting choices, you may need to use the Format Cells option.

There are also shortcut keys available for things like bolding (Ctrl + B), italicizing (Ctrl + I), and underlining (Ctrl +U) that give a third option for some basic formatting needs.

Aligning Your Text Within a Cell

By default, text within a cell is left-aligned and bottom-aligned. But at times you may want to adjust this. I often will center text or prefer for it to be top-aligned because it looks better to me that way when I have some column headers that are one line and others that are multiple lines.

To do this, highlight the cell(s) you want to change, and go to the Alignment section on the Home tab. You'll see on the left-hand side of that section six different images with lines in them. These are visual representations of your possible choices. The first row has the top aligned, middle aligned, and bottom aligned options. You can choose one of these three options for your cell. The second row has the left-aligned, centered, and right-aligned options. You can also choose one of these three options for your cell. So you can have a cell with top-aligned and centered text or top-aligned and right-aligned text or bottom-aligned and centered text, etc.

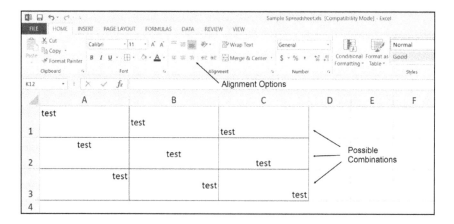

The angled "ab" with an arrow under it on the top row of the Alignment section also has a handful of pre-defined options for changing the direction of text within a cell. You can choose to Angle Counterclockwise, Angle Clockwise, Vertical Text, Rotate Text Up, and Rotate Text Down. (It also offers another way to access the Alignment tab of the Format Cells dialogue box which we'll talk about next. Just click on Format Cell Alignment at the bottom of the dropdown menu.)

Another way to change the text alignment within a cell(s) is to highlight your cell(s) and then right-click and choose Format Cells from the dropdown menu.

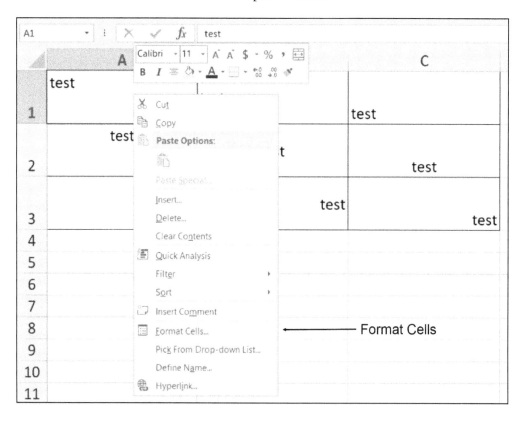

When the Format Cells dialogue box opens, go to the Alignment tab.

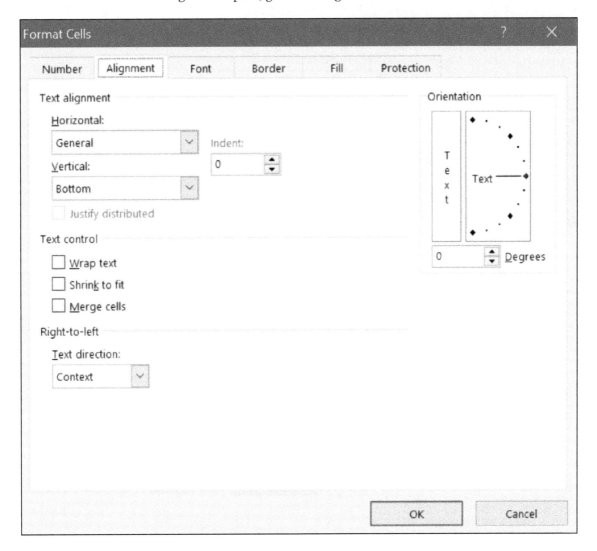

Choose from the Horizontal and Vertical dropdown menus to change the position of text within a cell (Top, Center, Bottom, Left, Right, etc.).

The Horizontal and Vertical dropdown menus have a few additional choices (like Justify and Distributed), but you generally shouldn't need them. (And be wary of Fill which it seems will repeat whatever you have in that cell over and over again until it fills the cell. Remember, if you do something you don't like, Ctrl + Z.)

You can also change the orientation of your text so that it's vertical or angled by entering the number of degrees (90 to make it vertical) or moving the line within the Orientation box to where you want it.

Bolding Text

You can bold text in a number of ways.

First, you can highlight the cell(s) you want bolded and click on the large capital B in the Font section of the Home tab.

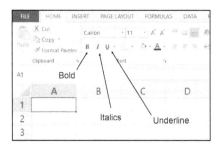

Second, you can highlight the cell(s) you want bolded and then type Ctrl and B at the same time. (Ctrl + B)

Or, third, you can highlight the cell(s) you want to bold and then right-click and choose Format Cells from the dropdown menu. Once you're in the Format Cells dialogue box, go to the Font tab and choose Bold from the Font Style options. If you want text that is both bolded and italicized, choose Bold Italic.

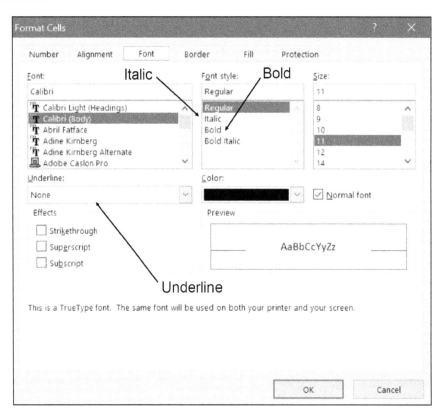

You can also bold just part of the text in a cell by clicking into the cell, highlighting the portion of the text that you want to bold, and then using any of the above methods.

To remove bolding from text or cells that already have it, highlight the bolded portion and then type Ctrl + B or click on the large capital B in the Font section of the Home tab. (If you happen to highlight text that is only partially bolded you may have to do it twice to remove the bold formatting.)

Borders Around Cells

It's nice to have borders around your data to keep the information in each cell distinct, especially if you're going to print your document.

There are two main ways to add borders around a cell or set of cells. First, you can highlight the cells you want to place a border around and then go to the Font section on the Home tab and choose from the Borders dropdown option. It's a four-square grid with an arrow next to it that's located between the U used for underlining and the color bucket used for filling a cell with color. Click on the arrow to see your available options, and then choose the type of border you want. (If you just want a simple border all around the cells and between multiple cells click on the All Borders option.)

With this option, to adjust the line thickness or line colors, see the options in the Draw Borders section, but be sure to choose your colors and line style before you choose your border type because the color and line type you choose will only apply to borders you draw after you choose them.

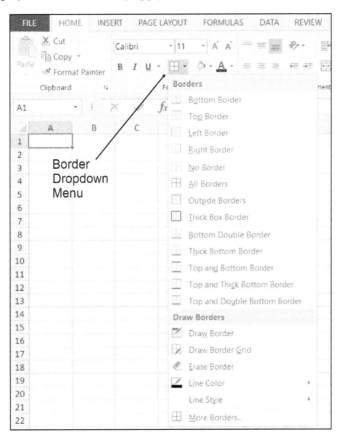

You can combine border types to get the appearance you want. For example, you could choose All Borders for the entire set of cells and then Thick Box Border to put a darker outline around the perimeter.

Your second choice is to highlight the cells where you want to place a border and then right-click and select Format Cells from the dropdown menu. Next, go to the Border tab and choose your border style, type, and color from there.

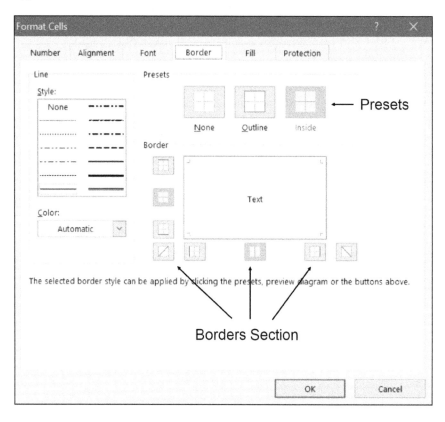

If you want one of the Preset options (outline or inside lines), just click on it. To clear what you've done and start over you can select None from the Presets section.

If you want only a subset of lines (for example, only the bottom of the cell to have a line), click on the choice you want from the Border section around the Text box. You can click on more than one of the lines in this section. So you could have, for example, a top and bottom border, but nothing else.

And, if you want to change the style of a line or its color from the default, you should do so in the Line section before you select where you want your lines to appear.

You can see what you've chosen and what it will look like in the sample box in the center of the screen.

Coloring a Cell (Fill Color)

You can color (or fill) an entire cell with almost any color you want. To do this, highlight the cell(s) you want to color, go to the Font section of the Home tab, and click on the arrow to the right of the paint bucket that has a yellow line under it. This should bring up a colors menu with 70 difference colors to choose from, including many that are arranged as complementary themes. If you want one of those colors, just click on it.

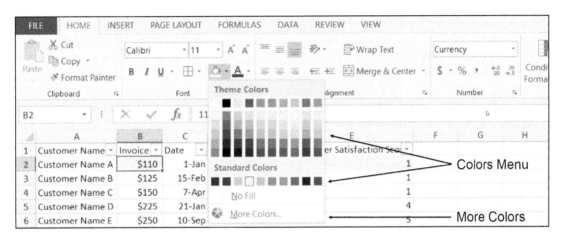

If none of those colors work for you, or you need to use a specific corporate color, click on More Colors at the bottom. This will bring up a Colors display box. The first tab of that box looks like a honeycomb and has a number of colors you can choose from by clicking into the honeycomb. The second tab is the Custom tab. It has a rainbow of colors that you can click on and also allows you to enter specific red, green, and blue values to get the exact color you need. (If you have a corporate color palette, they should give you the RGB values for each of the colors. At least my last employer did.)

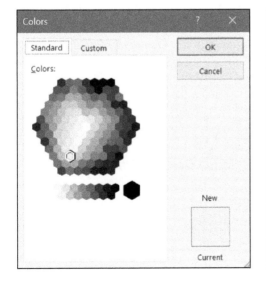
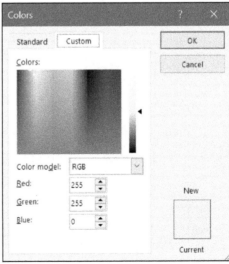

On the Custom tab, you can also use the arrow on the right-hand side to darken or lighten your color. With both tabs, you can see the color you've chosen in the bottom right corner. If you like your choice, click on OK. If you don't want to add color to a cell after all, choose Cancel.

Column Width (Adjusting)

If your columns aren't the width you want, you have three options for adjusting them.

First, you can right-click on the column and choose Column Width from the dropdown menu. When the box showing you the current column width appears, enter a new column width.

Second, you can place your cursor to the right side of the column name—it should look like a line with arrows on either side—and then left-click and hold while you move the cursor to the right or the left until the column is as wide as you want it to be.

Or, third, you can place your cursor on the right side of the column name and double left-click. This will make the column as wide or as narrow as the widest text currently in that column. (Usually. Sometimes this one has a mind of its own.)

To adjust all column widths in your document at once, you can highlight the entire worksheet and then double-left click on any column border and it will adjust each column to the contents in that column. (Usually. See comment above.)

To have uniform column widths throughout your worksheet, highlight the whole worksheet, right-click on a column, choose Column Width, and set your column width. Highlighting the whole worksheet and then left-clicking and dragging one column to the desired width will also work.

Currency Formatting

If you type a number into a cell in Excel, it'll just show that number. So, 25 is 25. $25 is $25. But sometimes you want those numbers to display as currency with the dollar sign and cents showing, too. Or you've already copied in unformatted numbers and now want them to have the same currency format.

To do this, highlight the cell(s) you want formatted this way, and then go to the Number section of the Home tab, and click on the $ sign.

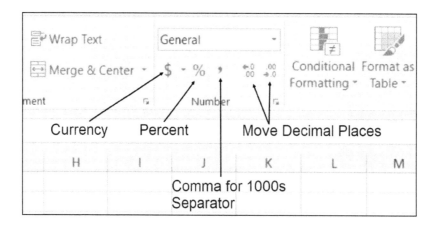

Another option is to highlight the cells you want formatted that way, go to the Number section of the Home tab, and use the dropdown to choose either Currency or Accounting.

You can also highlight the cell(s), right-click, choose the Format Cells option, go to the Number tab, and choose either Currency or Accounting from there.

Date Formatting

Sometimes Excel has a mind of its own about how to format dates. For example, if I type in 1/1 for January 1st, Excel will show it as 1-Jan. It means the same thing, but if I would rather it display as 1/1/2017, I need to change the formatting.

To do this, click on the cell with your date in it, go to the Number section on the Home tab, click on the dropdown menu, and choose Short Date. (You can also choose Long Date if you prefer that format.)

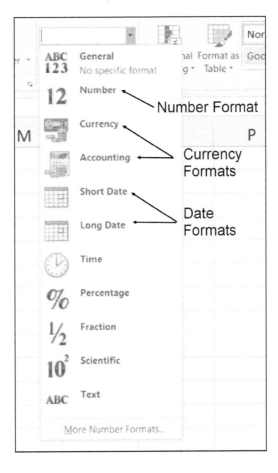

Another option is to highlight your cell(s), right click, choose Format Cells from the dropdown menu, go to the Number tab of the Format Cells dialogue box, and choose your date format from there by clicking on Date and then selecting one of the numerous choices it provides.

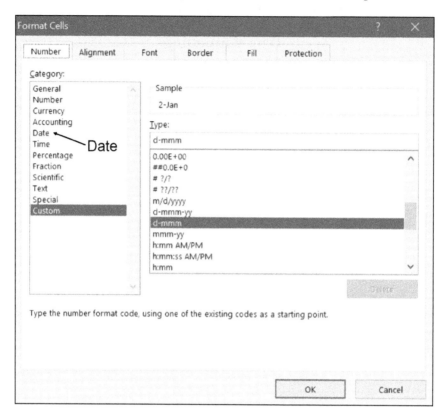

Note that if you just enter a month and day of the month like I did above, Excel will default to assuming that you meant the date to be for the current year and will store your date as MM-DD-YYYY even if you weren't trying to specify a year.

Font Choice and Size

In my version of Excel the default font choice is Calibri and the default font size is 11 point. You may have strong preferences about what font you use or work for a company that uses specific fonts for its brand or just want some variety in terms of font size or type within a specific document. In that case, you will need to change your font.

There are two ways to do this.

First, you can highlight the cells you want to change or the specific text you want to change, and go to the Font section on the Home tab. Select a different font or font size from the dropdown menus there.

You also have the option to increase or decrease the font one size at a time by clicking on the A's with little arrows in the top right corner that are next to the font dropdown box.

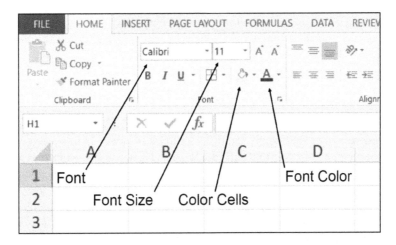

Second, you can highlight the cells or text you want to change, right-click, and choose Format Cells from the dropdown menu, and then go to the Font tab and choose your Font and Size from the listed values.

With either option, you can choose a font size that isn't listed by clicking into the font size box and typing the value you want.

Font Color

The default color for all text in Excel is black, but you can change that if you want or need to. (For example, if you've colored a cell with a darker color you may want to consider changing the font color to white to make the text in that cell more visible.)

You have two options. First, you can highlight the cells or the specific text you want to change, go to the Font section on the Home tab, and click on the arrow next to the A with a red line under it (see image above). You can then choose from one of the 70 colors that are listed, and if those aren't enough of a choice you can click on More Colors and select your color from the Colors dialogue box. (See Coloring a Cell for more detail about that option.)

Second, you can highlight the cell or text, right-click and choose Format Cells from the drop-down menu, go to the Font tab, and then click on the dropdown menu under Color which will bring up the same seventy color options and the ability to choose More Colors and add a custom color instead.

Italicizing Text

You do this by highlighting the cell(s) you want italicized and clicking on the slanted I in the Font section on the Home tab (see image under the Bolding description), or by highlighting the cell(s) and holding down the Ctrl key and the I key at the same time. (Ctrl + I)

Or, you can highlight the cell(s), right-click, choose Format Cells from the dropdown menu, go to the Font tab, and choose Italic from the Font Style options. (See image under the Bolding description.)

You can also italicize just part of the text in a cell by only selecting that portion and then using one of the methods above.

To remove italics from text or cells that already have it, you follow the exact same steps. (Highlight your selection and then type Ctrl + I or click on the slanted I in the Font section on the Home tab.)

Merge & Center

Merge and Center is a specialized command that can come in handy when you're working with a table where you want a header that spans multiple columns of data. (Don't use it if you plan to do a lot of data analysis with what you've input into the worksheet because it will mess with your ability to filter, sort, or use pivot tables. It's really for creating a finalized, pretty-looking report.)

If you're going to merge and center text, make sure that the text you want to keep is in the top-most and left-most of the cells you plan to merge and center. Data in the other cells that are being merged will be deleted. (You'll get a warning message to this effect if you have values in any of the other cells.)

You can merge cells across columns and down rows. So you could, for example, merge four cells that span two columns and two rows into one big cell while keeping all of the other cells in those columns and rows separate.

Highlight all of the cells you want to merge. Next, go to the Alignment section of the Home tab and choose Merge & Center. This will combine your selected cells into one cell and center the contents from the topmost, left-most cell that was merged across the selection.

You'll see on that dropdown that you can also choose to just Merge Across (which will just merge the cells in the first row) or to Merge Cells (which will merge the cells but won't center the text).

Also, if you ever need to unmerge those merged cells you can do so by selecting the Unmerge Cells option from that dropdown.

You can also Merge Cells by highlighting the cells, right-clicking, selecting the Format Cells option, going to the Alignment tab, and then choosing to Merge Cells from there. If you choose that option, you have to center the text separately.

Number Formatting

Sometimes when you copy data into Excel it doesn't format it the way you want. For example, I have a report I receive that includes ISBN numbers which are 10- or 13- digit numbers. When I copy those into Excel, it sometimes displays them in Scientific Number format (9.78E+12) as opposed to as a normal number.

To change the formatting of your data to a number format, you have two options.

First, you can highlight the cell(s) and go to the Number section of the Home tab. From the drop-down menu choose Number. (Sometimes General will work as well.) It will then convert it to a number with two decimal places. So 100.00 instead of 100. You can then use the zeroes with arrows next to them that are below the drop-down box to adjust how many decimal places display. The one with the right-pointing arrow will reduce the number of decimal places. The one with the left-pointing arrow will increase them. (See the Currency Formatting section for an image.)

Second, you can highlight the cell(s), right-click, select Format Cells from the dropdown, go to the Number tab, choose Number on the left-hand side listing, and then in the middle, choose your number of decimal places. You can also choose whether to use a comma to separate out your thousands and millions and how to display negative numbers at the same time.

Percent Formatting

To format numbers as a percentage, highlight the cell(s), and click on the percent sign in the Number section of the Home tab.

You can also highlight the cell(s), right-click, select Format Cells from the dropdown, go to the Number tab, choose Percentage on the left-hand side, and then in the middle, choose your number of decimal places.

Row Height (Adjusting)

If your rows aren't the correct height, you have three options for adjusting them. First, you can right-click on the row you want to adjust, choose Row Height from the dropdown menu, and when the box showing you the current row height appears, enter a new row height.

Second, you can place your cursor along the lower border of the row number until it looks like a line with arrows above and below. Left-click and hold while you move the cursor up or down until the row is as tall as you want it to be.

Third, you can place your cursor along the lower border of the row, and double left-click. This will fit the row height to the text in the cell. (Usually.)

To adjust all row heights in your document at once you can highlight the entire worksheet and then double-left click on any row border and it will adjust each row to the contents in each individual row. (Usually.) To have uniform row heights throughout your worksheet, you can highlight the whole sheet, right-click on a row, choose Row Height and set your row height that way or select the entire worksheet, right-click on the border below a row, and adjust that row to the height you want for all rows.

Underlining Text

You have three options for underlining text. First, you can highlight the cell(s) you want underlined and click on the underlined U in the Font section on the Home tab. (See the Bolding section for a screen shot.)

Second, you can highlight the cell(s) and type Ctrl and U at the same time. (Ctrl + U)

Third, you can highlight the cell(s), right-click, choose Format Cells from the dropdown menu, go to the Font tab, and choose the type of underlining you want (single, double, single accounting, double accounting) from the Underline drop down menu.

You can also underline part of the text in a cell by clicking into the cell, highlighting the portion of the text that you want to underline, and then using any of the above methods.

To remove underlining from text or cells that already have it, highlight the text and then use one of the above options.

Wrapping Text

Sometimes you want to read all of the text in a cell, but you don't want that column to be wide enough to display all of the text. This is where the Wrap Text option becomes useful, because it will keep your text within the width of the column and display it on multiple lines by "wrapping" the text.

(Excel does have a limit as to how many rows of text it will display in one cell, so if you have any cells with lots of text in them, check to make sure that the full contents of the cell are actually visible. You may have to manually adjust the row height to see all of the text.)

To Wrap Text in a cell, select the cell(s), go to the Alignment section of the Home Tab, and click on the Wrap Text option in the Alignment section.

Or you can highlight the cell(s), right-click, choose Format Cells from the dropdown menu, go to the Alignment tab there, and choose Wrap Text under Text Control.

* * *

One final formatting trick to share with you that is incredibly handy. (Maybe more so in Word than in Excel, but I use it frequently in both.)

Copying Formatting From One Cell To Another

In addition to the specific formatting options discussed above, if you already have a cell formatted the way you want it to, you can "Format Sweep" from that cell to other cells you want formatted the same way. You do this by using the Format Painter in the Clipboard section of the Home tab.

Highlight the cell(s) that have the formatting you want to copy (if the formatting is identical, just highlight one cell), click on the Format Painter, and then click into the cell(s) you want to copy the formatting to. The contents in the destination cell will remain the same, but the font, font color, font size, cell borders, italics/bolding/underlining, and text alignment and orientation will all change to match that of the cell that you swept the formatting from.

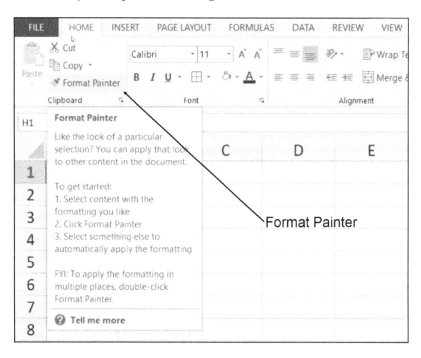

You need to be careful using the format sweeper because it will change *all* formatting in your destination cells. So, if the cell you're copying the formatting from is bolded and has red text, both of those attributes will copy over even if all you were trying to do was copy the bold formatting. (This is more of a problem when using the tool in Word than in Excel, but it's still something to watch out for especially if you have borders around cells.)

Also, the tool copies formatting to whatever cell you select next, which can be a problem if the cell you're copying from isn't next to the one you're copying to. Do not use arrow keys to navigate between the cells. You need to click directly from the cell with the formatting you want to the cell you're transferring the formatting to.

(Remember, Ctrl + Z is your friend if you make a mistake.)

If you have more than one isolated cell that you need to apply formatting to, you can double-click the Format Painter and it will continue to copy the formatting of the original cell to every other cell you click in until you click on the Format Painter again or hit Esc. (You'll know the tool is still in operation because there will be a little broom next to your cursor.)

You can copy formatting from multiple cells to multiple cells, so say the formatting for an entire row to an entire other row, but be sure to double-check the results since this is much more likely to result in unintended formatting.

Also, you can copy formatting from one cell to multiple cells at a time by simply highlighting all of the cells you want to copy the formatting to at once.

If you format sweep and then undo, you'll see that the cell(s) you were trying to format from are surrounded by a dotted border as if you had copied the cells. Be sure to hit the Esc key before you continue.

MANIPULATING YOUR DATA

Once you've entered your data into a worksheet, you might want to do something with it. Like sort it or filter it so you see only the entries that meet specific criteria, or analyze it using mathematical functions like addition or subtraction. This section will walk you through the basics of sorting, filtering, and analyzing your data.

Sorting

Sorting allows you to display your information in a specific order. For example, by date, value, or alphabetically. You can also sort across multiple columns, so you can, for example, sort first by date, then by name, then by amount.

To sort your data, select all cells that contain your information, including your header row if there is one.

If you set your data up with the first row as the header and all of the rest as data, you can just click in the top left corner of your worksheet to select all of the cells in the worksheet. Excel will then figure out the limits of your data when you choose to sort.

If you have a table of data that starts lower down on the page or that has a summary row or that is followed by other data, be sure to only select the cells in the data set you want to sort, because Excel will sort everything you select whether it makes sense to do so or not.

Once you've selected your data, go to the Editing section of the Home tab. Click on the arrow next to Sort & Filter, and choose Custom Sort. Your other option is to go to the Data tab and click on the Sort option there. Either path will bring you to the Sort dialogue box.

The first choice you need to make is to indicate whether or not your data has headers. In other words, does the first row of your data contain column labels? If so, click on that box in the top corner that says, "My data has headers." If you indicate that there is a header row, it will not be included in your sort and will remain the first row of your data.

When you do this, you'll see that your Sort By dropdown now displays your column labels. If you don't check this box, the dropdown will show generic column names (Column A, Column B, etc.) and all of your data will be sorted, including the first row.

Sometimes Excel tries to decide this for you and is wrong, so always make sure that your Sort By choices make sense given the data you selected, and that you check or uncheck the "My data has headers" box to get the result you want.

The next step is to choose your sort order.

What is the first criteria you want to sort by? Chose that column from the Sort By dropdown menu.

Next, choose *how* to sort that column of data. You can sort on values, font color, cell color, and icon. I almost always use values.

After that, choose what order to use. For text it's usually from A to Z to sort alphabetical or from Z to A to sort reverse alphabetical. I also sometimes use the Custom List option when I have a column with the months of the year or the days of the week in it. For numbers it's just Smallest to Largest or Largest to Smallest.

If all you want to sort by is one column, then you're done. Click OK.

If you want to sort first by the column you already entered and then by another column, you need to add the second column. Click on Add Level and select your next column to sort by and your criteria for that sort.

If you add a level you don't need, highlight it and choose Delete Level.

If you have multiple levels but decide that they should be sorted in a different order, you can use the arrows to the left of Options to move a sort level up or down.

The default is to sort top to bottom, but you can click on Options to sort left to right or to make your sort case sensitive.

When you're done with your sort options, click OK. If you change your mind, click Cancel. If you get a sort that has a mistake in it, remember to use Ctrl + Z to undo and try again.

A few things to watch out for with sort order. Be sure that you've selected all of the data you want sorted. If you only highlight three columns but have six columns of data, only the first three columns will be sorted. The other three columns will stay in their original order which will break the relationship between your data points.

Excel also offers quick-sort options (the ones that say Sort A to Z or Sort Z to A), but be wary when using them. Sometimes they work great, most times they sort in the wrong order for me or on the wrong column or miss that I have a header row. To save myself time and effort, I usually just use Custom Sort instead.

Filtering

Sometimes you want your data to stay right where it is, but you want to see only certain results that meet a specific criteria. For example, only customers located in Mozambique. Filtering allows you to do that. As long as your data is displayed in rows (and ideally with contiguous columns), you can use filtering.

To start, click on any cell in the header row of your data, and then in the Editing section of the Home tab, click on the arrow next to Sort & Filter and choose Filter.

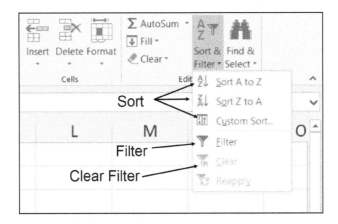

You should now see gray arrows to the right of each label in your first row.

One thing to note here is that the Filter function will only show arrows for columns that are touching. So if you have data in Columns A through D and then in Columns F through K, it will show the filter arrows for either Columns A through D OR Columns F through K, but not for both sets of columns at the same time. If you want to be able to filter on all of those columns at once, you need to remove any blank columns in between.

What I'm about to discuss applies to more recent versions of Excel, but not older versions. As I recall, older versions basically let you filter on one column and with limited criteria. You certainly couldn't filter by color until very recently. So if you have an older version of Excel you may be able to filter your results some, but not as well as with more recent versions. And if you save into an older version of Excel while your data is filtered, you may experience issues with how your data displays. If I recall correctly it keeps the filtering you had in place, but doesn't show all of the filtering choices you made. (I usually don't keep filters on my data. I use filtering to view my data while I'm working, but then I remove them before I close the file.)

Okay. Back to how to filter.

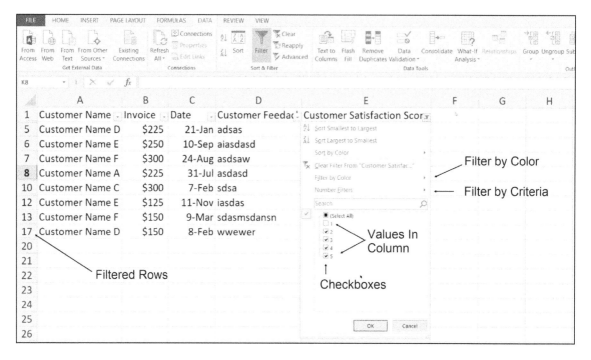

If you click on the arrow for any given column, you should see a list of all potential values in that column with checkboxes next to each value. For really long data sets (tens of thousands of rows) this may not be a complete listing. It definitely wasn't in older versions of Excel.

For basic filtering, you can use the checkboxes to set the criteria for what data to display. Simply uncheck the box for any values you don't want to see.

Or, if you want to see only one or two of the values, what you can do is click in the Select All box to unselect all of the values, and then click in the box for the one or two you want to see.

You can also type the name of the value you want to filter by into the Search field.

Or you can filter by criteria instead. Depending on the type of data you're filtering, the option will say Number Filters or Text Filters.

Click on the arrow and you should see options like "Equals" or "Does Not Equal" or "Begins With" or "Between" etc. The options differ depending on whether it's text or a number. You can use these filter criteria to select only the rows where those criteria are met. So, for example, you can filter to include only invoices over $500 or only customers in Canada.

Or, invoices over $500 for customers in Canada. Current versions of Excel allow you to filter on multiple columns at once.

If you've color-coded cells using Font color or Cell color, you can also filter by those criteria, using the Filter by Color option.

When cells in your worksheet are filtered, the row numbers in your worksheet will be colored blue, and you'll see that the row numbers skip since some rows won't be displayed. (In the screenshot above, rows 2, 3, 4, 9, 11, 14, 15, and 16 have been filtered out because they had customer satisfaction scores of 1.)

Columns where filtering is in place will show a funnel instead of an arrow on the gray dropdown next to the column name.

To remove filtering from a specific column, click on the gray arrow, and select Clear Filter from [Column Name].

To remove all filtering in a worksheet, go to the Editing section of the Home tab, click on Sort & Filter, and then choose Clear.

* * *

Alright, that was sorting and filtering. Let's talk functions now.

For any function, start with an equals sign (=) in the cell. That tells Excel that you're calculating something in this cell and to look for a function or mathematical symbol (like a * for multiplication).

Excel has hundreds of functions but the ones you'll probably use the most are the basic math functions, so we'll start there.

Basic Math Functions

Basic math functions in my definition are addition, subtraction, multiplication, and division. The below image shows simple formulas for each of the four basic math functions. The first column is when two values are involved, the second column is for when multiple values are involved. We'll walk through each one in a second, but note that for addition and multiplication there are named functions that you can use (SUM and PRODUCT, respectively) when multiple values are involved, but there are no named functions for subtraction or division.

While all of the examples I'm about to use focus on data in one worksheet, you can perform functions across worksheets. It's the same process, just click on the cell you want to use in the worksheet where it's located and Excel will take care of the rest.

D	E	F
	With Two Values	With Multiple Values
Addition	=A1+B1	=SUM(A1:B3)
Subtraction	=B1-A1	=B3-A2-B1
Multiplication	=A1*B1	=PRODUCT(A1:B3)
Division	=B1/A1	=B3/(B1/A1)

Alright, let's walk through each one in more detail.

Addition

If you just want to know what the value of some cells added together is, but you don't need it recorded in your worksheet, you actually don't even need to use a function. You can just highlight the cells you want to add together and then look in the bottom right corner of the worksheet. It should show you the average, the count, and the sum of the cells you have highlighted.

But if you want the results of that addition visible in a cell in the worksheet, then you need to use either the + sign or the SUM( ) function.

The + sign tells Excel to add the two values on each side of the sign together. So above where it says =A1+B1 that's telling Excel to add the values in cell A1 and cell B1. You can also write it as =25+35 and have Excel add 25 to 35. You don't have to use cell references, but remember that normally in Excel all you'll see displayed is the result of a calculation. The only way to know what values were combined is to click on the specific cell and look in the formula bar.

If you have more than one value to add together, you can use the SUM function. The easiest way to do this is to type

=SUM(

into your cell and then highlight the cells you want to add together. Excel will convert the cells you've highlighted into the proper notation.

As you can see above, the formula for the example is =SUM(A1:B3). This is adding cells A1, B1, A2, B2, A3, and B3 together. Rather than try to figure out the proper way to summarize that, it's best to let Excel do it. But if you want to do it yourself, basically a colon between cells (:) means "through" and a comma (,) means "and." So =SUM(A1,B3) would mean add A1 to B3.

Also, to reference an entire column leave out the row references. So =SUM(B:B) means sum all of the values in column B. And =SUM(B:C) means sum all of the values in columns B and C.

If you want to make sure that you entered your formula correctly, note that when you type a formula into Excel it will highlight the cells included in the formula.

To check the contents of a formula later, double-click on the cell with the formula and Excel will highlight the cells being used, and will color-code them as well. (Very helpful with nested IF functions, which are covered in the *Intermediate Excel* guide.)

With addition, you also have one other option. You can use the AutoSum option in the Editing section of the Home Tab. This is basically just another way to create your formula for you.

The AutoSum icon looks like the mathematical sum function (a big pointy E-like shape). Click in the cell either below or to the right of the numbers you want to add together, click on AutoSum, and Excel will highlight all contiguous numbers either above the cell or to the left of it, and create a SUM formula for you using those cells. The AutoSum option stops at blank lines, so if you need to sum across a blank space, you'll need to edit the formula for it to work.

Subtraction

There are no nifty shortcuts when it comes to subtraction. You basically just have to type in a formula using the negative sign. The basic format is =( )–( )–( ) where the parens represent your different values. So if I want to subtract the value in cell B1 from the value in cell A1 I would type =A1-B1.

If I want to subtract B1, C1, and D1 from A1 I could either type =A1-B1-C1-D1 or I could also use the SUM function and type =A1-SUM(B1:D1) since that gets the same result.

As with any type of subtraction, be sure you get the numbers in the right order. The number you're starting with goes on the left-hand side, the number you're taking away from that goes on the right-hand side.

Also, you can still click on the cells you need instead of typing the whole formula. So, start with =, click on the first cell you need, type - , and click on the next one. Not as useful for subtraction as it is for addition, because you can't really use it with multiple cells at once.

Multiplication

Multiplication basically works the same way as addition. You can use the function PRODUCT or you can use the star symbol (*) between two values you want to multiply together.

So if you want to multiply cell A1 by cell B1, you'd type =A1*B1 or =PRODUCT (A1:B1) or =PRODUCT (A1, B1). All three formulas will get you the same result.

For multiple values, it would be =A1*B1*C1 or =PRODUCT (A1:C1) or =PRODUCT(A1,B1,C1).

Division

Division, much like subtraction, is another one where order matters. In the case of division you use the right slash (/) to indicate that the number on the left-hand side should be divided by the number on the right-hand side.

So if I want to divide A1 by B1, I would type =A1/B1.

It's best not to divide multiple numbers in one cell, because it's prone to error and it's better to see your steps as you go, but if you do so, make sure to use parens to ensure that the correct numbers get divided since =(A1/B1)/C1 is different than =A1/(B1/C1).

Complex Formulas

As I just hinted, you can definitely do much more complex formulas in Excel. You just have to make sure you write it properly so that Excel knows which functions to perform first.

Put something in parens and Excel will do that before anything else. Otherwise it will follow standard mathematical principles about which actions to perform in which order.

According to the Excel help documentation (under Operator Precedence), Excel will first combine cells (B1:B3 or B1, B2), then create any negative numbers (-B1), then create percents, then calculate any exponentials (B2^2), then do any multiplication and division, then do any addition and subtraction, then concatenate any values, and then do any comparisons last.

All of this, of course, at least in the U.S., is done from left to right in a formula.

So, basically, Excel calculates starting on the left side of the equation and moves to the right, doing each of those steps above in that order throughout the entire formula before circling back to the start and doing the next step. Which means that multiplication and division are done first and then addition or subtraction.

Of course, anything in parens is treated as a standalone equation first. So if you have =3*(4+2), Excel will add the 4 and the 2 before it does the multiplication.

Basically, if you're going to write complex formulas they're definitely doable but you should be very comfortable with math and how it works. Also, be sure to test your equation to make sure you did it right. I do this by breaking a formula into its component steps and then making sure that my combined equation generates the same result.

Other Functions

Excel has a ton of available functions that can do all sorts of interesting things and not just with numbers.

To see what I'm talking about, go to the Formulas tab. There are seven different subject areas listed there (Financial, Logical, Text, Date & Time, Lookup & Reference, Math & Trig, and Other). Click on each of those dropdowns and you'll see twenty-plus functions for each one.

But how do you know if there's a function that does what you want to do? For example, is there a function for trimming excess space from a string of values? (Yes. It's called TRIM.) Or for calculating the cumulative principal paid on a loan between two periods? (Yes.)

So how do you find the function you want without hovering over each function to see what it does?

The simple way is to go to the Formulas tab and click on Insert Function. This will bring up the Insert Function dialogue box which includes a search function. Type a few words for what you're looking for.

For example, if I want to calculate how many days until some event occurs and I want to have this formula work no matter what day it is when I open my worksheet, then I need some way to set a value equal to today's date whatever day today is. So I search for "today" and get a function called TODAY that it says "Returns the current date formatted as a date." Perfect.

Or what if I have two columns of text and I want to combine them. If I search for "combine text" my second option is CONCATENATE which is described as "Joins several text strings into one text string." That'll work.

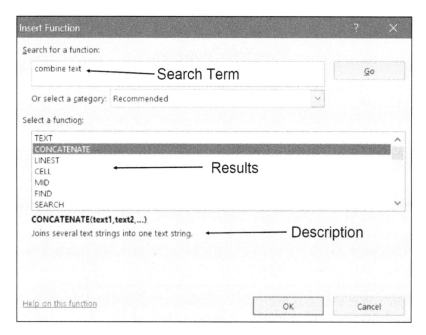

Once you've found a function you like, highlight it and click on OK. Excel will take you back to the worksheet and show you a Function Arguments dialogue box that tells you what inputs are needed to create that particular function.

So for CONCATENATE it shows me boxes for Text 1 and Text 2, because to write a concatenate function you need to at least write =CONCATENATE(A1, B1) where A1 and B1 are the two cells you're combining.

Sometimes selecting a function this way, even if you know what it does, is helpful because it shows you what order you need to put the information in and what form it needs to take. But you can also see this to a lesser degree when you start to type the function into your cell. Once you type the opening paren it will show you the components you need and their order. (Very helpful for things like SUMIF and SUMIFS that have different orders even though they do similar things.)

As a side note, TRIM, CONCATENATE, and SUMIFS are all discussed in further detail in *Intermediate Excel*.

Copying Cells With Formulas in Them

One of the nice things about working with formulas in Excel is that you don't have to type them over and over and over again. You can type a formula once and if you need to use it again, simply copy it to a new cell.

There are some tricks to copying formulas. So let's walk through those.

By default, formulas are relative. Meaning that if you have a formula that says =B1+C1 and you copy it (Ctrl + C) over to the right one cell it will become =C1+D1. If you copy it down one cell from that original location it will become =B2+C2. This is great when you have rows and rows of data with everything located in the same position and want to perform the exact same calculation on each of those rows. You can simply copy the formula and paste it down the entire column and it will perform that calculation on each and every row.

But sometimes you just want to move the calculation. Say it's in Cell B2 now and you want to put it in Cell A10. That's when you need to cut the formula (Ctrl + X) and move it instead of copy it. By cutting and moving the formula, it stays the exact same. If it said =B1+C1 it still does.

Another way to do this is to click into the cell, highlight all of the text in the cell, copy it, and tab (or Esc) out of the cell, and then click on the new location and paste it. (If you click into the cell, highlight all of the text, and try to click on where you want to paste it, you'll end up replacing your existing text in the source cell with a reference to the cell you clicked into.)

What if you want to copy the formula, but you want to keep some portion of it fixed. Either the row reference, the column reference, or the reference to an entire cell. (Useful when calculating different scenarios where you build a table with different values for variable x in one row and different values for variable y in one column and then calculate what value you get for each combination of x and y. So, hourly pay and hours worked, for example.)

You can fix a portion of a formula by using the $ sign. (We discussed it earlier with respect to inputting data, but I'll run through it again here.)

To fix the reference to a cell, put a $ sign before both the letter and the number in the cell name. So cell B2 becomes $B$2 in your formula. If you reference a cell that way ($B$2), no matter where you copy that formula to it will continue to reference that specific cell. This is useful if you have a constant listed somewhere that's used in a calculation performed for a number of rows. So say you're selling widgets and they're all priced at $100. You might list Widget Price at the top of your worksheet and put 100 in a cell at the top and then calculate how much each customer owes by multiplying their units purchased by that fixed value.

If you want to keep just the column the same, but change the row reference, put the dollar sign in front of the letter only. So $B2 when copied would become $B3, $B4, etc.

If you want to keep the row the same, but change the column reference, you'd put the dollar sign in front of the number only. So B$2. When copied, that portion of the formula would change to C$2, D$2, etc.

One more thought about copying formulas. I usually just highlight all of the cells where I want to copy the formula to and then paste, but there's a shortcut that you can sometimes use that's faster when you have many many rows of data.

If you have a formula in a cell and want to copy it downward and the column where that cell is located is touching another column of data that has already been completed (so you have a full column of data next to the column where you want to put your formula), you can place your cursor on the bottom right corner of the cell with the formula and double-left click. This should copy the formula down all of your rows of data.

It doesn't work if the other column of data hasn't been filled in yet. Excel only knows how far to copy the formula based on the information in the other column. But it can be a handy shortcut in a table with lots of completed information where you're just adding a calculation.

Select All

Another little trick that comes in handy when I'm working with data I've already added to my worksheet is the ability to select all of the contents of the worksheet at once. To do this, click on the top left corner of the sheet where the rows and columns meet. In this version of Excel the bottom half of the square is light gray.

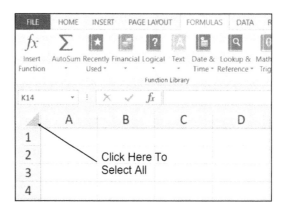

Doing this will select all of the rows and columns in the worksheet and allow you to easily copy the contents so you can move them to another worksheet. Usually I do this when I want to use the Paste Special – Values option to remove any formulas from the worksheet. I Select All, Copy, Paste Special-Values and that overwrites the entire worksheet with just that values that were in the cells.

PRINTING

Alright. That was the basics of manipulating your data. Now on to printing. You might not think that printing needs its own chapter, but it does. Not because clicking on Print is so hard to do, but because you need to format your data well to get it to print well. If you just hit print without thinking about how that information in your worksheet will appear on a page, you'll likely end up with pages worth of poorly-formatted garbage.

Now, it's possible you have no intent of printing anything, in which case, skip this chapter. But if you are going to print, let's try and waste as little paper as possible for you.

First things first. To print, go to the File tab and select Print. If you don't want to clean anything up, you can then just click on the big Print button right there on the page and be done with it.

Typing Ctrl and P at the same time (Ctrl + P) will also take you to the print screen which looks like this:

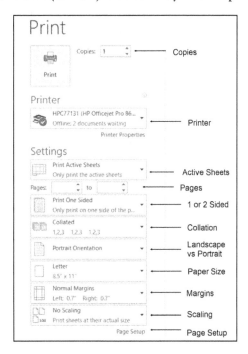

There are a number of things you can do on this page, so let's just walk through them starting at the top and working our way down.

Print

Once you're ready to print your page, you can click on the button on the top left with the image of a printer that says Print.

Number of Copies

If you want to print more than one copy, change your number of copies using the up and down arrows next to the Print button.

Printer

It should display your computer's default printer, but if you want to use a different printer than that one, click on the arrow next to the printer name and choose from the listed options. If the printer you want isn't listed, choose Add Printer and add the printer.

Print Active Sheets / Print Entire Workbook / Print Selection

My version of Excel defaults to Print Active Sheets. This will generally be the worksheet you were working in when you chose to print. However, you can select more than one worksheet by holding down the Control key and then clicking on another worksheet's name. When you do this, you'll see that the names of all of your selected worksheets are highlighted, not just one of them.

I would only print multiple worksheets if you're satisfied that each one is formatted the way you want it formatted. Also, choosing to print more than one sheet at a time either with Print Active Sheets or Print Entire Workbook, results in strange things happening to your headers and footers. For example, your page numbering will occur across worksheets. If you mean each worksheet to be a standalone report with numbered pages specific to that report, then you need to print each worksheet separately.

As I just alluded to, the Print Entire Workbook option prints all of the worksheets in your workbook.

Print Selection allows you to just print a highlighted section of a worksheet or worksheets. (I happened to have three worksheets selected at once and when I highlighted the first twenty cells in one of those worksheets, the selection it was ready to print was those twenty cells in each of the three worksheets.)

Print Selected Pages

Just below the Print Active Sheets section is a row that says Pages and has two boxes with arrows at the side. You can choose to just print a specific page rather than the entire worksheet. To figure out which page to print, look at your preview (which should be taking up most of the screen).

Print One Sided / Print on Both Sides (long edge) / Print on Both Sides (short edge)

The default is to just print on one side of your paper. If you have a printer that can print on both sides of the page you can change your settings to do so. You want the long-edge option if your layout is going to be portrait-style and the short-edge option if your layout is going to be landscape-style. (See below.)

Collated / Uncollated

This only matters if what you're printing has more than one page and if you're printing more than one copy. In that case, you need to decide if you want to print one full copy at a time, x number of times or if you want to print x copies of page 1 and then x copies of page 2 and then x copies of page 3 and so on until you've printed all pages of your document. In general, I would choose collated, which is also the default.

Portrait Orientation / Landscape Orientation

You can choose to print in either portrait orientation (with the short edge of the page on top) or landscape orientation (with the long edge of the page on top). You can see the difference by changing the option in Excel and looking at your print preview.

Which option you choose will depend mostly on how many columns of data you have.

Assuming I'm dealing with a normal worksheet with rows of data listed across various columns, my goal is to fit all of my columns on one page if possible. Sometimes changing the layout to landscape allows me to do that because it allows me to have more columns per page than I'd be able to fit in portrait mode.

If I have just a few columns of data, but lots of rows I'll generally stick with portrait orientation instead.

You'll have to decide what works best for you and your specific data.

Letter / Legal / Statement / Etc.

This is where you select your paper type. Unless you're in an office or overseas, chances are you'll leave this exactly like it is. I'm sure my printer could print on legal paper, but I don't have any for it to use so it's a moot point for me. In an office you may have the choice of 8.5"x11", legal paper, and even other larger sizes than that.

Normal Margins / Wide Margins / Narrow Margins / Custom Margins

I would expect you won't use this, but if you need to then this would be where you can change the margins on the document. The normal margins allow for .7" on each side and .75" on top and bottom. If you have a lot of text and need just a little more room to fit it all on one page, you could use the narrow margin option to make that happen. I generally use the scaling option instead.

No Scaling / Fit Sheet on One Page /
Fit All Columns on One Page / Fit All Rows on One Page

I use this option often when I have a situation where my columns are just a little bit too much to fit on the page or my rows go just a little bit beyond the page. If you choose "Fit All Columns on One Page" that will make sure that all of your columns fit across the top of one page. You might still have multiple pages because of the number of rows, but at least everything will fit across one page.

Of course, depending on how many columns you have, this might not be a good choice. Excel will make it fit, but it will do so by decreasing your font size and if you have too many columns you're trying to fit on one page your font size may become so small you can't read it.

So be sure to look at your preview before you print. (And use Landscape Orientation first if you need to.)

Fit All Rows on One Page is good for if you have maybe one or two rows too many to naturally fit on the page.

Fit Sheet on One Page is a combination of fitting all columns and all rows onto one page. Again, Excel will do it if you ask it to, but with a large set of data you won't be able to read it.

Page Setup

The Page Setup link at the very bottom gives you access to even more options. As with everything else in the more modern versions of Excel, the most obvious options are the ones that are readily visible that we already discussed, but there are other options you have in formatting your page. If you click on the Page Setup link you'll be taken to the Page Setup dialogue box which is another way to choose all your print options. A few things to point out to you that I find useful:

1. **Scaling**
   On the Page tab you can see the scaling option once more. But the nice thing here is that you can fit your information to however many pages across by however many pages long. You're not limited to 1 page wide or 1 page tall. So say you have a document that's currently one page wide and four pages long but the last page is just one row. You can scale that document in the Page Setup dialogue box so that the document that prints is one page wide by three pages long and that last row is brought up onto the prior page.

2. **Center Horizontally or Vertically**
   On the Margins tabs there are two check boxes that let you center what you're printing either horizontally or vertically or both. I will often choose to center an item vertically. If I don't do that, it tends to looks off balance.

3. **Header/Footer**
   We're going to talk about another way to do this in a moment, but if you want to setup a header and/or a footer for your printed document you can do so here. The dropdown boxes that say (none) include a number of pre-formatted headers and footers for you to use. So if you just want the page number included, there should be a pre-formatted one that lets you do that. Same with including the worksheet name or file name in the header

or footer. As you look at each one it will show you examples of the actual text that will be included. You also have the option of customizing either the header or footer.

4. Sheet

The sheet tab has a couple of useful options, but I'm going to show you a different way to set these options because I find it easier to set them when I'm in the worksheet itself.

* * *

Page Layout Tab

If you exit out of the print option and go back to your worksheet, you'll see that one of the tabs you have available to use is called Page Layout. There are certain attributes that I set up here before I print my documents. Let's walk through them.

(Also, note that you can change margins, orientation, and size here just as easily as in the print preview screen.)

1. Print Area

If you only want to print a portion of a worksheet, you can set that portion as your print area by highlighting it, and then clicking on the arrow next to Print Area and choosing Set Print Area.

Only do it this way (as opposed to highlighting the section and choosing Print-Selection) if it's a permanent setting. Once you set your print area it will remain set until you clear it. You can add more data to your worksheet but it will never print until you change your print area or clear the setting.

I use this when I have a worksheet that has either a lot of extra information I don't want to print or where the formatting extends beyond my data and Excel keeps trying to print all those empty but formatted cells.

2. Breaks

You can set where a page break occurs in your worksheet. So say you have a worksheet that takes up four pages and you want to make sure that rows 1 through 10 are on a page together and then rows 11 through 20 are on a page together even though that's not how things would naturally fall. You can set a page break to force that to happen.

Personally, I find page breaks a challenge to work with, so I usually try to get what I need some other way.

3. Print Titles

This one is incredibly valuable. When you click on it, you'll see that it brings up the Page Setup box and takes you to the Sheet tab.

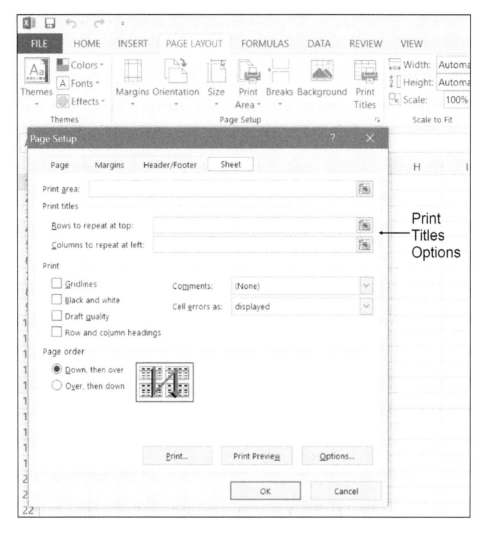

The first valuable thing you can do here is set the rows you want to repeat at the top of the page. Say you have a worksheet with a thousand rows of data in it that will print on a hundred pages. How do you know what's in each column on each page? You need a header row. And you need that header row to repeat at the top of each and every page.

"Rows to repeat at top" is where you specify what row(s) is your header row. Click in that box and then click on the row number in your worksheet that you want to have repeat at the top of each page.

The second valuable thing you can do here is set a column(s) you want to repeat on the left-hand side of each page. I need this one less often, but I do still sometimes use it. Say, for example, that you had a list of students, one per row, and their test scores across fifty tests, and that when you printed that information it printed across two pages. Well, without listing the student's name in the left-hand column on every page, you wouldn't know whose scores you were looking at after the first page. So you'd need to set that name column to repeat on each page.

To do so, click in the box that says "Columns to repeat at left", and then click on the letter for the column(s) you want to repeat on each page.

You'll see that Excel converts your choices to standard notation, so if you feel comfortable enough you can just type it in yourself, but I almost never do.

Do be careful if you're going to choose more than one row or column to repeat that you don't end up selecting so many rows or columns that you basically just print the same thing over and over and over again.

CONCLUSION

There you have it. A beginner's guide to Excel. This wasn't meant to be a comprehensive guide to Excel, but to instead give you the basics you need to do 95% of what you'll ever want to do in Excel. I hope it did that.

If something wasn't clear or you have any questions, please feel free to reach out to me at mlhumphreywriter@gmail.com. I don't check that email daily, but I do check it regularly and am happy to help.

Also, if there was something I didn't cover that you want to know about, the Microsoft website has a number of tutorials and examples that I think are very well-written and easy to follow at www.suppport.office.com. I usually find what I need with a quick internet search for something like "bold text Excel 2013" and then choose the Microsoft link

I find their web-based help much more useful than the Help options available within Excel, but you can try those, too. Click on the question mark in the top right corner and search for what you need. Or you can hold your mouse over the tasks listed on the various tabs and you'll usually see a brief description of what the item does. A lot of the descriptions also have a "tell me more" link at the bottom of the description that will take you directly to the help screen related to that item.

If you want to explore more advanced uses of Excel and liked the way I present information, then check out *Intermediate Excel* which explores topics such as pivot tables, charts, conditional formatting, IF functions, and a lot more. (The full list is included in the introduction to the book.)

I've also published a few hands-on guides that might interest you.

The *Juggling Your Finances: Basic Excel Primer* focuses on how to use addition, subtraction, division, and multiplication to manage your personal finances and walks you through a number of sample calculations. The focus there is just on those four functions and how to use them.

Excel for Writers and *Excel for Self-Publishers* are geared towards writers and assume that you're comfortable with Excel. They walk users through exactly how to create things like a word count and time tracker or a two-variable analysis grid right down to how to format the cells to match the examples and what each formula needs to be in each cell. Sometimes the challenge with Excel is in figuring out how to use it to do what you want and that's what those guides cover.

Again, if there's something specific you want to know how to do, just ask. Happy to point you in the right direction.

And thanks for reading this guide. Excel is an incredibly powerful tool and now that you have the foundation you need to use it effectively, I hope you'll see just how incredible it can be.

Also, if you want to test your knowledge of this material check out *The Excel for Beginners Quiz Book* which contains quizzes for each section of this book as well as five exercises that will allow you to apply what you've learned here in real-world scenarios.

Intermediate Excel

EXCEL ESSENTIALS BOOK 2

M.L. HUMPHREY

CONTENTS

INTRODUCTION

In *Excel for Beginners* we covered almost all of what you need to know to work in Excel on a daily basis. But there are additional things that I use Excel for that weren't covered there, mostly because I think sometime it just gets overwhelming when you're trying to learn something new to have everything thrown at you all at once. So the beginner's guide was meant to let you master the basics. Things like how to input data, how to format it, some basic ways to manipulate it, and how to print the results.

In this guide, which I'm calling *Intermediate Excel*, we're going to take all of that base knowledge one step further. It still doesn't cover all of Excel, but by the time we're done here I think you'll know 98% of what you'll ever want to know about Excel and probably some that you never wanted to know.

So what specifically are we going to cover?

1. Conditional Formatting
2. Inserting Symbols
3. Pivot Tables
4. Subtotaling and Grouping Data
5. Charts
6. Removing Duplicate Entries
7. Converting Text to Columns
8. The CONCATENATE function
9. The IF function
10. The COUNTIFS function
11. The SUMIFS function
12. The TEXT function
13. How to Limit the Input Choices in a Cell
14. Locking Cells or Worksheets
15. Hiding a Worksheet
16. Creating a Two Variable Analysis Grid

Also, we'll discuss how to find the answer when you want to do something I haven't covered. (I suspect that will mostly occur when you're dealing with a specific function since there are hundreds of them and I'm only covering the ones I use most often.)

This isn't a hands-on guide like *Excel for Writers*, *Excel for Self-Publishers*, or the *Juggling Your Finances Basic Excel Primer*. We're not going to put these techniques to real-world use or build the worksheets I show you as examples. But there will be lots of screenshots so you can see exactly how it all works and, me being the talkative person I am, I'll mention for each one how I've used it in the past or am currently using it.

One more thing to point out before we begin. This guide is written using Excel 2013. If you're using a version of Excel prior to Excel 2007 some of what I'm going to cover will not be available to you or it will work differently. This wasn't as much of an issue with *Excel for Beginners* as it is here, so even if you managed to get through that guide with an older version of Excel, you may not make it through this one without challenges. For example, the COUNTIFS and SUMIFS functions were introduced with Excel 2007 and Pivot Tables and Charts have definitely become easier to use in newer versions of Excel.

Alright. Let's review our basic terminology and then we'll dive into the fun stuff.

BASIC TERMINOLOGY

Column

Excel uses columns and rows to display information. Columns run across the top of the worksheet and, unless you've done something funky with your settings, are identified using letters of the alphabet.

Row

Rows run down the side of the worksheet and are numbered starting at 1 and up to a very high number.

Cell

A cell is a combination of a column and row that is identified by the letter of the column it's in and the number of the row it's in. For example, Cell A1 is the cell in the first column and first row of a worksheet.

Click

If I tell you to click on something, that means to use your mouse (or trackpad) to move the arrow on the screen over to a specific location and left-click or right-click on the option. (See the next definition for the difference between left-click and right-click).

If you left-click, this selects the item. If you right-click, this generally creates a dropdown list of options to choose from. If I don't tell you which to do, left- or right-click, then left-click.

Left-click/Right-click

If you look at your mouse or your trackpad, you generally have two flat buttons to press. One is on the left side, one is on the right. If I say left-click that means to press down on the button on the left.

If I say right-click that means press down on the button on the right. (If you're used to using Word or Excel you may already do this without even thinking about it. So, if that's the case then think of left-click as what you usually use to select text and right-click as what you use to see a menu of choices.)

Spreadsheet

I'll try to avoid using this term, but if I do use it, I'll mean your entire Excel file. It's a little confusing because it can sometimes also be used to mean a specific worksheet, which is why I'll try to avoid it as much as possible.

Worksheet

This is the term I'll use as much as possible. A worksheet is a combination of rows and columns that you can enter data in. When you open an Excel file, it opens to worksheet one.

Formula Bar

This is the long white bar at the top of the screen with the $f\chi$ symbol next to it.

Tab

I refer to the menu choices at the top of the screen (File, Home, Insert, Page Layout, Formulas, Data, Review, and View) as tabs. Note how they look like folder tabs from an old-time filing system when selected? That's why.

Data

I use data and information interchangeably. Whatever information you put into a worksheet is your data.

Select

If I tell you to "select" cells, that means to highlight them.

Arrow

If I say that you can "arrow" to something that just means to use the arrow keys to navigate from one cell to another.

A1:A25

If I'm going to reference a range of cells, I'll use the shorthand notation that Excel uses in its formulas. So, for example, A1:A25 will mean Cells A1 through A25. If you ever don't understand exactly what I'm referring to, you can type it into a cell in Excel using the = sign and see what cells Excel highlights. So, =A1:A25 should highlight cells A1 through A25 and =A1:B25 should highlight the cells in columns A and B and rows 1 through 25.

With Formulas Visible

Normally Excel doesn't show you the formula in a cell unless you click on that cell and then you only see the formula in the formula bar. But to help you see what I'm referring to, some of the screenshots in this guide will be provided with formulas visible. All this means is that I clicked on Show Formulas on the Formulas tab so that you could see what cells have formulas in them and what those formulas are.

Unless you do the same, your worksheet will not look like that. That's okay. Because you don't need to have your formulas visible unless you're troubleshooting something that isn't working.

Dialogue Box

I will sometimes reference a dialogue box. These are the boxes that occasionally pop up with additional options for you to choose from for that particular task. Usually I include a screen shot so you know what it should look like.

Paste Special – Values

I will sometimes suggest that you paste special-values. What this means is to paste your data using the Values option under Paste Options (the one with 123 on the clipboard). This will paste the values from the cells you copied without also bringing over any of the formulas that created those values.

Dropdown

I will occasionally refer to a dropdown or dropdown menu. This is generally a list of potential choices that you can select from. The existence of the list is indicated by an arrow next to the first available selection. I will occasionally refer to the list of options you see when you click on a dropdown arrow as the dropdown menu.

CONDITIONAL FORMATTING

Alright then. Let's dive right in with a conversation about conditional formatting.

What is it and why would you want to use it?

At its most basic, conditional formatting is a set of rules you can apply to your data that help you see when certain criteria have been met. I, for example, use it in my budget worksheet where I list my bank account values. I have minimum balance requirements on my checking and savings accounts, so both of the cells where I list those values are set up with conditional formatting that will color those cells red if the balance in either account drops below the minimum requirement. This helps remind me of those requirements, because I'm not always thinking about it when I move money around.

Conditional formatting is also useful when you have a set of data and want to easily flag certain results as good or bad. You can combine conditional formatting with filtering so that you first apply your conditional formatting to your data to color the ones you want to focus on and then filter the data using Cell Color or Font Color.

The easiest way to see how conditional formatting works is to walk through an example.

	A	B	C	D	E	F	G	H	I	J
1	Sale Price	$ 4.99				Conditional Formatting (Red<$1500, Green>$3500)				
2	Payout	70%								
3						Monthly Sales Per Title				
4						15	30	60	150	250
5					1	$ 52.40	$ 104.79	$ 209.58	$ 523.95	$ 873.25
6					2	$104.79	$ 209.58	$ 419.16	$1,047.90	$ 1,746.50
7					3	$157.19	$ 314.37	$ 628.74	$1,571.85	$ 2,619.75
8					4	$209.58	$ 419.16	$ 838.32	$2,095.80	$ 3,493.00
9					5	$261.98	$ 523.95	$1,047.90	$2,619.75	$ 4,366.25
10					6	$314.37	$ 628.74	$1,257.48	$3,143.70	$ 5,239.50
11					7	$366.77	$ 733.53	$1,467.06	$3,667.65	$ 6,112.75
12					8	$419.16	$ 838.32	$1,676.64	$4,191.60	$ 6,986.00
13					9	$471.56	$ 943.11	$1,886.22	$4,715.55	$ 7,859.25
14					10	$523.95	$1,047.90	$2,095.80	$5,239.50	$ 8,732.50
15										
16										

(Column C, rotated text: Number of Titles)

This one is pulled from *Excel for Self-Publishers* and is a two-variable analysis grid that looks at the various combinations of number of titles and monthly units sold per title to project a monthly income number. (It actually uses four variables because it's set up so you can also change the assumed list price and payout in the top left corner, but the grid itself is comparing the combinations of titles and number sold. We'll talk about how to build a generic two-variable grid like this one later.)

I've applied conditional formatting to the results to flag in red any cell where the monthly income would be less than $1,500 and to flag in green any cell where the monthly income would be over $3,500.

To color the cells green if the amount is over $3,500, I highlighted the cells I wanted to apply conditional formatting to (in this case E5:I14), then went to the Styles section of the Home tab and clicked on the dropdown arrow next to Conditional Formatting. I then choose Highlight Cells Rules and Greater Than.

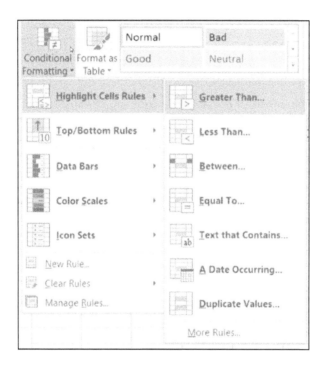

This brought up the Greater Than dialogue box where I entered 3500 in the left-hand field and chose Green Fill with Dark Green Text from the right-hand dropdown.

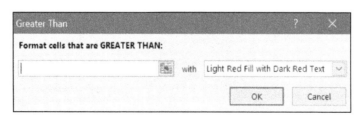

After I clicked OK any cell where the value was greater than $3,500 was colored green with green text.

To color the cells red if the amount was under $1,500 I did the same thing except I chose Less Than under Highlight Cells Rules and entered 1500 in the left-hand field of the Less Than dialogue box..

To sum it up: Highlight your cells, go to the Styles section of the Home tab, click on Conditional Formatting, choose the option you want, set your parameter, and choose your desired formatting.

With the Highlight Cells Rules, you can set parameters using Greater Than, Less Than, Between, Equal To, Text that Contains, A Date Occurring, or to flag Duplicate Values.

I should note that the duplicate values option doesn't discriminate between different values. So if you have a 7, 8, and 9 repeated twice in a list it will color all of the 7s, 8s, and 9s in the list the same color. (We'll talk later about how to remove duplicate values from a list if you need to.)

The date option is a bit odd as well. It lets you flag a date occurring yesterday, today, tomorrow, in the last seven days, last week, this week, next week, last month, this month, or next month. Depending on what you want to use it for, those options could be very useful or very limited.

With the highlight cells rules I usually stick with the default formatting options of Light Red Fill with Dark Red Text, Yellow Fill with Dark Yellow Text, Green Fill with Dark Green Text, Light Red Fill, Red Text, or Red Border. But note that there is also an option at the bottom of that dropdown menu to apply a custom format. When you click on that option it brings up the Format Text dialogue box. With that you can basically format the cell however you want. I was just able to choose to format my text with a purple font and in italics.

There are other options available to you other than the Highlight Cells Rules. The next one on the list is Top/Bottom Rules. You can format values that fall in the top X of your range, the bottom X of your range, the top X% of your range, the bottom X% of your range, above the average for the range, or below the average for the range. (While the options are labeled Top 10 Items, Top 10%, etc. when you click on them you'll see that you can adjust the number to whatever you want to use.)

The next option you have is to add Data Bars to your cells. With data bars, the higher the value, the longer the bar within the cell. It creates a quick visual representation of relative value.

Color Scales are another way to show the relative value of cells within a range. With Color Scales the color moves from red for smaller values through yellow and to green for the larger values.

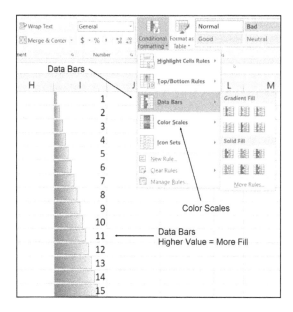

In the Data Bars example above, I had the values in order so you could easily see the bars getting bigger as the numbers increased in size. Here's an example of Data Bars and Color Scales with the data in order versus in a random configuration:

I	J	K	L	M
Ordered By Size			Random Order	
Data Bars	Color Scales		Data Bars	Color Scales
1	1		1	1
2	2		2	2
3	3		5	5
4	4		9	9
5	5		10	10
6	6		11	11
7	7		12	12
8	8		6	6
9	9		7	7
10	10		8	8
11	11		13	13
12	12		14	14
13	13		3	3
14	14		4	4

Your last option is Icon Sets which insert a colored symbol into each cell based on its relative value within the range. (See image below for an Icon Set that uses a non-filled, half-filled, or fully-filled star to demonstrate relative value.)

If you want to use Data Bars, Color Scales, or Icon Sets but you want to set absolute limits for when a color is applied (as opposed to letting Excel look at the data and divide it equally), you can do so by highlighting the cells you've applied the conditional formatting to and going to Manage Rules under Conditional Formatting in the Styles section of the Home tab and then choosing Edit Rule. This will let you set the parameters for each criteria.

In the examples below you can see that I've edited the default criteria:

You can always remove any conditional formatting from a range of cells or a worksheet by going to the Conditional Formatting dropdown, choosing Clear Rules, and then choosing to clear all rules from a range of cells or from the entire worksheet.

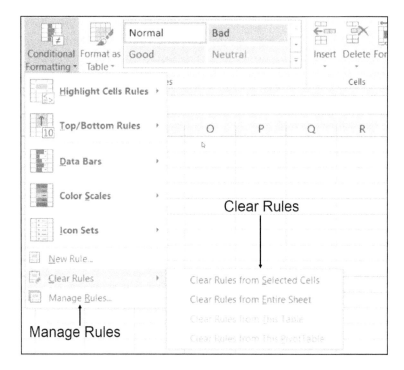

If you think there might be conditional formatting you want to keep and you just want to remove one rule, go to Manage Rules instead, which will show you all of the conditional formatting rules that are in place on the worksheet. (You can choose to display all rules for the worksheet using the dropdown at the top of the dialogue box.)

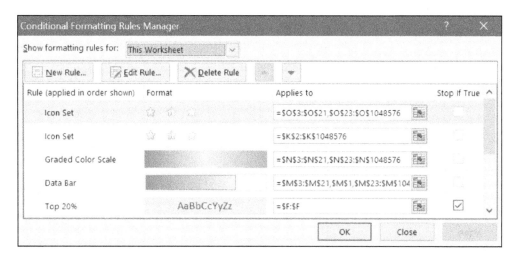

You can also change the order of the rules, edit them, or create new ones from here.

Be careful if you have multiple rules running that could conflict with one another that they're set to run in the correct order and that you've considered whether or not to check the "Stop if True" box. (If that box is checked, then the minute that criteria is met in that cell, none of your other rules will run on that cell.)

And, last but not least, you can also go to New Rule from the Conditional Formatting dropdown to add any type of rule you want to add, including all of the ones we just discussed. This will bring up the New Formatting Rule dialogue box. It's probably the best place to go to create complex rules with custom parameters, but it won't be as user-friendly as the dropdowns. (Like with all things in Excel, the options you can access from the dropdowns on the tabs are what you'll need most often, the dialogue boxes are where you go to do everything else.)

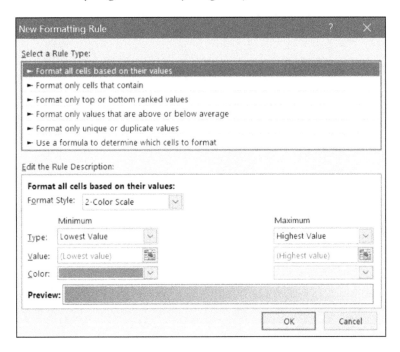

Finding which option you want will be the biggest challenge, but after that it's just a matter of making your choices from the dropdowns and specifying your limits and thresholds in the provided fields.

Now on to something much simpler: Inserting Symbols.

INSERTING SYMBOLS

This doesn't come up often, which is why I included it in this book instead of the beginner book. But I do occasionally want to insert a symbol into a field. For example, maybe I want to use the € sign for Euros or the £ sign for British Pounds. There are shortcuts you can type that will insert them, but I don't do it often enough to know them.

Another time I've used symbols is in my tracking of my short story submissions which I covered in *Excel for Writers*. In that case I used stars and exes to indicate which stories had received personal rejections from a market and which had received form rejections.

Inserting a symbol is a very straight-forward process. You can either insert a symbol into its own cell or as part of text within a cell. Like this:

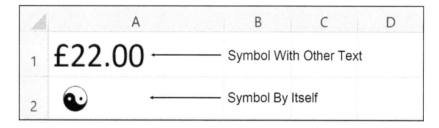

In Cell A1 I inserted a symbol and then clicked into the cell and typed my additional text. (I could've just as easily done so in the opposite order.) In Cell A2 I simply inserted my chosen symbol.

Once a symbol is there, you can treat it just like text and change the font size or the font color. DO NOT change the font, though. For a lot of these that's what determines the symbol you're seeing. For example, that yin yang symbol is actually what a [looks like in the Wingdings font.

So how do you do this?

Simple. First, click into the cell where you want to add the symbol. (If there's already text in that cell, then click into the spot within that text in the formula bar where you want to add the symbol.) Next, go to the Insert tab and click on Symbol in the Symbols section. This will bring up the Symbol dialogue box:

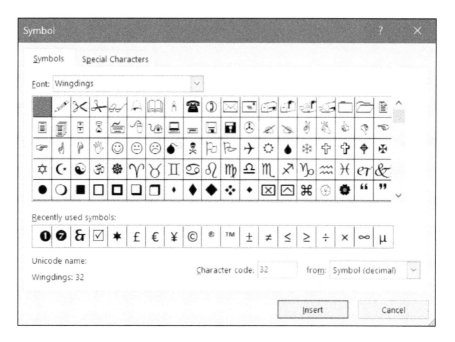

If you've recently used the symbol you're looking for it will be under Recently Used Symbols at the bottom of the dialogue box. Otherwise, you can scroll through the displayed symbols which will give you most language-based symbols like Greek and Coptic, Cyrillic, Armenian, Hebrew, and Arabic as well as currency symbols and arrows and a lot of other basic choices.

If that doesn't have what you're looking for, change the Font in the dropdown menu. Wingdings fonts are the ones that tend to have images like scissors, mailboxes, smiley faces, Zodiac symbols, etc.

Note that there's also a Special Characters tab where you can find things like the copyright symbol, trademark symbol, and paragraph symbol.

When you find what you're looking for, click on the symbol so that it's highlighted and then click on Insert at the bottom of the dialogue box. In the cell where you inserted the symbol you will see the symbol as an image, but in the formula bar it will appear as the normal text symbol it is in a font like Times New Roman. So for example, below I inserted an asterisk but in the font Ennobled Pet. In the Cell it appears as a paw print with an asterisk in the center. In the formula bar you just see the asterisk.

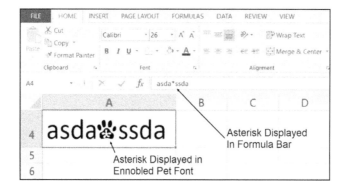

That's it. It's that simple. Just remember that a lot of the symbols you'll insert are driven by the font choice, so if you do insert symbols into your file be very careful about using the Format Painter or selecting all and changing the font, because you may end up erasing any symbol you inserted.

PIVOT TABLES

Alright. Now that we had a breather, let's dive back into one of the most useful things you can do in Excel, which is create a pivot table of your data. A pivot table takes rows and rows of data and puts it into nice summary reports based on the criteria you set. I use these all the time. If you only learn one thing from this guide, let it be pivot tables.

If you're self-published, they're great for summarizing the Amazon daily and monthly sales reports. In less than a minute you can see what sales you have by title or how much you've earned in each currency or how many page reads you've had. I also use it to see my ad spend by title, month, or author.

If you're not self-published, pivot tables can be used on any listing of data where you have more than one entry per customer or product or whatever. So, say you run a small business and had 1,000 sales this year and now you want to know who your best customer was and all you have is those 1,000 entries. You could sort by customer and then manually add up sales for each one, which could take hours. Or you could create a pivot table that calculates total sales for each customer and then sort to see who's at the top and be done in less than five minutes.

Sounds great, right? So how do they work? What do you do?

First, you need your information organized in the right format. There needs to be one row that contains the labels for each column. (I sometimes call this the header row.) Directly below that you need to list your information with one row per entry and nothing else other than the data.

The mistake a lot of people make (and Amazon used to do with their monthly reports which they have now fortunately changed) is that they'll list information in one row and then below that row list a subset of information. So maybe Row 5 is the customer information and then below that they list the transactions for that customer in Rows 6-10 and then Row 11 is another row of customer information and below that are the transactions for that customer.

The problem with that approach is that you can't easily manipulate that data. You can't sort it, filtering it is a challenge, you can't use pivot tables with it, and you can't create charts from it either. It's information that's there for display purposes not analysis.

Don't do that.

At least not in your source worksheet.

Always have one place where you simply list your information. You can then use that worksheet to create your summary reports and analysis. But always have that one document that is just the information.

Also be sure not to have any blank rows or columns in your data set and to have only one type of data (date, currency, text) per column. (Blank rows aren't a deal-breaker, but Excel will treat them as valid sources of data so you'll end up with blank entries in your summary tables. Blank columns will generate an error message when you try to create the pivot table.)

To understand the proper way to display your data, let's look at an example:

	A	B	C	D
1		**BAD DATA LAYOUT**		
2	**Albert Jones**			
3		8/1/2015	1 widget, 1 other	$25.00
4		8/30/2015	10 widgets	$250.00
5		9/1/2015	3 whatchamacallits	$45.00
6				
7	**Richard Martinez**			
8		3/7/2016	10 who knows what	$35.00
9		4/7/2016	20 whatsits	$30.00

G	H	I	J	K	L
	GOOD DATA LAYOUT				
Customer	Date of Transaction	Quantity	Item	Unit Price	Total
Albert Jones	8/1/2015	1	Widget	$ 20.00	$ 20.00
Albert Jones	8/1/2015	1	Other	$ 5.00	$ 5.00
Albert Jones	8/30/2015	10	Widget	$ 25.00	$ 250.00
Albert Jones	9/1/2015	3	Whatchamacallit	$ 15.00	$ 45.00
Richard Martinez	3/7/2016	10	Who knows what	$ 3.50	$ 35.00
Richard Martinez	4/7/2016	20	Whasit	$ 1.50	$ 30.00

On the top is a display of information that you can't do anything with. Look at customer Albert Jones. How many units has he bought total? How many widgets vs. whatchamacallits? And overall, how many widgets have you sold this year? And to whom? You'd have to physically calculate those numbers because of the way they were recorded. (This is fine for a final report, but it shouldn't be how you store that information initially.)

In contrast, look at the bottom example. It's the same information. But now if we want to know how many widgets Mr. Jones has bought we can just filter that list by customer and widget. (Or we can create a pivot table which we'll do in a moment.) Same with overall number of units sold for the year. Just add a quick formula and you have your answer.

So what are the rules? How should you structure your data to get the most use out of it?

To the extent you can, when you're listing information, have a separate column for anything you might want to analyze or use to separate your data. So here, for example, we have customer name, date, and item in separate columns, because we may want to use those to separate our data. We also have quantity of each item, unit price, and total paid in separate columns because we might want to use each of those values to calculate numbers such as how much customers spend or how much they pay per unit on average.

Also, try to standardize entries to the extent you can. (Later we'll talk about using data validation to limit the allowed values within a cell.) A widget should always be called a widget. Don't let it be called a blue widget sometimes and a red widget other times or enter it as widget once and widgets the next time. (If colors matter, create a column for color or use a product code to distinguish the two.)

And don't have extra summary lines or columns mixed in with your raw data. So don't have a row inserted in the midst of your sales entries that totals up the values for Customer A. (All of that should happen in another worksheet. This should just be where you store your raw data.)

Use one row, ideally Row 1, to label each of your columns and identify what that column contains, and then one row for each transaction with all the details you want to track in that one row. This may mean you repeat information, such as customer name in multiple rows. That's fine. (Just be sure it's standardized and Customer A is always written the same way.)

The analysis you can perform depends one hundred percent on how you structure your data.

Okay, then. Assuming you have a good set of data to work with, it's time to create a pivot table.

Highlight your data. (If it's the entire worksheet, you can Select All by clicking in the top left corner. If the data starts lower down in the worksheet, be sure to highlight the header row as well as the data rows.)

Go to the Insert tab and choose Pivot Table.

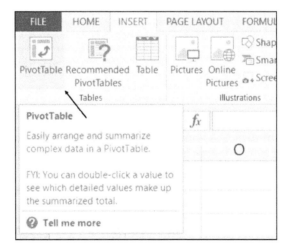

Choose to add your Pivot Table to a new worksheet. (I always do this because I don't want my source data and my pivot table to interfere with one another.) After you do so, you should see a blank pivot table on the left-hand side and a listing of the available pivot table fields on the right-hand side.

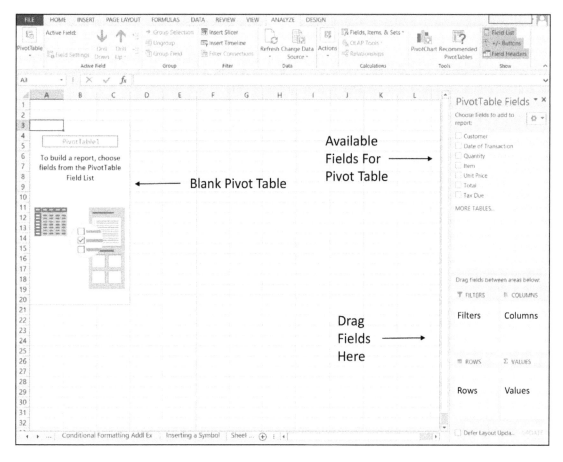

Click on the name of each of the fields you want to use and either drag each field to the table on the left or to the area in the bottom right corner where it says "Drag fields between areas below." I prefer to drag them downward, but both ways work.

In this example I dragged Customer to the Rows section and Quantity and Total to the Values section. This gave me a pivot table where I could see quantity bought and total paid by customer.

	A	B	C
1			
2			
3	**Row Labels**	**Sum of Quantity**	**Sum of Total**
4	Albert Jones	15	$320.00
5	Richard Martinez	30	$65.00
6	**Grand Total**	**45**	**$385.00**
7			

For any field you drag to the Values section, be sure that the correct function is being performed on the data. I have some data sets (Amazon's) that I work with where the default is to Count numbers instead of Sum them. If you need to change the function being performed on the data, click on the arrow next to the field name and choose Value Field Settings.

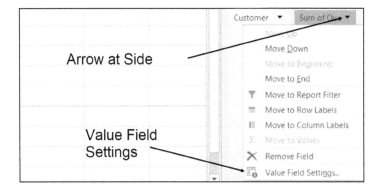

This will bring up the Value Field Settings dialogue box where you can choose to display the results as a Sum, Count, Average, Minimum, Maximum, Product, Count Numbers, or Standard Deviation. You can also choose on the Show Values As tab to show the result as a % of the Grand Total, % of the Column Total, % of the Row Total, and many other options.

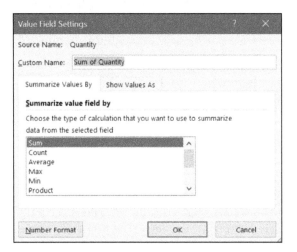

In the Value Field Settings dialogue box you can also choose how to format the values in that column of the table by clicking on the Number Format box at the bottom. (You can also format the cells by highlighting them and using the Number section of the Home tab to choose your format or by highlighting them, right-clicking, and choosing Format Cells.) In this example, I've set up the Quantity column to display as % of Column and formatted the Total column as Currency.

If you want to perform two (or more) calculations with the same field, just add it more than once and specify for each instance the function you want performed.

You can also add variables to go across the top of the table as well. Below I've added Item into the Columns section of the pivot table. Since I had two entries listed in the Values section, it creates two columns for each Item.

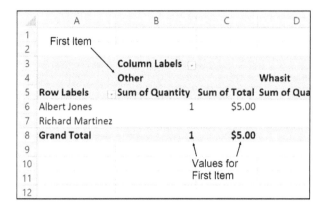
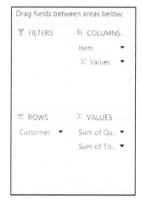

If you don't like the order that your entries are in, you can right-click on an entry and use the Move option to change the display order. You can do this within the values for each variable (so I could move Other to the end in the above example) or when you have multiple column or row variables.

If I remove Unit Price from Values, then it's a much simpler table to view. Here we have Item across the top, customer down the side, and the units of each item bought by each customer in the table:

Sum of Quantity	Column Labels					
Row Labels	Other	Whasit	Whatchamacallit	Who knows what	Widget	Grand Total
Albert Jones	1		3		11	15
Richard Martinez		20		10		30
Grand Total	1	20	3	10	11	45

You can also filter the results in your pivot table so that it's specific to a subset of your data. To apply a filter, you move the field you want to filter by into the Filters section and then choose the values you want from the drop down menu. Uncheck any values you don't want included in the table.

For example, here I moved Item to the Filters section and then unchecked all items except Whatchamacallits. (The easy way to do this is click the box next to (All) so that all values are unselected and then choose the one you want.)

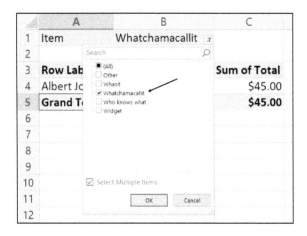

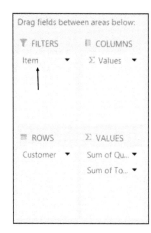

There are a number of other things you can do with pivot tables using the Analyze tab under PivotTable Tools. (If you aren't seeing PivotTable Tools, click on the pivot table in the worksheet.)

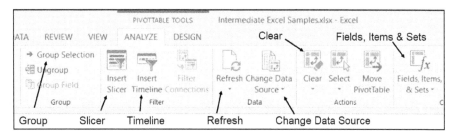

* * *

You can create an artificial grouping of entries by clicking on each of the items you want to include in the group while holding down the Ctrl key and then choosing Group Selection from the Group section of the Analyze tab. To remove a grouping, click on the Group name and then choose Ungroup.

Once you've grouped a set of results (say books in a series or related customer accounts), you can click on the minus sign next to the group name and that will hide the individual entries that make up that group and only display the totals for the group.

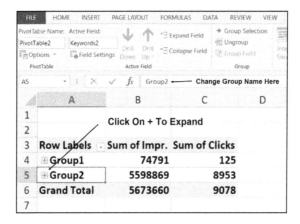

To rename a group, click on its name and then change the group name in the formula bar.

Clicking on Collapse Field in the Active Field section of the Analyze tab will collapse all grouped entries into their summary row. Clicking on Expand Field will expand all of them.

* * *

I've never used Insert Slicer before, but it seems to basically work like a filter option, without being a filter. So you can choose to insert a slicer, click on the field you want to slice by, and then click on the values for that field that appear in the slicer box and it will narrow your pivot table down to just the results that match that criteria. To undo your slice, click on the funnel image in the top right corner of that box.

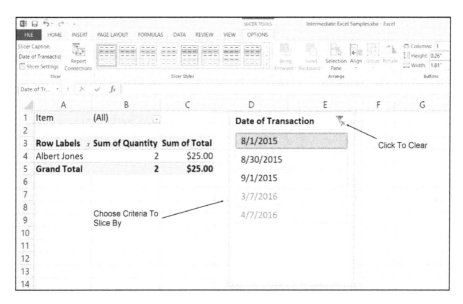

* * *

Insert Timeline is another one I've never used before. It appears to use any date provided in your data and let you narrow it down by month, quarter, year, or day. This is very handy for data where you have just the date (8/9/15) but want to see the data by month or year without having to add new fields to your original data source. (And certainly beats my old method of filtering by date and then checking/unchecking boxes.)

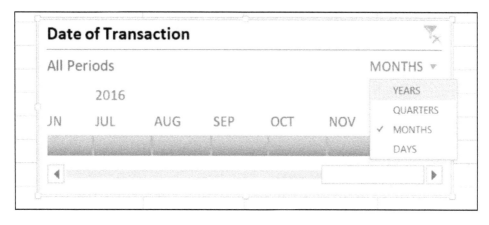

* * *

You can use Refresh to update the table if your source data changes. For example, you might find that customer Albert Jones was entered as Albert Jones and Albert R. Jones so is showing as two different entries. After you go back to your source data and update one of the entries, click on Refresh to have Excel regenerate the table to reflect the change.

* * *

You can also use Change Data Source to change the data the pivot table includes. For example, if you've added additional entries since it was last generated. Click on Change Data Source and then Change Data Source in the dropdown menu and it will take you to the page with your source data as well as highlight the cells contained in that range. The easiest way to update the range is to use your cursor to select all of the cells you want in range. If you have thousands of rows of data, you can select the top section of the data and then click into the box and change the final number to correspond to the last row of your data. (If you try just updating the cell references by typing in the data field, it sometimes gets messed up and tries adding cell ranges within your existing range, so I usually avoid that approach.)

* * *

If you want to keep the pivot table but start over fresh by removing all fields and settings, you can click on Clear, and choose Clear All. To clear just the filters you've applied to the table, click on Clear and choose Clear Filters.

* * *

If you want to add a new calculation to the table (for example, I usually want to place a dollar value on my page reads which requires multiplying them by a constant), you can do so using Fields, Items, & Sets. Click on it and choose Calculated Field. You'll see a dialogue box where you can name the field and build a calculation using existing fields and/or other numbers. Here I've calculated a tax due amount using a 5.75% tax:

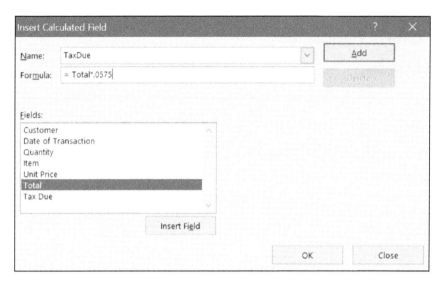

When you're done, click on OK. The field should be listed in your Pivot Table Fields and may already be shown in your table. If it isn't showing in your table, drag it to where you want it to be and change any value field settings you need to change. (So that, for example, it sums the values instead of counts them.)

* * *

The Design tab under Pivot Table Tools allows you to choose how the table displays. You can change the color, add a blank row after every entry in the table, choose when and how to display subtotals, choose when and how to display grand totals, and change the formatting of the row and column headers. It basically allows you a number of options to refine your table results to display according to your preferences. For example:

Customer	Item	Sum of Quantity	Sum of Total	Sum of Tax Due
Albert Jones	Other	1	$5.00	$ 0.29
	Whatchamacallit	3	$45.00	$ 2.59
	Widget	11	$270.00	$ 15.53
Richard Martinez	Whasit	20	$30.00	$ 1.73
	Who knows what	10	$35.00	$ 2.01
Grand Total		45	$385.00	$ 22.14

Here I've chosen to change the color, add a line between entries, display the column grand totals, not display subtotals or row totals, and I've kept the bolded row and column headers.

What else?

To remove a field you didn't want to add to the table, click on the arrow next to the field name in the bottom right corner and choose Remove Field. You can also right-click in a cell in a column in the table and choose Remove [Column] to remove a column from the table. Or right-click on a row value and choose Remove [Row] to remove a row from the table. (I use brackets there because the option will actually name the row or column you're allowed to delete. So, it'll say "Remove Units" for the Units variable.)

If you have multiple entries under Row, Column, or Values and want to change their order, left-click and drag the field to where you want it.

To undo something you just did and didn't like, click anywhere in the worksheet and use Ctrl + Z. (It won't work until you've clicked into the worksheet for whatever strange reason.)

One thing to be cautious of when working with pivot tables is that they're dynamic. The number of rows is not set and the number of columns can easily change based upon your choices of what to include or not include in the table. This is the reason I tend to build them as I need them but not keep them long-term. If you do set one up that you want to repeatedly run, which I can see doing if you get fancy with your settings, just be careful that (a) you always have all the data you want to include selected and (b) that you don't add other text or calculations around the table that could be overwritten or become inaccurate when the table is refreshed. (You'll see if you try to write a formula referencing an entry in a pivot table that it isn't just referencing that cell, it's referencing the pivot table and an entire subset of the data in the table based upon the listed criteria. So you might write a formula in Row 6 that corresponds to Customer Jones who is currently listed in Row 6 but then refresh your table and Customer Jones is now in Row 8 but the formula is still in Row 6 and still refers to Customer Jones.)

My advice if you want to do additional calculations on your data is to either copy the entire table and paste special-values and then do your analysis on that pasted table, or to build the calculations into the table itself as discussed above. Don't mix the two. Don't create a pivot table and then do external computations on those values while it's still a pivot table.

Alright.

Hopefully that was a good, solid beginning with respect to pivot tables. If you want to go further with them, your best bet is the Microsoft website at https://support.office.com.

(The big topic I didn't cover here is how to link multiple tables of data to create one pivot table. That's very close to what you do in Access, and it would probably require an entire book of its own. I muddle my way through in Access, but it's not something I'd feel comfortable teaching, so we're going to put that one under the heading Advanced Excel Topics, a book I will never write.)

SUBTOTALING AND GROUPING DATA

While pivot tables are a great way to analyze a table of data, they're not the only way. In a moment we'll talk about charts, which are a visual way of analyzing data. But first let's talk about something much more simple: the ability to subtotal data.

I like to use this for my monthly income numbers. I have a table that lists month, year, units sold, and amount earned. With subtotals I can easily take that listing and see what I earned and sold for each calendar year.

You could just as easily use subtotals to get summary information by customer or product.

The Subtotal option is located in the Outline section of the Data tab.

To subtotal your data, first sort it by the criteria you want to use to group your data. Here's our sample data:

	A	B	C	D
1	**Month**	**Year**	**Units**	**Amount Earned**
2	August	2013	1,234	$ 346.51
3	September	2013	2,345	$ 426.21
4	October	2013	3,456	$ 524.23
5	November	2013	23,454	$ 1,199.90
6	December	2013	24,565	$ 32,932.77
7	January	2014	25,676	$ 40,507.30
8	February	2014	26,787	$ 1,475.88
9	March	2014	4,567	$ 1,815.33
10	April	2014	5,678	$ 2,232.86
11	May	2014	6,789	$ 644.81
12	June	2014	7,900	$ 793.12
13	July	2014	13,455	$ 975.52

I want to subtotal my data by year, so I've sorted it to make sure that all of the 2013 entries are together, all the 2014 entries are together, and all the 2015 entries are together. (I actually sorted by year and then by month because I'm compulsively anal like that, but sorting by year was all that was needed.)

If you don't sort your data before you try to subtotal it, you'll end up with something like this when you do subtotal:

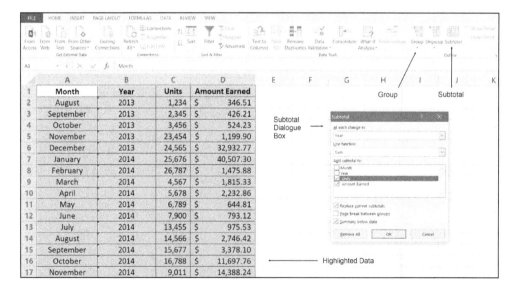

There are two entries for 2014 and 2015 because the data wasn't sorted by year, so I had a couple of rows of 2015 data interspersed with my 2014 data. Each time the year changed, Excel treated it as a new group.

So remember, with subtotals *you always need to sort your data first.*

Alright. Now that your data is sorted, select all the fields with data in them and click on Subtotal in the Outline section of the Data tab. This should bring up the Subtotal dialogue box.

First, under "at each change in" choose which column you want to group on using the dropdown menu to select that column's name. (You can have subtotals of multiple columns, but you can only group the data by one column.)

Next, choose what function you want to use for subtotaling the other columns. (Usually the function I want is Sum, but you can also choose Count, Average, Max, Min, Product, etc.)

Finally, under "add subtotal to" check which columns you want that function to be performed on. In this case, we want it to be for units and earnings.

Once you've done that, you can then choose whether you want each grouping to appear on its own page by checking the box for "page break between groups", whether you want the summary of the entire column at the very bottom by checking "summary below data", and (if you had existing subtotals), whether you want to replace any existing subtotals by checking "replace current subtotals."

Once you're satisfied with your choices, click OK.

You should end up with something like this:

	A	B	C	D
	Month	Year	Units	Amount Earned
1				
2	August	2013	1,234	$ 346.51
3	September	2013	2,345	$ 426.21
4	October	2013	3,456	$ 524.23
5	November	2013	23,454	$ 1,199.90
6	December	2013	24,565	$ 32,932.77
7		2013 Total	55,054	$ 35,429.62
8	January	2014	25,676	$ 40,507.30
9	February	2014	26,787	$ 1,475.88
10	March	2014	4,567	$ 1,815.33
11	April	2014	5,678	$ 2,232.86
12	May	2014	6,789	$ 644.81
13	June	2014	7,900	$ 793.12
14	July	2014	13,455	$ 975.53
15	August	2014	14,566	$ 2,746.42
16	September	2014	15,677	$ 3,378.10
17	October	2014	16,788	$ 11,697.76
18	November	2014	9,011	$ 14,388.24
19	December	2014	10,122	$ 17,697.54
20		2014 Total	157,016	$ 98,352.89
21	January	2015	11,233	$ 21,767.97
22	February	2015	12,344	$ 4,155.06
23	March	2015	17,899	$ 5,110.72
24	April	2015	19,010	$ 6,286.19
25	May	2015	20,121	$ 7,732.01
26	June	2015	21,232	$ 9,510.37
27	July	2015	22,343	$ 26,774.61
28		2015 Total	124,182	$ 81,336.93
29				

Group Levels

F8

See those numbered columns on the left-hand side? Those are your group levels. In the image above, we're looking at all of the rows of data.

If I click on the 2 in the top-left corner, I will only see one row per year without any of the detail rows showing. Like this:

	A	B	C	D
1	Month	Year	Units	Amount Earned
7		2013 Total	55,054	$ 35,429.62
20		2014 Total	157,016	$ 98,352.89
28		2015 Total	124,182	$ 81,336.93
29		Grand Total	336,252	$ 215,119.45
30				

And if I were to click on the 1 I would only see the Grand Total row. What we've done here is taken a table of data and grouped it by year and subtotaled the units sold and earnings for each of those years.

To remove subtotals, go back to the Subtotal option and click on Remove All in the Subtotal dialogue box.

If you want to keep the subtotals, but remove the groupings on the left-hand side, you can either click on Ungroup in the Outline section of the Data tab and then select Ungroup once more. (This will remove one level of grouping at a time.) Or you can click on Ungroup and then choose Clear Outline, which will remove all levels of grouping.

* * *

Alright, that was Subtotals. Now on to Groups.

The Group option allows you to group rows or columns so that you can easily hide them or show them once again by simply clicking a plus or minus sign.

This is similar to hiding columns or rows in terms of what it does, but it's much more useful for situations where you have columns or rows that you'll be routinely hiding and unhiding.

So how to do it:

The columns or rows you group have to be adjacent. (So this doesn't work the same as with pivot tables.)

Select all of the rows or columns you want grouped, choose Group from the Outline section of the Data tab, and then choose Group again from the dropdown.

When you've successfully grouped columns or rows you'll see a section above or to the side of the worksheet with numbers for each group level and a minus sign. (If you close the group, that minus sign will become a plus sign.)

Here I've grouped my first two columns and you can see the minus sign above them when they're visible and the plus sign above Column C when they're not. You can hide or unhide those columns by clicking on the plus or minus sign. It's that easy.

	A	B	C	D
1	**Month**	**Year**	**Units**	**Amount Earned**
2	August	2013	1,234	$ 346.51
3	September	2013	2,345	$ 426.21
4	October	2013	3,456	$ 524.23
5	November	2013	23,454	$ 1,199.90
6	December	2013	24,565	$ 32,932.77

← Click To Hide Group

	C	D	E
1	**Units**	**Amount Earned**	
2	1,234	$ 346.51	
3	2,345	$ 426.21	
4	3,456	$ 524.23	
5	23,454	$ 1,199.90	
6	24,565	$ 32,932.77	

← Click To Show Group

To remove all grouping from a worksheet use Clear Outline under Ungroup in the Outline section of the Data tab.

One final note: Ctrl + Z and Ctrl + Y did not always work for me when I was subtotaling and grouping data while writing this section. I had two Excel files open at the time and when I tried to undo something related to subtotaling or grouping it sometimes undid something in the other worksheet instead of the subtotaling or grouping I'd just done. So my advice is use the Remove All and Clear Outline options instead when dealing with subtotaling and grouping.

CHARTS – DISCUSSION OF TYPES

Charts are a great way to visualize your data. There's nothing like a nice bar chart or pie chart to see exactly what's going on. You know what they say, a picture's worth a thousand words. And seeing one big chunk of color dominating all the others tells you everything you need to know about who your best customer is or what your biggest expense is.

Just like with pivot tables, your data needs to be arranged properly before you can use charts. Specifically, for most of the charts we're going to discuss, you need one set of labels across the top and one set down the side with values listed in the cells where those two intersect.

Here are two examples:

	G	H	I	J	K	L	M	N	O	P	Q	R	S	T
		DATA TABLE OPTION 1								DATA TABLE OPTION 2				
		Amazon	Createspace	ACX	Con Sales				201701	201702	201703	201704	201705	201706
201701		$100.00	$37.00	$23.50	$10.00			Amazon	$100.00	$107.00	$114.49	$122.50	$131.08	$140.26
201702		$107.00	$39.59	$25.15				Createspace	$37.00	$39.59	$42.36	$45.33	$48.50	$51.89
201703		$114.49	$42.36	$26.91				ACX	$23.50	$25.15	$26.91	$28.79	$30.80	$32.96
201704		$122.50	$45.33	$28.79	$25.00			Con Sales	$10.00			$25.00		$8.00
201705		$131.08	$48.50	$30.80										
201706		$140.26	$51.89	$32.96	$8.00									

This is fictitious sales data for each month for various sales platforms. In the first example, the sales channels are listed across the top and the months are listed along the side with the intersection of those two showing the dollar value of sales for that sales channel for that period.

In the second example, each month is listed across the top and each of the sales channels is listed down the side.

(My version of Excel will work with your data in either configuration, but I'm pretty sure that's not how it used to be.)

To create a chart from your data, highlight the cells that contain your labels and values. In the examples above that would either be G1:K7 or M1:S5.

Go to the Insert tab and click on the Chart type you want. (See next section for a detailed discussion of chart types.) As soon as you place your mouse over each chart selection you'll see the chart appear. When you click on that selection, the chart will be inserted into your worksheet.

We'll discuss each chart type in detail next, but the general rule is that for time series data like the examples above that include multiple variables (your sales channels) across multiple time periods (each month), the best choices are column charts, bar charts, and line charts. For data where you have multiple variables but no time component, a better choice is a pie or doughnut chart. Scatter charts are good for random data points where you're looking at the intersection of two or three variables to see if there's any sort of relationship between them.

Excel does offer additional chart types like bubble charts and radar charts, but we're not going to cover them in this guide.

Okay, time to discuss Column Charts, Bar Charts, Line Charts, Pie and Doughnut Charts, and Scatter Charts in more detail.

Column Charts

The top-left chart option in the Charts section of the Insert tab is Column Charts. It's the image with the upright bars.

There are seven possible column charts that you can choose from, but I'm going to focus on the top set of choices, which are the 2-D versions since most of the 3-D versions are the same except three-dimensional.

For 2-D, you can choose from clustered columns, stacked columns, and 100% stacked columns. Here is an example of all three using the exact same data:

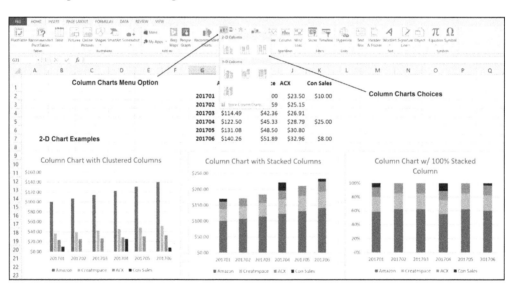

The difference between the clustered columns and the stacked columns is that the clustered columns version puts the results for each variable side-by-side for each time period. You can easily see the height difference between different results, but it can quickly become too busy if you're dealing with a large number of variables. For example, I have nine sales channels I track. Having nine columns side-by-side for each of twelve months would be overwhelming.

In that case, the stacked columns option is a better choice. Like with clustered columns, stacked columns have different column heights for each variable based on their value, but the columns are stacked one atop the other instead of side-by-side for each time period. So you end up with only one column per time period.

The stacked columns option lets you see the overall change from time period to time period based on the total height of the column.

The 100% stacked columns option presents all of the information in one column just like stacked columns does. But instead of basing each section's height on its value, it shows the variable's percentage share of the whole. While you lose any measurement of value (a column chart with values of 2:5:5 will look the exact same as one with values of 20:50:50 or 200:500:500), you can better see changes in percentage share for each variable. (A variable that goes from 10% share to 50% share will be clearly visible.)

As mentioned above, the first three 3-D column chart options are the same as the 2-D options. The only difference is that the bars are three-dimensional instead of two-dimensional. (And really that's more of a gimmick for Powerpoint presentations than anything else. Remember: Charts should be as clean and simple as you can make them while still presenting all necessary information.)

The final 3-D option is a more advanced chart type that creates a three-variable graph, and we're not going to cover that in this guide. (Consider it an Advanced Excel Topic.)

Bar Charts

Bar charts are the next chart type you see under the Charts section of the Insert tab. They're just like the column charts, except on their side, with a clustered, stacked, and 100% stacked option available in both two-dimensional and three-dimensional versions.

Here are examples of the 2-D versions:

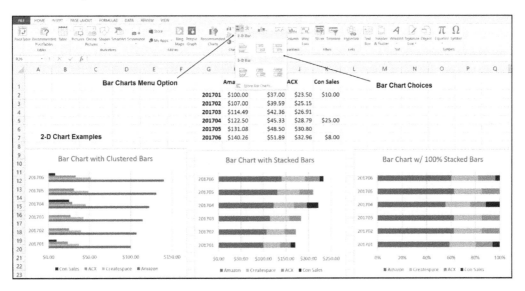

Line Charts

Line charts are the first chart type shown in the second row of choices. There are seven options listed, but you should only use the first choice on the left for each of the 2-D rows of choices.

This is because the other four 2-D options really aren't viable for a line graph. They're meant to do what the stacked columns graphs do and show relative values, but people just don't read line graphs that way. You expect that if there's a line drawn on a graph that it's showing actual values for that particular variable not relative values or cumulative values

The 3-D option is a more advanced chart type that creates an actual three-variable line graph and we're not going to cover it in this guide. (Consider it an Advanced Excel Topic.) You can use it to create a two-variable line graph with a three-dimensional line, but don't. Keep it simple.

Here are examples of the basic line chart and the line chart with markers:

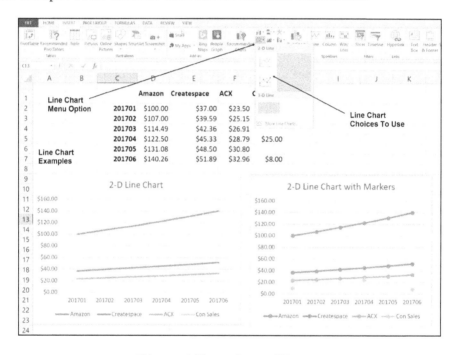

Pie and Doughnut Charts

Next we have pie and doughnut charts. These are best used when you have one set of variables for one period of time. So I've built the below examples using just the total values for each of the sales channels.

(To select a subset of your data, like I've done here, you can use Ctrl and your mouse to highlight just the sections you want before you choose your chart type. Or you can select all of the data, choose your chart type, and then go to Select Data and remove the data you don't want to use.)

There are three two-dimensional pie chart options and one doughnut chart option. The three-dimensional pie chart option is the same as the basic pie chart except in three-dimensions.

Here are examples of the two-dimensional pie charts and the doughnut chart:

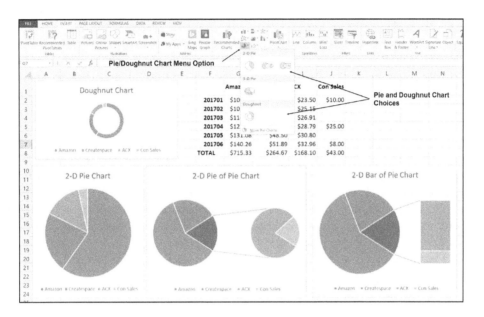

For the pie charts, you can choose between a standard pie chart, a pie of pie chart, or a bar of pie chart

If you're only focused on who or what accounts for the biggest share, then you should just use the standard pie chart or the doughnut chart.

If you want to be able to clearly see the results for all of your segments, even the smallest ones, then the pie of pie chart or the bar of pie chart are potentially better choices.

The pie of pie chart creates one main pie chart in which it combines a number of the smaller results to form one segment of the chart. It then breaks out those smaller results into their own pie chart where they each take up their proportion of that smaller part of the pie.

So, for example, in the sample we're seeing here, ACX and Con Sales were combined in the left-hand pie chart but were the only ones in the right-hand pie chart. In the left-hand chart, together they are 18% of the total. In the right-hand chart they are 78% and 22% *of that 18%*. (If you were to insert labels on this chart, the labels would be the share that each one had of the overall whole, so the smaller pie chart would show 14% and 4% as the labels. It's a bit confusing.)

The bar of pie chart does something similar except it creates a bar chart with the smaller values instead of a smaller pie chart. In order to avoid confusion, the bar of pie chart is probably the better choice of the two, but honestly I wouldn't use either one if you could avoid it. (The best charts can be read without explanation and I'm not sure that would be true for either of these for your average user.)

Scatter Charts

Scatter charts (or scatter plots) are the second option on the bottom row of the chart types.

Scatter charts plot the value of variable A given a value for variable B. For example, if I were trying to figure out if gravity is a constant, I might plot how long it takes for a ball to reach the ground when I drop it from varying heights. So I'd plot time vs. distance. From that I could eventually see that the results form a pattern which does indicate a constant. (Thanks high school physics teacher for making physics fun.)

There are five scatter plot options. The first one is a classic scatter plot. It takes variable A and plots it against variable B, creating a standalone data point for each observation. It doesn't care what order your entries are in, because there's no attempt to connect those entries to form a pattern.

The other four scatter plot options include lines drawn through each plotted point. The two smooth line options try to draw the best curved line between points. The straight line options just connect point 1 to point 2 to point 3 using straight lines between each point. The charts with markers show each of the data points on the line, the charts without markers do not.

Excel draws the line from the first set of coordinates you provide to the second to the third, etc. This introduces a time component into your data since the order you list the data points in impacts the appearance of the line. If you have data where the order of the measurements doesn't matter and you still want to draw a line through the points (like my example of dropping a ball from varying heights where it doesn't matter which height you drop it from first), then you'll want to sort your data by one of the variables before you create your scatter plot.

Here is an example of a scatter plot and a scatter plot with a line for five measurements of the time it takes for a ball dropped from different heights to reach the ground:

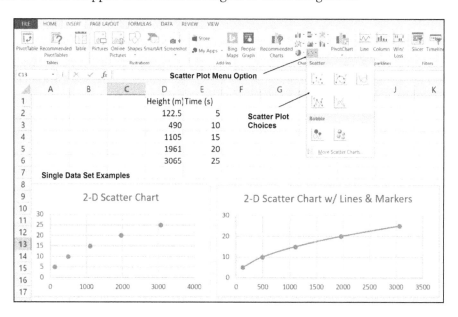

Because I sorted the data before I plotted it, we can see a nice trend line that indicates some sort of exponential relationship exists there.

You can also use scatter plots to chart more than one set of results. You just need to list the results side-by-side with the criteria you want as the horizontal axis listed first. Like this:

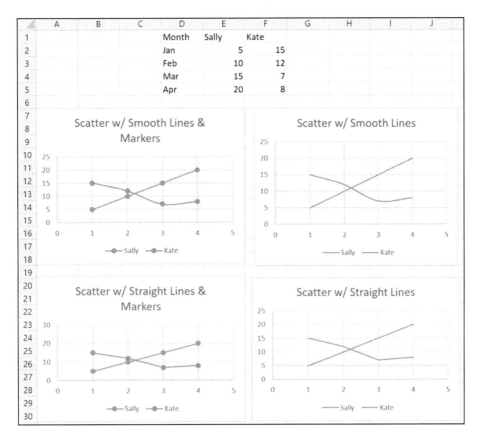

In this case we're charting the results for some measurement for two different people over the course of four months. See how the smooth line plots have lines that curve whereas the straight line plots don't? The more drastic the changes between points, the more noticeable that would become.

Note that you can also map multiple sets of data in a basic scatter plot without the lines, but including the lines makes it easier to see any difference between the data sets.

* * *

Now that you understand the basic chart types, let's talk about how to edit your charts to get them to look exactly like what you want.

CHARTS – EDITING

Chances are, once you've created a chart you'll want to edit it. With the sample charts I showed you in the last chapter I edited the name of each one, resized them, and moved them. But you can do much more than that. Like label each axis, change the legend, label your data, change the chart colors, etc. So let's walk through some of that.

* * *

We'll start with a few fixes for if the chart doesn't seem to be working the way you expected it would. These involve using Switch Row/Column, Select Data, and Change Chart Type in the Design tab under Chart Tools.

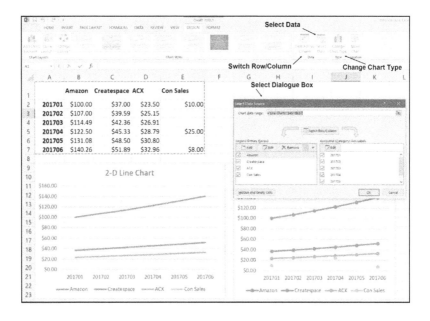

Switch Row/Column

Once you've created your chart you may find that the data you wanted along the bottom is along the side and the data you wanted along the side is along the bottom. The easiest way to fix this is to click on Switch Row/Column in the Data section of the Design tab under Chart Tools. (If you can't see the Chart Tools tabs, click onto the chart somewhere and they should appear.)

Select Data

You may also find that the data being charted isn't the data you wanted to chart. To change your data selection go to Select Data in the Design tab under Chart Tools. This will bring up the Select Data Source dialogue box. (See above.)

To remove a series of data, uncheck its box or highlight it and then click on Remove.

To add a series, click on Add, name the series, and then select the data to include from your worksheet.

To edit a series, select the series you want to edit, click on Edit, and then change the selected cells to what you want.

To change the order of the series elements, click on one of the elements and use the up and down arrows.

To remove an unwanted axis label, uncheck the box next to it.

You can also expand or reduce the data covered by a chart by clicking in the chart, going to the data table which should now be highlighted, and then left-clicking in the bottom right corner, and dragging the border of the highlighted area to either expand or contract the selection. (If you do this, just be sure that the highlight also expands for the data labels, too. It should, but if it doesn't you'll need to do so manually.)

Change the Chart Type

If you decide that you want a bar chart instead of a column chart or a column chart instead of a line chart you can click on the chart and then go to the Insert tab and choose the new chart type.

Or you can go to the Design tab under Chart Tools, click on Change Chart Type, and choose from there.

* * *

Once you have the chart you want and the data points in the places they should be, the next step is to make sure that the chart elements you want are present. For example, that data labels are included on a pie chart or a legend is included on your bar chart.

There are two easy ways to do this using Chart Styles or Quick Layouts. You can also easily change the color palette using Change Colors. All three are located in the Design tab under Chart Tools. (Be sure to click on your chart to see the Chart Tools.)

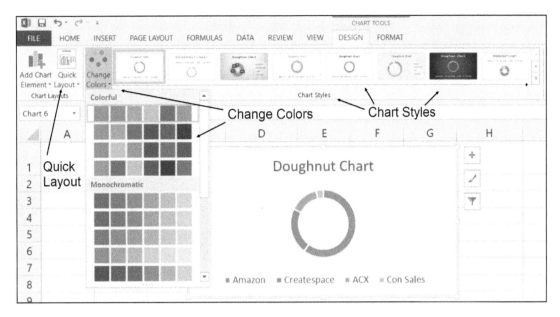

Choosing a Chart Style

Excel provides a number of pre-defined Chart Styles to choose from. The number of choices varies depending on the type of chart, but there are usually a variety with different colors and chart elements included or excluded.

To select one, click on your chart and go to the Design tab under Chart Tools. You'll see the available options in the Chart Styles section of the tab. If there are more than seven available, you can see the rest of them by using the arrows on the right-hand side of the box.

To see what a style will look like, hold your cursor over the style image. To pick a style, click on it.

(You can choose a Chart Style and then customize it further using Chart Elements and the formatting options we'll discuss in a minute, so if you see a style that's close to what you want, pick it.)

Using a Quick Layout

The Quick Layout dropdown is also in the Design tab under Chart Tools but in the Chart Layouts section. It provides a variety of layout options to choose from. The exact number will again depend on the chart type you've chosen.

The layouts include various configurations of data labels, axis labels, legends, and grid lines. (One option for scatter charts even includes an r-squared calculation.) To use a quick layout, click on your chart and then click on the one you want. If you hover over each one you can see what it will look like before you make your choice.

If you use a Quick Layout after you choose a Chart Style the color scheme and background colors will stay the same as the Chart Style, but the layout will update. If you choose a Quick Layout and then a Chart Style, the Chart Style will override your Quick Layout, so if you want to combine the two start with your chart style.

Using Change Colors

The easiest way to change the colors in your chart is to use one of the pre-defined color palettes available under Change Colors. Just click on Change Colors in the Design tab and then select the palette you want.

* * *

Add Chart Element

If you want more control over which chart elements are included and where they're positioned, but still want to work with pre-defined options, use the Add Chart Element dropdown menu in the Design tab.

The options available will vary by chart type. For example, as you can see below, Data Table, Lines, and Up/Down Bars are not available for scatter plots.

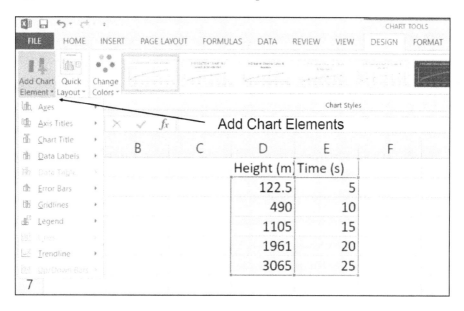

To see the possible choices for each chart element, highlight the name and a secondary dropdown menu will appear. For each of the options shown in the secondary dropdown menu, you can hover your mouse over the option to see what it will look like before you click on it and make the change.

Let's walk through what each element represents:

1. **Axes**

    Axes allows you to add (or remove) data point labels to each axis.

2. **Axis Titles**

    Axis Titles allows you to add (or remove) a title to each axis.

3. **Chart Title**

Chart Title allows you to either (a) remove the chart title entirely, (b) place it at the top of the chart, or (c) place it in a centered overlay position.

4. **Data Labels**

You can use Data Labels to label each of the data points in your chart. (I find this particularly useful with pie charts, although I usually have to move the labels from their default locations, something we'll discuss how to do in the next section.)

5. **Data Table**

Data Table allows you to add or remove a table below your chart that shows the data that was used to create the chart.

6. **Error Bars**

You can add bars that show the standard error, standard deviation, or percentage error in your data. (Usually you would use these if you had a data set that was predicting values and you wanted to show your potential error range. I wouldn't recommend using these on a chart unless you're dealing with data of that type and know what you're doing.)

7. **Gridlines**

Gridlines allows you to add (or remove) horizontal or vertical lines to your chart. These can make it easier to identify the approximate value of a specific point in the chart.

8. **Legend**

Legend allows you to determine the position of the legend (the listing of what each color in the chart stands for) within the chart. If you choose top and bottom, the legend elements will be in a row. If you choose right or left, they'll be displayed in a column. You can also remove the legend, although I generally wouldn't recommend that.

9. **Lines**

Lines allows you to add high-low lines or drop lines to a line chart.

10. **Trendline**

You can use Trendline to add a line onto your data to see if it fits a pattern like a linear or exponential relationship. (I'll note, though, that when I tried it on the data I purposefully constructed to follow an exponential pattern that it imposed a curve in the wrong direction. Honestly, I wouldn't use this unless you have a very good reason to do so.)

11. **Up/Down Bars**

You can add Up/Down bars to a line graph. Another one I wouldn't use unless you have a very specific reason for doing so.

* * *

Now that you have all of the elements in place, time to discuss how to change the aesthetics of the chart. Things like size, position, and colors.

Changing the Chart Size

If you click onto a chart you've created you'll see white squares appear at each of the corners as well as in the middle of each side. Hover your mouse over each of these squares and you'll see that the cursor turns into a two sided arrow. Left-click and drag and you can increase or decrease the size of your chart. All of the elements within the chart will resize themselves automatically to fit the new size.

Moving a Chart

If you want to move a chart within your worksheet, left-click on an empty space within the chart, hold and drag. (Don't click on an element within the chart, like the title, because that will just move that element around. If you do that, like I sometimes do, just Ctrl +Z to put the element back where it was and try again.)

If you want to move a chart to another worksheet or even another file (including a Word file or PowerPoint presentation), you can click onto an empty space within the chart and use Ctrl + C to copy it or Ctrl + X to cut it, and then Ctrl + V to paste it into the new location.

Moving Elements Within a Chart

You can manually move any of the elements within a chart by left-clicking on the element and dragging it to its new location.

Renaming a Chart

To change the name of a chart, left-click on the Chart Title. You should see the title is now surrounded by a box with blue circles in each corner. You can now highlight the existing text, delete it, and then add your own text.

Renaming a Data Field as Displayed in the Legend

To change the data labels used in the legend, you need to do so in the data table. As soon as you do that, the chart legend will update as well.

Changing the Color of Chart Elements

The easiest way to change the color of the chart elements is to use Change Colors, which we discussed above. If those colors aren't sufficient, you can use the Format tab under Chart Tools to change the color of each separate element in the chart one-by-one.

To do so, double-click on the element with the color you want to change, go to the Format tab under Chart Tools, and click on either the Shape Fill dropdown or the Shape Outline dropdown. You'll use Shape Fill for bar, column, and pie graphs and Shape Outline for 2-D line graphs. (Be careful with the 3-D line graphs, because if you use Shape Outline you'll only be changing the color on the edges of the line, not the entire line.)

Once you've clicked on the dropdown for Shape Fill or Shape Outline you can use one of those provided colors or go to More Fill Colors and choose a custom color from there.

Be sure that you've only selected the elements you want to change or you may end up changing the color of all of the elements in the chart. (Something that kept happening to me when dealing with the pie charts. If that happens, just Ctrl + Z to undo and try again.)

When you click on an element, it should by default select all of the elements in the chart that relate to that variable. If it doesn't, try again rather than manually changing each one.

Another way to change the color of a chart element is to use Shape Styles in the Format tab under Chart Tools. Be sure, as above, to only select the elements you want to change. Click on the element first and then click on the style that you want.

Using the Formatting Task Pane

The box on the right-hand side of the screen that appears when you're working in a chart gives yet another way to change your formatting. (If it isn't there, double-click on the chart or an element in the chart and that should bring it up.)

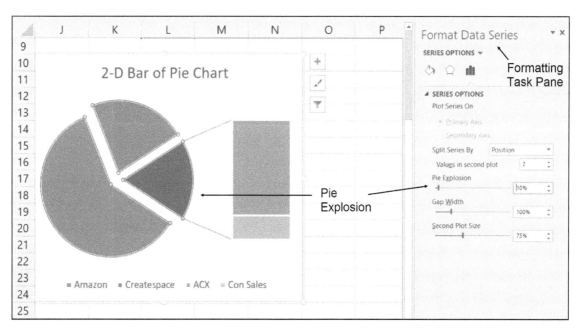

The options you'll be given vary depending on the type of chart and where you've clicked within that chart. You can do things like edit the fill style for chart elements, change the chart border, specify the size of the chart, choose how the text within the chart displays, etc.

For example, with a basic pie chart this is where you'd go to expand the pie pieces outward from the center so that the pieces have separation (pie explosion) or to rotate the pie so that the pie slice you want displayed at the top is (angle of first slice).

Changing Font Properties

If you want to change the font, font color, font size, or font style (italic, bold, underline), you can also click on the text element and then go to the Home tab and change the font options there just like you would with ordinary text in a cell.

* * *

There you have it. How to create a chart and customize for your needs. Let's move on to something a little easier now, Removing Duplicates.

REMOVING DUPLICATE ENTRIES

Sometimes I find myself with a data set that has values listed more than once, but all I really care about is the unique values. For example, you might have a listing of client transactions and want to extract from that a list of your client names. But you don't need John Smith listed three times and going through and manually deleting those duplicate entries is painful. (I'm pretty sure I used to have to do that using subtotals to help me find them...)

Anyway. It's very easy to remove duplicate entries in Excel using the Remove Duplicates option.

To do this, highlight the column of data you're working with, go to the Data tab, and click on Remove Duplicates and you'll then see the Remove Duplicates dialogue box which lets you choose which columns to remove duplicates from and to indicate whether or not your data has headers.

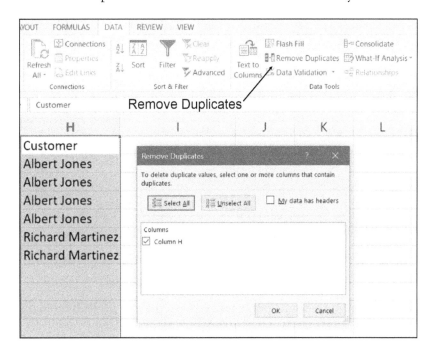

If you indicate that your data has headers, the first row of data will be excluded from the analysis. Once you've made your selections, click OK.

You'll see above that I was removing duplicates from Column H. In the results below, you can see that the multiple entries for Albert Jones and Richard Martinez were removed and that Excel condensed the entries so that they form a new list with one entry per customer and no blank lines in between.

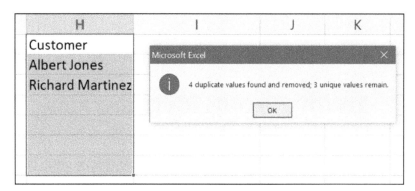

You can also use multiple columns to determine if duplicates exist. For example, you could use Customer Name and Customer State to identify duplicates in a situation where you want to keep both ABC Corp in Nevada and ABC Corp in New York as separate entries.

Whether you're using one column or more than one column, best practice is to isolate the columns you want to use into a new worksheet. The reason for this is that if you have six columns of data and only use two of those columns to remove duplicates, data in the other columns will also be deleted at the same time that Excel removes the duplicates. Which means that you only end up with one row of data per unique value set even if that's not what you wanted. And Excel won't condense that data into the remaining row. You lose that information entirely.

Here's an example of what happens. In the data set below I have five columns of data and I'm going to use two of them, Customer and Item, to remove duplicates.

	A	B	C	D	E	F
1	Customer	Date of Transaction	Quantity	Item	Unit Price	Total
2	Albert Jones	8/1/2015	1	Widget	$ 20.00	$ 20.00
3	Albert Jones	8/1/2015	1	Other	$ 5.00	$ 5.00
4	Albert Jones	8/30/2015	10	Widget	$ 25.00	$ 250.00
5	Albert Jones	9/1/2015	3	Whatchan	$ 15.00	$ 45.00
6	Richard Martinez	3/7/2016	10	Who knov	$ 3.50	$ 35.00
7	Richard Martinez	4/7/2016	20	Whasit	$ 1.50	$ 30.00
8						

I should end up with three entries for Albert Jones and keep the two for Richard Martinez.

And I do. But look at what happened with the Albert Jones entries. I originally had an 8/1/15 and an 8/30/15 entry where he bought Widgets. I now only have the 8/1/15 entry.

	A	B	C	D	E	F
1	Customer	Date of Transaction	Quantity	Item	Unit Price	Total
2	Albert Jones	8/1/2015	1	Widget	$ 20.00	$ 20.00
3	Albert Jones	8/1/2015	1	Other	$ 5.00	$ 5.00
4	Albert Jones	9/1/2015	3	Whatchan	$ 15.00	$ 45.00
5	Richard Martinez	3/7/2016	10	Who knov	$ 3.50	$ 35.00
6	Richard Martinez	4/7/2016	20	Whasit	$ 1.50	$ 30.00
7						
8						
9						
10						
11						
12						

Microsoft Excel ✕

ⓘ 1 duplicate values found and removed; 5 unique values remain.

OK

The other entry was removed entirely and there's no obvious way to see that that happened in the remaining data.

So, again, best practice here is to only have the columns you're going to use to remove duplicates. If you leave in other columns you will have bad data. You will either lose entire rows of information, like in the example above, or, if you choose to not expand the selection, your data will no longer match up because the columns you selected will be shorted when the duplicates are removed but none of the surrounding columns will.

Remove Duplicates is a fantastic tool. *If used properly.*

This is a good point in time to repeat one of the key rules to data analysis: Keep your source data untouched. Always work with a copy. You never know when something you do will introduce an error and you won't realize it right away. You need that clean source file to go back to when that happens.

Okay. On to Converting Text to Columns.

CONVERTING TEXT TO COLUMNS

Converting text to columns allows you to take information that's all in one cell and split it out across multiple columns. The most basic use of this is when you have something like comma-delimited data where all of the data is listed as one long entry with commas separating each piece of information, often found in a .csv file. If you want to put each piece of information into its own column, you can often just paste that data into Column A, run text to columns on it, and you'll have what looks like a normal table of data in less than a minute.

Comma-delimited data is special because it's literally built to have commas as the separator. (Sometimes it does get messy if the data entries also have commas in them, so you need to look at your data when you're converting it to see if this will be an issue for you. We'll talk about delimiters more in a second.)

I use text to columns in a very different way.

I like to use it to rearrange data or strip out information I don't need.

For example, I was recently given a listing of employees where the entire employee name for each employee was in one cell with first name followed by last name. So "Bob Smith," "Alfred Jones," "Katie Clark," etc. Because there was some variation in people's first names (Jim instead of James or a guy whose legal first name was Albert but who went by Dave), I wanted to change that list to one I could sort by last name. Text to columns allowed me to easily do that by taking those name entries and splitting each one into one column for first name and one column for last name.

Let's walk through how I did that:

First, make sure that there isn't any data in the columns to the right of the data you want to convert. Excel will overwrite any existing data you have in those other columns. If you do have data in the columns to the right of the column you're converting, you can insert columns to make space for the conversion. I'd recommend inserting a few more columns than you think you'll need. (All it takes is one Alfred David Jones, Jr. in your list to create havoc.)

Next, highlight the cells with the data you want to convert, go to the Data tab, and in the Data Tools section click on Text to Columns. This will bring up the Convert Text to Columns Wizard dialogue box which walks you through the conversion process.

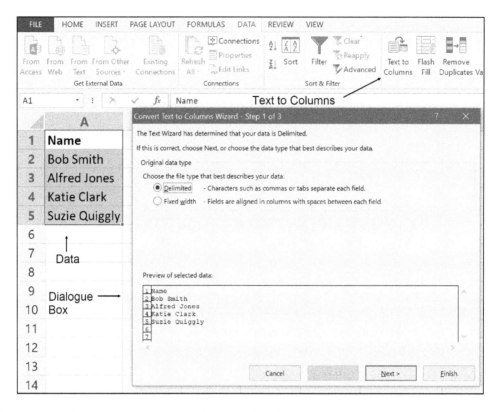

You have two options on the first screen: Delimited or Fixed Width.

Fixed Width lets you split your data into columns based upon number of characters/spaces without any consideration for what the actual content is.

Fixed Width conversion is useful when you have standardized entries that are all built the same way and you need to separate out a portion of those entries. For example, if your company uses a customer ID where the first three letters are a location identifier, you could use the fixed width option to separate the location identifier from the rest of the customer ID.

Delimited allows you to specify a character or characters that separate your data elements. (That's what I used for this example since my first and last names are of varying lengths but are separated with a space.)

Once you've selected between Fixed Width and Delimited, click on Next. This will take you to the second screen where you can set the break locations for Fixed Width or specify the delimiter(s) for Delimited.

Below is the second screen for the Fixed Width option. You can see that in the data preview section in the bottom half of the dialogue box Excel shows a sample of what the data will look like. Breaks can be of any size. Click on the data preview to place a break line, double-click to remove it, click and drag to change its position.

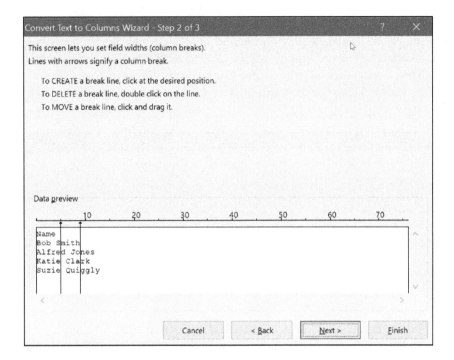

Below is the second screen for the Delimited option:

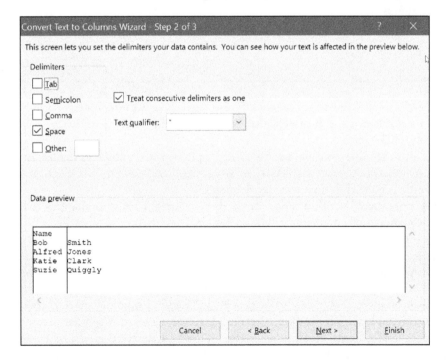

You can choose one or more of the listed options as your delimiter or specify your own delimiter using the Other option. The data preview section at the bottom shows how your data will be separated. Any delimiters that you specify will be deleted from the final data. In this example, that means there will be no spaces left in either of the two columns that are going to be created.

On the third and final screen you can specify how each of your new columns should be formatted.

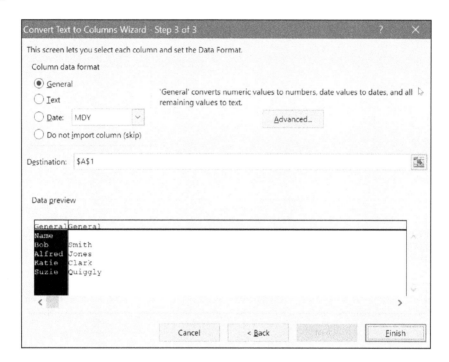

If they don't need special formatting just click Finish. If you do want to specify formatting (General, Text, Date, or do not import), you can click on that column and then select the formatting you want. Once that's done, click Finish.

You should now see that your entries have been split across multiple columns. In our example, "Bob Smith" in column A becomes "Bob" in Column A and "Smith" in Column B. The space between the words is gone since that was our delimiter.

Converting "Bob Smith" to "Bob" and "Smith" is very straight-forward and easy to do.

Not every scenario you'll encounter will be so simple.

If the names in that list had been written as "Smith, Bob" instead, then I would've had to choose both commas and spaces as my delimiters. Otherwise, if I'd just chosen commas as the delimiter it would have keep that space between the two words and I would've ended up with "Smith" in Column A and both a space and the word Bob in Column B.

Some data is even more challenging to work with and requires multiple steps to convert.

For example, if you have "Smith, Bob, electrical engineer, Colorado" as your text string, you can't just specify space and comma as your delimiters. That will separate electrical engineer into two columns. You'd end up with "Smith", "Bob", "electrical", "engineer", and "Colorado" all in separate columns. If that same set of data also had an entry for "Jones, Mark, auditor, Nevada" you'd have a problem. Your state entry for Mark Jones would be lined up with the second part of the title entry for Bob Smith. Like below in Rows 17 and 18:

	A	B	C	D	E	F	G	H	I	J	K	L	M
13													
14													
15													
16	**Example**				**Specify Comma and Space as Delimiter**								
17	Smith, Bob, electrical engineer, Colorado				Smith	Bob	electrical	engineer	Colorado				
18	Jones, Mark, auditor, Nevada				Jones	Mark	auditor	Nevada					
19													
20					**Specify Comma As Only Delimiter**					**Apply TRIM Function to Remove Extra Space**			
21					Smith	Bob	electrical engineer	Colorado		Smith	Bob	electrical engineer	Colorado
22					Jones	Mark	auditor	Nevada		Jones	Mark	auditor	Nevada
23													

All Excel knows is what you tell it. If you tell it that spaces and commas are delimiters, that's all it thinks about. It doesn't understand that that third entry is a title listing and that those words need to be kept together.

The better option, although it's also a two-step process, is to separate the data into columns using just the comma as your delimiter. That gives you entries that at least line up, but you'll still have an extra space in them like you see in Cells E21:H22 above.

But that's an easy fix. You can remove extra spaces around text using the TRIM function.

To trim the extra spaces from Cell E21 you can just type =TRIM(E21) in a cell. That's what I did above in Cell J21. I then copied the formula to cells J21:M22.

You can see that the extra spaces that were there in Cells F21:H22 are now gone.

To finish it off, copy cells J21:M22 and paste special-values so that the formulas are gone and all that's left is your listing of last name, first name, occupation, and location for each employee.

* * *

Always check your data after you convert it. Sometimes converting data is easy and all your entries convert without a hitch. But all it takes is one "Mark David Jones, III" in your list to throw things off.

THE CONCATENATE FUNCTION

Let's say what you really wanted to do was convert those "Bob Smith" entries to a "Smith, Bob" format. How would you do that? Or how would you take a column with first names in it and combine that with a column with last names in it to make an entry like "Smith, Bob"?

Enter the CONCATENATE function. The CONCATENATE function lets you combine multiple elements, including data across multiple columns, into one cell. How?

Let's just dive in and show you an example.

Below we have our first names and last names in separate columns and now we want to bring them together in the order "last name" + a comma + a space + "first name" where the last name is in Cell B2 and the first name is in Cell A2.

The formula for that is: =CONCATENATE(B2,", ",A2) which I've placed in Cell F2. I can now copy it down to Cells F3:F5 and we get:

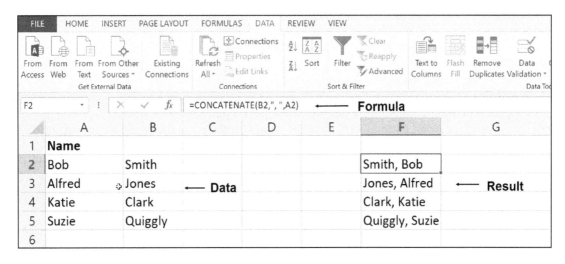

Right now all of the entries in Column F are still formulas. If we delete the contents of Columns A and B, we'll lose our values in Column F. So after I use CONCATENATE like this, I copy the cells where I used the formula and paste special – values to replace the formula with just the results of the formula so that doesn't happen.

Let's go back to that formula and break it down a bit, because it's important that you see what I did in that middle portion.

There are three elements that we're combining with that formula. First, the contents of Cell B2. Next, a comma and a space. And, finally, the contents of Cell A2.

To include the contents of a cell, you just list the cell name like I did with B2 and A2 in the formula.

To include text you need to use quotation marks around the text you want to include. In this example, I have a comma and a space within quotes for my second element.

So the formula is:

$$=\text{CONCATENATE(}$$

$$\text{B2}$$

$$,$$

$$","$$

$$,$$

$$\text{A2}$$

$$)$$

If that's still a bit confusing to you, just try it a few times. Start with =CONCATENATE (B2, A2) which will give you SmithBob and then go from there to try and fix it.

Once you get the hang of it, CONCATENATE is very easy to use. The biggest challenge is remembering to include those text elements between cells when they're needed.

And you can put anything in between those quotes. If I need to include a / mark or a star or whatever else, I can.

Just remember: Excel will treat it as text.

If I write =CONCATENATE("=",A11,"*",B11) where A11=2 and B11=3, Excel will display that as =2*3. That's a text entry, not a formula, though. To turn it into a formula, you have to paste special-values and then click into the cell, copy the contents, and paste them into a new cell. So this is definitely not a shortcut for building formulas.

Bottom line: CONCATENATE lets you combine the values in different cells as well as text elements to create a single entry.

Now on to one of my favorite functions, the IF function.

THE IF FUNCTION

I love the IF function. I really do. That probably indicates a need for therapy, but it's true. I just…love it. It's so useful. Especially when you can nest IF functions. It's like building one of those complex flow charts, but in one cell.

So how do they work?

An IF function basically says, if A is true, then do B. If it isn't true, then do C.

When you nest IF functions, you can set something up that says if A is true then do B, if it isn't true then if C is true do D, and if that isn't true then if E is true do F, and if none of that is true do G. You can just keep going and going and going. It's awesome.

But you have to get it right.

So let's start with a basic IF function that looks at whether or not to charge shipping on an order. Let's say that all customers who buy more than $25 worth of product get free shipping and anyone who buys $25 or less worth of product has to pay a 5% charge for shipping.

Here's our data and our IF function:

In Column A we have the cost of the customer's order. In Column B we have our IF function. For Row 2 it is =IF(A2>25,0,A2*0.05). In Column C we have the customer's total cost which is just Column A plus Column B.

Let's walk through the IF function.

The formula starts with IF A2 > 25. That's the condition we're evaluating. Did the customer spend more than $25?

The next portion of the function is 0. That's the outcome to return if the answer to the question we asked in the first part of the function is true. If our customer spent more than $25 then we want to return a result of zero.

The final portion of the function is A2*0.05. That's the outcome to return if the answer to the question is false. If your customer DID NOT spend more than $25 then we want to return a value equal to 5% of what they spent.

You can think of an IF function as walking through an if-then-else or if-then-otherwise process where each of the sections of the function is one of those steps. So: =IF(If, Then, Else)

IF A2>25, THEN 0, ELSE A2*.05.

That was just a simple IF function. Let's make it more complex. (This is where it gets fun.)

Let's say that we want to provide customers with a discount based upon how much they spend. Spend up to $25, no discount, over $25 and up to $50, $5, etc. To apply this discount, we can build a nested IF function. Here we go:

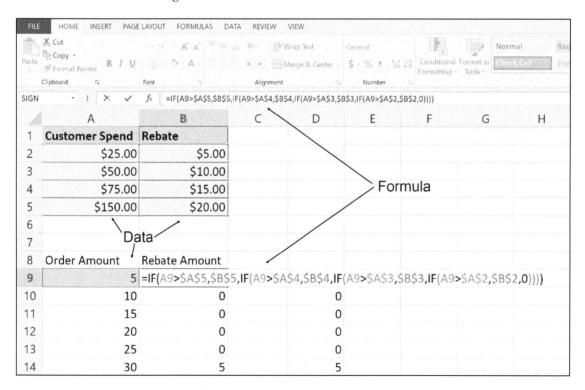

The table we want to use to determine our discount is in Cells A1:B5.

Our formula for an order amount that's listed in Cell A9 is:

=IF(A9>$A$5,$B$5,IF(A9>$A$4,$B$4,IF(A9>$A$3,$B$3,IF(A9>$A$2,$B$2,0))))

That looks insanely complicated, I know, but let's break it down. It's all just logical steps.

We start with IF A9>A5. Is the order amount over the value in Cell A5? (We use the $ signs here so we can copy the formula down to other cells and keep the references to the table constant.)

If that's true, then B5. That's our discount when the purchase amount is over the value listed in A5. So, if the customer paid more than $150 they'll get $20 off.

If that's not true, then...

We look to see if A9>A4. Instead of closing out the function with an alternate value, we start another IF function. This is the next step in our analysis. We know our purchase amount isn't greater than A5, but is it greater than A4?

If so, then B4. If it's not greater than A5 but is greater than A4, we apply the discount listed in B4. So all purchases for more than $75 and up to $150 receive a $15 discount.

If that's not true, then...

We look to see if A9>A3. Once more, instead of closing out the IF function, we start another one. Our value isn't greater than A5 or A4, but is it greater than A3?

If so, then B3. If it's not greater than A5 or A4 but is greater than A3, we apply the discount for purchases that are more than $50 and up to $75.

If that's not true, then...

Is A9>A2. This is our final threshold, so no more IF functions after this one. If our purchases is less than A5, A4, and A3 but still greater than A2...

Then, B2. We apply the discount for purchases over $25 and up to $50.

Otherwise 0. Because at that point the purchases is for $25 or less and there's no discount to apply.

Here it is again:

=IF(A9>$A$5,$B$5,IF(A9>$A$4,$B$4,IF(A9>$A$3,$B$3,IF(A9>$A$2,$B$2,0))))

* * *

It's kind of insane to walk through, right? It can seem overwhelming.

Draw it out if you need to. It's just IF-THEN-ELSE over and over again. The only difference is that the ELSE steps start over with a new IF-THEN-ELSE set of steps.

Sometimes, when I need to break an IF function like this down to figure out why it isn't working, I take out each of the individual IF functions and look at them separately. I start with the first IF function and ask what it's doing and why and if that makes sense. So what we had was:

=IF(A9>$A$5,$B$5,IF(A9>$A$4,$B$4,IF(A9>$A$3,$B$3,IF(A9>$A$2,$B$2,0))))

What if this wasn't working? How would you figure out where it's going wrong?

Start with the first IF function =IF(A9>$A$5,$B$5,OTHER) where OTHER is everything else that needs to happen after that.

Ask yourself, "Does it make sense that if A9 is greater than A5 we return a value of B5? And, if so, does it also make sense that if A9 is not greater than A5 that we do something else?"

When I originally was writing this IF function, I started with the lowest threshold instead of the highest. So I had =IF(A9>$A$2,IF(A9>$A$3,IF....and had ended with $B$2 as my last value. Take out all the garbage in between and I had IF(A9>A2,OTHER,B2). Meaning if A9 wasn't greater than A2 I was going to return a discount of $5. That was wrong. But to see it, I needed to get everything else out of the way.

For the curious, here's what it looks like to write an IF function that starts with the lowest threshold instead and works its way up.

=IF(A22>$A$2,IF(A22>$A$3,IF(A22>$A$4,IF(A22>$A$5,IF(A22>$A$5,$B$5),$B$4),$B$3),$B$2),0)

I prefer not to write IF functions like this one, because my mind doesn't follow the logic as well. In the example we walked through where you start with the highest discount, each IF function is completed before the next one starts. That's much easier to follow than this second approach where you're basically saying IF, IF, IF, IF, IF before you ever start in on your THEN, ELSE steps.

You can do it either way. And if you get stuck you can isolate each IF function to see what's wrong, but I just find the IF(A, B, IF(C, D,E)) approach an easier one to follow.

In addition to just getting the logic wrong, another error I commonly commit when building nested IF functions is failing to put enough parens or putting them in the wrong place. A few rules to remember:

1. Always have an opening paren after an IF.
2. Always have a closing paren after the last item for each IF function.

See this example again:

=IF(A22>$A$2,IF(A22>$A$3,IF(A22>$A$4,IF(A22>$A$5,IF(A22>$A$5,$B$5),$B$4),$B$3),$B$2),0)

See how after each of the price thresholds (B5, B4, B3, B2), we have a closing paren?
But it's different if you build it this way:

=IF(A9>$A$5,$B$5,IF(A9>$A$4,$B$4,IF(A9>$A$3,$B$3,IF(A9>$A$2,$B$2,0))))

In this case, each IF function is only closed out when the prior IF function is, so you end up with all of your closing parens at the very end.

We have four IF functions so need four closing parens.

Excel makes it easy to see if you have your parens in the right place. If you click into the formula bar and arrow through your equation Excel will highlight not only the paren you're on but it will also briefly bold the corresponding paren.

Also, Excel uses distinct colors for each set of parens, but those can be harder to see.

* * *

That was probably a lot to take in. So let's try to bottom line it:

- IF functions follow an IF-THEN-ELSE pattern.
- You can nest IF functions by replacing the THEN or the ELSE portion of an IF function with another IF function.
- If you get an error message that says you've entered too many arguments, the more likely cause is a misplaced paren.
- Always test your IF function after you've written it to make sure it's doing what you want it to do.
- If you're referencing a table of values that drive your IF function (like with our sales discount example), be sure to use $ signs to fix the cell references.

Alright, let's move on to COUNTIFS, another function I love. (Although not as much as I love SUMIFS which we'll cover after that.)

THE COUNTIFS FUNCTION

I probably use the SUMIFS function more than I use COUNTIFS, but I couldn't cover SUMIFS without also covering COUNTIFS.

For users of older versions of Excel, I know for a fact that the COUNTIFS and SUMIFS functions did not exist (before I believe Excel 2007) because I once used one of them on a work project and then had to go back and redo the entire worksheet when it turned out our client didn't have as recent a version of Excel as I did. So you may not have this function available if you're working in a pre-2007 version of Excel.

But I digress. (Again. Always.)

Let's get down to it.

What does COUNTIFS do?

If you use it on only one range of data, it will count the number of entries in that range that meet your criteria. If you use it on more than one range of data, for example, three columns, it will count the number of entries that meet all three of your criteria.

Let's look at a real-world example.

Here's our data and our calculations:

	A	B	C	D	E
1	Customer	Country	Units	Item	
2	A	USA	23	Whatsits	
3	B	USA	21	Whatsits	
4	C	USA	25	Whatchamacallits	
5	D	Zimbabwe	43	Whatchamacallits	
6	E	Zimbabwe	32	Whatsits	
7					
8					
9	**Customers From Zimbabwe**			**All Cells In Cells A2 through B6 With An "e"**	
10	=COUNTIF(B2:B6,"Zimbabwe")		2	=COUNTIFS(A2:B6,"*e")	3
11	=COUNTIFS(B2:B6,"Zimbabwe")		2		
12					
13	**Customers From Zimbabwe who Bought Whatsits**			**All Cells in Cells C2 through C6 With a Value Over 25**	
14	=COUNTIFS(B2:B6,"Zimbabwe",D2:D6,"Whatsits")		1	=COUNTIFS(C2:C6,">25")	2
15					

If you want to know how many customers you have in Zimbabwe, you can apply COUNTIFS to the column where you list the country for each customer, column B, using the equation:

$$=COUNTIFS(B2:B6,"Zimbabwe")$$

This basically says, look at the range from B2:B6 and count each time Zimbabwe appears.

(You could also use the COUNTIF function and get the same result, but might as well use COUNTIFS since it can be expanded to include more than one criteria.)

What if instead you want to know how many customers you have in Zimbabwe who also ordered Whatsits? Then you'd need to use COUNTIFS and set criteria for both Columns B, where you list country, and Column D, where you list product.

The equation is:

$$=COUNTIFS(B2:B6,"Zimbabwe",D2:D6,"Whatsits")$$

What you're saying here is, look at Cells B2:B6 and identify every time the value is Zimbabwe. For each row where the value in Column B is Zimbabwe, then look at the corresponding cell in Column D and see if that value is Whatsits. If it is, count it.

Both criteria must be met to be counted.

The COUNTIFS function isn't limited to exact word matches. You can use wildcards like the * in your count criteria. For example, =COUNTIFS(A2:B6,"*e*") will look for all cells where there's an entry with an e in it within the range and count it. In this case, that returned a value of 3, the two Zimbabwe entries as well as Customer E.

Note, too, that I had it count across rows and columns in that example. If you have multiple count criteria, though, they have to be the same size and orientation. You couldn't have A2:B6 and A3:A5, because those wouldn't match up in terms of size. And you couldn't have C2:C5 and A3:C3 together because they don't match up in terms of orientation. But you could have A1:B2 and C1:D2.

You can also use count criteria that are numeric. The function =COUNTIFS(C2:C6,">25") counts all entries in the range that have a value greater than 25. In this case, 2.

Another thing to keep in mind with COUNTIFS is that each range you specify needs to be unique. You can't use this to count entries where, for example, customers bought Whatchamacallits or Whatsits since in our example those are both listed in the same range.

If you select columns of data for your analysis then COUNTIFS will look across each individual row in that column to see if the criteria are met.

If you select rows of data for your analysis then COUNTIFS will look down each individual column to see if all criteria are met.

Here's another example of how it all works using three students and their scores on three exams.

	F	G	H	I	J	K	L	M
1		Student	Grade 1	Grade 2	Grade 3			
2		A	92	82	88			
3		B	93	94	93			
4		C	93	92	93			
5								
6								
7								
8		Result		Formula				
9	Total Scores Over 90	7		=COUNTIFS(H2:J4,">90")				
10	# Test with All Over 90	1		=COUNTIFS(H2:J2,">90",H3:J3,">90",H4:J4,">90")				
11	# Student All Over 90	2		=COUNTIFS(H2:H4,">90",I2:I4,">90",J2:J4,">90")				
12								

The formula in Cell G9, =COUNTIFS(H2:J4,">90"), is applying the COUNTIFS function across the entire range from H2 to J4 and counting any instance where the value is over 90. (I've copied the text of each of the formulas and pasted it into the cells in Column I using a ' to make it appear as text so you can see the formula and the result at the same time.)

The formula in Cell G9 returns a count of 7 because there were 7 test scores over 90.

The formula in Cell G10, =COUNTIFS(H2:J2,">90",H3:J3,">90",H4:J4,">90"), is applying the COUNTIFS function by rows to see how many tests there were where all three students scored over a 90. As you can see in the data, the only column where all three students scored over a 90 is for Grade 1 and that's the count it returns.

The formula in Cell G11, =COUNTIFS(H2:H4,">90",I2:I4,">90",J2:J4,">90"), is applying the COUNTIFS function by columns to see how many students had over a 90 on all three tests. As you can see in the data, this is true for students B and C which is why the count is 2.

COUNTIFS is very powerful, but as with a lot of these functions, it's easy to set it up wrong. One of the things I do when I'm building a worksheet using formulas like this is start small with data I can evaluate visually. I confirm that my function works the way I think it should before applying it to a larger data set where I can't easily confirm the result.

Once you have the basic framework down, you can then expand your formulas to cover a broader range of cells or to be more complex.

Start small. Test. Be sure you understand the concept and how it works. And then expand.

Alright, now on to SUMIFS which I use on a regular basis.

THE SUMIFS FUNCTION

Have I told you how much I love the SUMIFS function? Because I do. I use it all the time, primarily for tracking pending payments.

When I have sales of my books on Amazon it takes two months before I'm paid for those sales. In the meantime, I know that I'm owed X U.S. Dollars for sales in the U.S., Y Canadian Dollars for sales in Canada, Z British Pounds for sales in the UK, etc. I've had months where I had pending payments in at least six different currencies. Because of conversion rates, I can't just add those numbers together to see my total pending payments. 1 U.S. Dollar does not equal 1 Canadian Dollar and it certainly does not equal 1 Indian Rupee.

What I do to deal with this is use the SUMIFS function to sum all pending payments in each currency. I then apply a conversion rate to those amounts to see what I might actually be owed in U.S. Dollars. (Since currency exchange rates are constantly moving there's no actual guarantee that's what I'll receive in two months when I'm paid but at least it gives me a nice estimate. If you ever get big enough for those shifts to matter, look into currency hedging. I am not even close to worrying about that, though, so let's get back to the point.)

What does SUMIFS do?

It works much like COUNTIFS in that it looks to see if one or more criteria that you specify have been met. But where it differs is in what it does next. Instead of counting how many times all of those criteria are met it sums the values in a separate range of cells that you specify.

Let me show you how I use it. (Keeping in mind these are complete garbage numbers and not reflective of my actual earnings.)

	A	B	C	D	E	F	G	H
						F2 =SUMIFS(B$2:B$22,D$2:D$22,"USD",E$2:E$22,"")		
1	Month	Income	Source	Currency	Paid	Total Outstanding		
2	June 2017	$ 123.45	Amazon Brazil	BRL		$ 7,770.73	USD	$ 7,770.73
3	June 2017	$ 345.67	ACX	USD	X	$ 124.12	CAD	$ 93.46
4	June 2017	$ 546.78	Createspace	USD	X	$ 125.68	GBP	$ 177.71
5	June 2017	$ 124.68	D2D	USD	X	$ 1,246.35	EUR	$ 1,392.17
6	June 2017	$ 163.98	Nook	USD		$ 123.56	AUD	$ 92.79
7	June 2017	$ 698.43	Kobo	USD		$ 124.56	INR	$ 1.87
8	June 2017	$ 124.12	Authors Republic	USD	X	$ 123.45	BRL	$ 1.85
9	June 2017	$ 345.12	Google	USD	X			
10	June 2017	$ 125.23	Pronoun	USD				
11	July 2017	$ 124.47	ACX	USD	X	Outstanding in USD		$ 9,530.59
12	July 2017	$ 784.45	Createspace	USD				
13	July 2017	$ 31.25	D2D	USD				
14	July 2017	$ 315.27	Kobo	USD				
15	July 2017	$3,169.25	Nook	USD				
16	July 2017	$1,234.12	Pronoun	USD				
17	July 2017	$1,248.75	Amazon US	USD				
18	July 2017	$ 125.68	Amazon UK	GBP				
19	July 2017	$1,246.35	Amazon DE	EUR				
20	July 2017	$ 124.56	Amazon India	INR				
21	July 2017	$ 124.12	Amazon Canada	CAD				

What you're seeing here is a listing of payments from sales channels. We have the sales month, the amount earned, the sales channel, the currency for the pending payment, and whether it's been paid yet. If you were to add all those values up they'd equal to 11249.29, but that number is useless. It means nothing because of the various currencies involved. Also, some of those amounts have already been paid so they're no longer outstanding.

Enter the SUMIFS function. In Cell F2 I have the formula:

=SUMIFS(B$2:B$22,D$2:D$22,"USD",E$2:E$22,"")

What that formula is saying is, for each row between 2 and 22 sum the values in Column B (amount earned) when the value in Column D (currency) is USD and the cell in Column E (Paid) is blank. Because I used $ signs to lock the cell references, I can copy that formula down and then just change the currency reference for each of the currencies in Column F.

The formula for Cell F6, for Australian Dollars, becomes:

=SUMIFS(B$2:B$22,D$2:D$22,"AUD",E$2:E$22,"")

Once I've broken out my pending payments by currency, I can then multiply them by the conversion rate for that currency to calculate an estimated amount that's outstanding in U.S. Dollars. That's what's happening in Column H.

And then, last, but not least, I can add all those values together to get a total estimate of outstanding payments in USD.

That's not the only way I use SUMIFS. I also use it to track bills I've paid for the month and to calculate how much I still have due so I can make sure enough money is in my bank account.

You could also use this to sum, for example, the amount of payables you have outstanding from customers who are more than 30 days past due. Or the amount you've earned from customers who are in Zimbabwe. Or who are in Zimbabwe, whose account was opened by Salesman George, and where the account was opened within the last year.

Unlike with COUNTIF and COUNTIFS where you could use them interchangeably when dealing with one variable, the SUMIF and SUMIFS functions require you to enter your information in a different order, so you have to know which one you're using to write the function correctly. Since SUMIFS can handle anything SUMIF can, it's best to just stick with SUMIFS.

Also, like the COUNTIFS function, you can apply SUMIFS to ranges of cells, just be sure that the size and dimension of the ranges for each of the arguments (what to sum, what to evaluate) are the same or it won't work.

THE TEXT FUNCTION

I'll admit, I have not used the TEXT function a lot. It was never really on my radar until I recently had to figure out a way to convert a date to a day of the week so that I could recreate something I do in a more manual way as a pivot table. (For the time and word count tracking that's included in *Excel for Writers*.) But I have to say what I saw of it was very impressive.

According to Excel, the TEXT function "converts a value to text in a specific number format." That sounds pretty boring, doesn't it? You'd read that and think, "So what?"

But when you dig into it, it's far more interesting than that boring description would have you believe. It can do all sorts of things with formatting as well as providing detailed information about dates.

The basic way it works is you specify the cell to make into text and then provide the formatting you want. That cell you reference needs to be a number or a date for this to work, so it isn't a substitute for using CONCATENATE but they can do similar things.

At its most basic, TEXT can specify a format for a number.

You list the cell and then specify the format you want applied to the number in that cell. So =TEXT(E10,"$0.00") formats a number as currency with a dollar sign in front and with two decimal places.

There are a few tricks for formatting numbers:

Using a zero forces a specified number of decimal places to show even if the number doesn't require them. So, #.00 will display up to two decimal places even if that means displaying 2.00 or 2.50.

Using the pound sign (#) will display up to that number of decimal places, but will not force that many decimal places if the last number would be a zero. So, #.## would force 2.123 to be 2.12 but would leave 2.5 as 2.5.

Using a question mark (?) makes Excel insert spaces to align the decimal point across rows of numbers. You can substitute the question mark for a zero or combine it with zeroes to get the desired number of total decimal points to display. (But be careful. I used #.?0 and ended up with a number where the space was added to the question mark's location and it was then followed by a 0. Better to use #.0? instead to avoid that problem.)

Including a period in the text format will include a period with the number. Even when one isn't needed. So #.## applied to 2 gives you 2. which is not what you really want.

Here are some examples. The left- hand columns are sorted by number with white and gray bands to separate each one. The right-hand columns are sorted by format with white and gray bands to separate each format.

B2		⌄ : ✕ ✓	fx	=TEXT(A2,"#.0#")		

	A	B	C	D	E	F	G
1	**Original Value**	**Converted Value**	**Format**		**Original Value**	**Converted Value**	**Format**
2	1	1.0	#.0#		1	1	#
3	1	1.00	#.00		1.2	1	#
4	1	1.	#.?		1.7	2	#
5	1	1	#		2.356	2	#
6	1	1			1	1.	#.?
7	1	1. 0	#.?0		1.2	1.2	#.?
8	1.2	1.2	#.0#		1.7	1.7	#.?
9	1.2	1.20	#.00		2.356	2.4	#.?
10	1.2	1.2	#.?		1	1. 0	#.?0
11	1.2	1	#		1.2	1.20	#.?0
12	1.2	1.2			1.7	1.70	#.?0
13	1.2	1.20	#.?0		2.356	2.36	#.?0
14	1.7	1.7	#.0#		1	1.0	#.0#
15	1.7	1.70	#.00		1.2	1.2	#.0#
16	1.7	1.7	#.?		1.7	1.7	#.0#
17	1.7	2	#		2.356	2.36	#.0#
18	1.7	1.7			1	1.00	#.00
19	1.7	1.70	#.?0		1.2	1.20	#.00
20	2.356	2.36	#.0#		1.7	1.70	#.00
21	2.356	2.36	#.00		2.356	2.36	#.00
22	2.356	2.4	#.?		1	1	
23	2.356	2	#		1.2	1.2	
24	2.356	2.356			1.7	1.7	
25	2.356	2.36	#.?0		2.356	2.356	

See how using just the # sign to format a number results in that number being rounded up to the nearest whole number? (In Cells F2:F5)

Or how adding a ? after the period, but not including any zeroes in the format means you can end up with a whole number with a period after it? (In Cell F6)

Or how using "#.?0" adds a blank space between the period and the zero for a number like 1 to ensure that the decimal places line up? (In Cell F10)

And how using "#.00" forces a number to have two decimal places no matter what? (Cells F18:F21)

You can force pretty much any basic number formatting you want. But the additional benefit to using the TEXT function is that it also allows you to include text with that number formatting by using the & symbol.

For example,

=TEXT(E10,"$0.00") & " per unit"

converts the numeric value in Cell E10 to a currency format with a dollar sign and two decimal places and then adds to that a space and the words "per unit". (If you want that space, it has to be within the quotes.)

That's very handy for when you have a series of numbers and you want to make them more presentation worthy.

But what has me really excited about the TEXT function is how it handles dates and times. Specifically, what it can do with months and days. You can take a date like 1/8/17 and using TEXT you can convert that into the name of the day of the week or the month. How cool is that?

Here's a list of examples:

L5		:	×	✓	f_x	=TEXT(K5,"mmmm")	

	K	L	M
1	**Original Value**	**Converted Value**	**Format**
2	1/8/2017	1	m
3	1/8/2017	01	mm
4	1/8/2017	Jan	mmm
5	1/8/2017	January	mmmm
6	1/8/2017	8	d
7	1/8/2017	08	dd
8	1/8/2017	Sun	ddd
9	1/8/2017	Sunday	dddd
10	1/8/2017	17	yy
11	1/8/2017	2017	yyyy
12	2:15:00 AM	2	h
13	2:15:00 AM	02	hh
14	2:09:00 AM	2:9	h:m
15	2:09:00 AM	2:09	h:mm
16	2:09:00 AM	2 AM	h AM/PM
17			

In Cell L4 I've taken the date 1/8/17 and used the formula =TEXT(K4,"mmmm") to display the long version of the name of the month that corresponds to that date.

In Cell L8 I've used the formula =TEXT(K8,"dddd") to display the long version of the day of the week that corresponds to that date.

I don't know how often you'll need this, but it is pretty nifty and I did end up needing it for that pivot table. (Internet searches are your friend when you think something should be possible in Excel but have no idea how to make it work. Turns out there are no new problems under the sun, it's just a matter of knowing how someone else might phrase the question so you can find where it was already asked and answered.)

LIMITING ALLOWED INPUTS INTO A CELL

One of the biggest challenges with analyzing older data sets is that a lot of them didn't use standardized values. For example, one of the data sets I worked with started with paper forms that people completed by hand and that data was then input into a database exactly as it was written. Which meant that for a field like country you ended up with USA, U.S., Unites States, America, and all sorts of creative spellings of those words. When that happens, it becomes an incredible challenge to do any sort of analysis on that data set. You can't just say, count all entries where country is United States, because you'll miss all those other entries.

That's why if you're building any sort of tracking or input form you should limit the allowed values to the extent possible. Things like State and Country are obvious examples. But in the financial services industry you might also limit financial objective or income or net worth to pre-defined values or numeric ranges. Or, if you want exact numbers, at least limit the input field so that only numbers can be provided. If you don't, you'll end with someone somewhere who puts something like, "Refused to Disclose" in a net worth field.

So ask yourself, with the data you're dealing with, what can you standardize? Once you know that, if you're using Excel to track this kind of information, you can impose limits on those cells. You do this with Data Validation which can be found on the Data tab under Data Tools.

Let's walk through how to do it.

First, if you're going to have a list of acceptable values, you need to create it and have it available in Excel. I'd recommend putting it in another worksheet in the same Excel file. (We'll talk about how to hide that worksheet and lock it from editing later.)

Now that you have the list of accepted values (or if there is no list and you just want to limit the cells to a specific input type), highlight the cells you want to limit.

Next, click on Data Validation in the Data Tools section of the Data Tab and then Data Validation again.

You'll now see the Data Validation dialogue box.

If you're working with a list of accepted values, select List from the dropdown menu under Allow, and then click in the Source box and highlight your list of accepted values. You should end up with something like this:

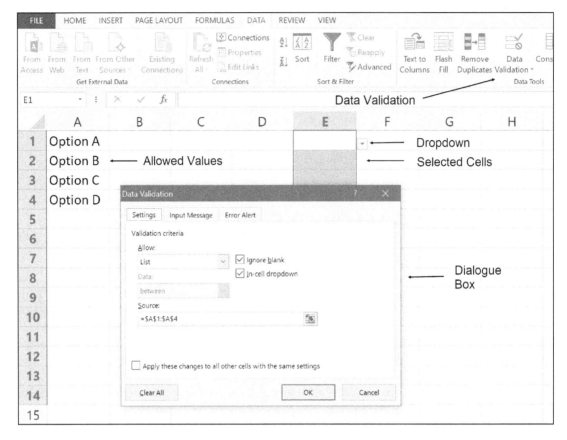

If you don't have a list of accepted values, you can choose under Allow to limit the formatting in those cells to Whole Numbers, Decimals, Dates, Times, a specific text length, or a custom format. When you choose one of those options it will require you to enter an allowed range of values. If you don't care what the range is, you can enter something like a minimum of 0 and a maximum of 1,000,000. (Although that example would force a positive number, so think through the implications of any range you choose.)

Click OK once you've made your choices.

For the list option, you'll see that the cells where you applied data validation now have a dropdown arrow. When you click on that arrow the only available choices will be the ones you specified. If someone tries to enter a different value in one of those cells, they'll receive an error message telling them the value they've entered is not valid.

The cells with number or text formatting limits won't have the dropdown arrow, but will generate an error message for any entry that doesn't meet your specifications.

You can add a message that will display when people click on any of the cells with data validation. Do so by using the Input Message tab in the Data Validation dialogue box.

You can also customize the error message by using the Error Alert tab.

To remove data validation, highlight the same set of cells, pull up the Data Validation dialogue box (by clicking on Data Validation and then Data Validation again under Data Tools in the Data tab), and choose Clear All in the bottom left corner.

One caution about using data validation. Be sure before you limit the inputs into a cell that you've thought through all the possible options. There is nothing more annoying than trying to input valid information and getting an error message and having no way to work around it.

I worked on a large project where we were trying to come up with these sorts of lists and when you really dig in, it isn't always as straight-forward as it seems. There are standardized lists out there for country, U.S. state, and currency code, for example, but sometimes the decision of which one to use is political. For example, do you list Burma or Myanmar? Where do you list Puerto Rico? How about including countries that no longer exist?

All I'm saying is think it through before you roll it out to your users, test it with them once you do, and then be open to making changes as needed. Unless there's a good reason not to, I like to include an Other option with a free-text field when I'm rolling out a new list. I then monitor to see what gets entered in that field so I can either update the list with an entry I missed, provide education to those misusing the Other field, or accept that there are sometimes one-off situations that will require that Other option to always exist.

LOCKING CELLS OR WORKSHEETS

Since we just talked about setting up a worksheet for someone else to use, it occurred to me you should also know how to lock a range of cells or hide a worksheet altogether. For example, I had a worksheet I created once for work where users input values into the first five or six columns and then those values were used in formulas that made up the rest of the worksheet. Because I didn't want anyone to change those formulas, I locked those cells down.

To lock a range of cells, first select the cells you want to lock, right-click, and choose Format Cells. In the Format Cells dialogue box, go to the Protection tab and click the Locked box. Then click on OK.

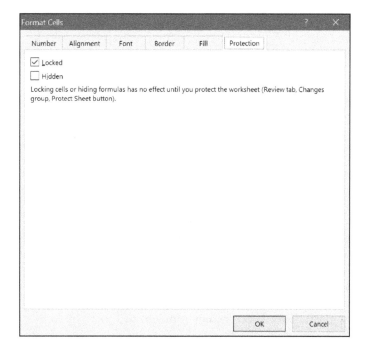

(If you also don't want users to even be able to see the formulas or values within those locked cells, you can also click on Hidden.)

The cells won't be locked at this point. You now need to add protection to the worksheet. To do that, go to the Cells section of the Home tab and click on Format. You should see an option to Protect Sheet. Select it and you'll see the Protect Sheet dialogue box.

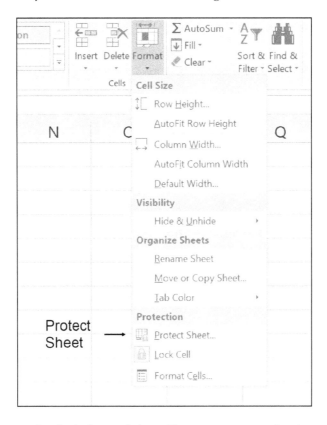

You need to use a password to lock the worksheet. Be sure you remember it.

There are a number of options for what you can allow users to do even when a worksheet is protected.

It's a little backwards since you're choosing what you're willing to allow instead of what you're not willing to allow, but there you have it.

The default is to allow people to select cells in the worksheet. Unless they shouldn't be copying the information for any reason, this is fine to keep.

I can also see an argument for allowing people to format columns in case they enter a value that's too big for the current column width, which I've had happen with users in the past. (It's very annoying to enter a number, see ### instead, and not be able to widen the column.)

What to allow from the rest of that list is a judgement call. I try to lock down as much as I can without interfering with functionality, so I'd probably lock too much and then wait for complaints and fix it then. It very much depends on the environment you work in. Is it better to allow users to do most everything and then find out that they do crazy things like delete the most important column in the worksheet? Or is it better to lock it down too tight and have to fix it when someone complains, which may damage your department's reputation and could, if you have the wrong kind of boss, lead to your boss yelling at you?

That's why beta testing is so important. Make your best choice and then give it to a bunch of users to test for you before you give it to everyone. See what they complain about and adjust from there. (That's the ideal scenario.)

Once you've protected a sheet, you'll see that the options that you didn't allow are no longer available in the menus and dropdowns.

To remove protection from a worksheet just go back to the Format dropdown, select Unprotect Sheet, and provide your password.

You can also add or remove protection on a worksheet or for an entire Excel file (workbook) on the Review tab in the Changes section using Protect Sheet or Protect Workbook.

HIDING A WORKSHEET

To hide an entire worksheet so that other users don't see it when they open the file (for example, if you have dropdown lists and you want to use one worksheet for storing them), right-click on the worksheet name and select Hide.

To unhide a hidden worksheet, right-click on the name of any worksheet that's visible, choose Unhide, and then select which of the hidden worksheets you want to unhide.

If you combine hiding a worksheet with protecting the workbook, no one will be able to access that hidden worksheet unless they have the password and can unprotect the workbook first.

CREATING A TWO-VARIABLE ANALYSIS GRID

This isn't a function within Excel, it's just something I find incredibly useful and often use Excel to do, so I figure it's worth sharing. It sounds far fancier than it is, too.

A two-variable analysis grid takes one variable (for example, hours worked) and another variable (for example, hourly wage) and creates a table showing the results of combining those two variables. I use it to look at potential income from consulting, to analyze income at different sales and price levels for my books, to calculate what I could earn if I sold my house at different prices and sales commissions, etc.

When you combine it with conditional formatting, it's even more powerful.

Let's look at an example using hourly wage and hours worked to see how just a little bit more income per hour can really add up.

	A	B	C	D	E	F	G	H
1		Weekly				Hours Worked		
2			10	20	30	40	50	60
3		$ 8.50	$ 85.00	$ 170.00	$ 255.00	$ 340.00	$ 425.00	$ 510.00
4	Wages	$ 9.00	$ 90.00	$ 180.00	$ 270.00	$ 360.00	$ 450.00	$ 540.00
5		$ 9.50	$ 95.00	$ 190.00	$ 285.00	$ 380.00	$ 475.00	$ 570.00
6		$ 10.00	$ 100.00	$ 200.00	$ 300.00	$ 400.00	$ 500.00	$ 600.00
7		$ 10.50	$ 105.00	$ 210.00	$ 315.00	$ 420.00	$ 525.00	$ 630.00
8								
9		Monthly				Hours Worked		
10			10	20	30	40	50	60
11		$ 8.50	$ 340.00	$ 680.00	$ 1,020.00	$ 1,360.00	$ 1,700.00	$ 2,040.00
12	Wages	$ 9.00	$ 360.00	$ 720.00	$ 1,080.00	$ 1,440.00	$ 1,800.00	$ 2,160.00
13		$ 9.50	$ 380.00	$ 760.00	$ 1,140.00	$ 1,520.00	$ 1,900.00	$ 2,280.00
14		$ 10.00	$ 400.00	$ 800.00	$ 1,200.00	$ 1,600.00	$ 2,000.00	$ 2,400.00
15		$ 10.50	$ 420.00	$ 840.00	$ 1,260.00	$ 1,680.00	$ 2,100.00	$ 2,520.00
16								
17		Yearly				Hours Worked		
18			10	20	30	40	50	60
19		$ 8.50	$4,420.00	$ 8,840.00	$13,260.00	$17,680.00	$22,100.00	$26,520.00
20	Wages	$ 9.00	$4,680.00	$ 9,360.00	$14,040.00	$18,720.00	$23,400.00	$28,080.00
21		$ 9.50	$4,940.00	$ 9,880.00	$14,820.00	$19,760.00	$24,700.00	$29,640.00
22		$ 10.00	$5,200.00	$10,400.00	$15,600.00	$20,800.00	$26,000.00	$31,200.00
23		$ 10.50	$5,460.00	$10,920.00	$16,380.00	$21,840.00	$27,300.00	$32,760.00
24								

Here I've created three grids, one that only looks at a week, one that looks at a month, and one that looks at an entire year. On the last one I've then applied conditional formatting to highlight any cells that are greater than $20,000. (I went with numbers close to the minimum wage, but obviously, you'd want to do this with numbers that were relevant to your own situation.)

This grid is incredibly easy to create. (I usually don't bother with all the fancy formatting.) All you need is to write your formula once in the first cell of the grid and then copy it to the other cells in the grid.

The formula I used in Cell C3 is =$B3*C$2

The formula I used in Cell C11 is =$B11*C$10*4

The formula I used in Cell C19 is =$B19*C$18*52

That's what you'd earn in a week, what you'd earn in four weeks, and what you'd earn in fifty-two weeks at that wage if you worked that number of hours.

Using the $ sign in front of the B makes sure that Column B continues to be the column referenced even when we copy the formula to the right. And using the $ sign in front of each of the row numbers (2, 10, and 18) makes sure that that's the row referenced even when we copy the formula down to other rows.

If I'd left those $ signs out and tried to copy the formula it wouldn't have worked when I copied it to other cells in the grid. All the other cells would have been referencing the wrong row or column. You could write each formula by hand, but why do that when you don't need to?

Here are the grids with formulas showing for the first two column options:

	A	B	C	D
1		Weekly		
2			10	20
3		8.5	=$B3*C$2	=$B3*D$2
4	Wages	9	=$B4*C$2	=$B4*D$2
5		9.5	=$B5*C$2	=$B5*D$2
6		10	=$B6*C$2	=$B6*D$2
7		10.5	=$B7*C$2	=$B7*D$2
8				
9		Monthly		
10			10	20
11		8.5	=$B11*C$10*4	=$B11*D$10*4
12	Wages	9	=$B12*C$10*4	=$B12*D$10*4
13		9.5	=$B13*C$10*4	=$B13*D$10*4
14		10	=$B14*C$10*4	=$B14*D$10*4
15		10.5	=$B15*C$10*4	=$B15*D$10*4
16				
17		Yearly		
18			10	20
19		8.5	=$B19*C$18*52	=$B19*D$18*52
20	Wages	9	=$B20*C$18*52	=$B20*D$18*52
21		9.5	=$B21*C$18*52	=$B21*D$18*52
22		10	=$B22*C$18*52	=$B22*D$18*52
23		10.5	=$B23*C$18*52	=$B23*D$18*52
24				

That's it. It's that easy, but so powerful as an analysis tool. And, as you saw when we were talking about conditional formatting, you can incorporate additional fixed variables either in the formulas themselves (like I did here with the number of weeks) or by using a cell reference in the formula to point to the cells where you've entered them.

WHAT I HAVEN'T COVERED AND
HOW TO LEARN IT ON YOUR OWN

There are plenty of things you can do in Excel that I haven't covered here and didn't cover in *Excel for Beginners*. For example, there are hundreds of functions available in Excel and I've only covered maybe a dozen of them, all told. I could've provided a chapter on every single one, but most of what I would cover wouldn't be useful to most readers. I don't know anyone who has used all the function in Excel. I haven't and I've been using it as part of my day job for twenty-plus years.

What I've tried to do between this guide and *Excel for Beginners* is cover 99% of what the average reader will need in Excel. And, hopefully, give you a strong enough understanding of Excel that you can find the rest of what you need yourself.

Let me walk through how to do that.

Most of the options on the Excel toolbar have a description of what they do. All you have to do is hold your cursor over the option and it usually provides a one or two paragraph summary as well as a name for the option. Also, if there's a Ctrl shortcut, it lists that with the name. For example, Cut on the Home tab in the Clipboard section says "Cut (Ctrl+X)" and then has a description "Remove the selection and put it on the clipboard so you can paste it somewhere else."

If that isn't enough information, some of the options in Excel also have a "Tell me more" blue question mark at the bottom of that description. For example, Text to Columns in the Data Tools section of the Data Tab:

Text to Columns

Split a single column of text into multiple columns.

For example, you can separate a column of full names into separate first and last name columns.

You can choose how to split it up: fixed width or split at each comma, period, or other character.

❓ **Tell me more**

I consider this the best way to get into the Excel help screen for a given option. For some reason, when I try to search Excel help directly using the question mark in the top right corner of the screen it never seems to bring up what I want. But that is also another option. You can click on that question mark or press F1 and it will bring up the Excel Help box where you can enter a search phrase and then explore the suggested help topics to find what you want.

For functions, the best way to find more information is through the Insert Function dialogue box. To bring it up, go to the Formulas tab and select Insert Function.

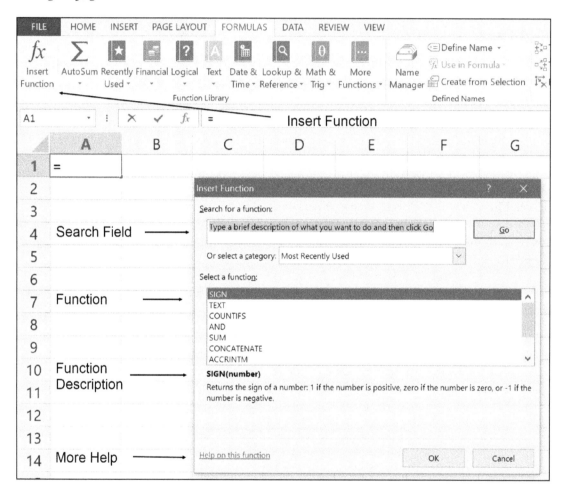

If you don't know the function you need, use the "search for a function" field. Type what you're trying to do into that box and click on Go and Excel will bring up a list of possible functions. For example, if I search for "merge text", CONCATENATE is on the list Excel provides.

Or you can use the dropdown menu below the search box to narrow your results to a specific type of function. (Financial, Math & Trig, Date and Time, Statistical, Lookup & Reference, Database, Text, Logical, Information, Engineering, Cube, Compatibility, Web, Most Recently Used)

If you do know the function, you can also type it in the search box.

For each function that Excel lists as a result of your search, when you highlight the function there will be a brief description of the function as well as, in the bottom left corner, a "help on this function" link.

If you need a better understanding of how the function works, choose the help link. This will bring up the Excel Help screen for that function.

Double-clicking on the function name will bring up a Function Arguments dialogue box that will walk you through how to build the function and will even show you a sample result.

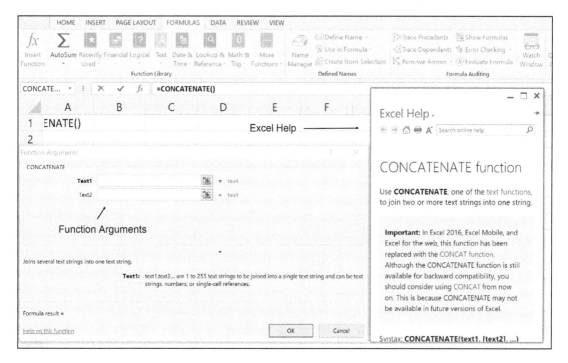

Sometimes (often) none of the above will be enough to answer your question.

When I need to better understand a functionality within Excel, I usually use an internet search to get me to the correct page on the Microsoft website (support.office.com). I'll search for something like "pivot tables excel 2015" and then choose the search result for support.office.com. Don't ask me why, but the help Microsoft provides on its website is far superior to what it provides within Excel itself. There are sample data sets, step-by-step instructions, video tutorials, and all sorts of other learning aids. (A little late to tell you this now, but you could've probably worked your way through all of them and you'd know more than I've taught you. But no one ever does that. I certainly don't. I just go there when I'm stuck.)

What the Microsoft website isn't good at is telling you if something you want to do is possible or how to use a specific function for a specific purpose. So, for example, my two-variable analysis grid above. Microsoft, I don't believe, unless it's coincidental, isn't going to provide help on building something like that.

But someone somewhere has probably already asked if that's possible on an Excel forum. Something like, "I want to model the outcome of different combinations of two variables. How can I do that in Excel?" You can benefit from that by doing a quick internet search for something like "table combination two variables excel" and see what comes up. It isn't always perfect. Sometimes you have to adapt what someone else needed to your own purposes or wade through a bunch of arguments and incorrect answers to get what you need, but it's usually out there. (Don't click on any links provided in those answers, though. I don't trust that they aren't from scammers. If someone can't explain it right there in the forum, move on.)

You could also post your questions on one of those forums, but be prepared for some rough treatment if you do. Chances are you'll forget to mention the version of Excel you're working in or something else that the person answering your question considers essential, and instead of being polite about it they'll make some rude comment. And heaven forbid you post in the wrong forum…But if you tough all that out and give them what they need, you'll usually get a solution to your question.

Of course, you can also email me at mlhumphreywriter@gmail.com. I don't check that account daily, but I do check it regularly. If I know or can find the answer quickly, I will definitely help out. (Just don't ask me to build your entire tracking worksheet for you, not unless you're prepared to pay my consulting rate which is not cheap.)

CONCLUSION

That's it. That's *Intermediate Excel*. If you want to go beyond this to things like using macros or SQL, I'm afraid you're on your own. But I do hope that at this point you feel pretty confident that you can use Excel for day-to-day purposes and to do some more complex data analysis if nothing else.

I'm pretty sure I mentioned this in *Excel for Beginners*, but let me mention it again. If you're ever troubleshooting a formula or function, you can double-click on the cell that contains it and Excel will highlight all of the cells used by the function. It's often very easy to see that a function is referencing a blank cell, for example, instead of the one it needs to. You may not know how to fix that (although I'd like to think you will at this point), but at least you'll know enough to tell someone who can fix it what isn't working. Another thing to note about that is that Excel color codes the cell highlight and the cell reference within the function so you can see that a blank cell is being referenced and then look at the formula/function and see where that happens within the formula.

Anyway.

My other big piece of advice on all off this is two-fold.

First, remember that you can almost always undo things. Ctrl + Z is your friend. Don't be scared to try something. You can almost always undo it if it goes wrong.

Also, if you are building a worksheet with a lot of moving parts, be sure to save interim versions of it. So let's say I figure out how to get the calculation in Column A working perfectly and am now starting on a new calculation for Column B. I might save a version of my file and title it File20170830.xls and then keep working on Column B. That way if I mess things up so bad I can't fix them (it happens), I can just go back to that older file and start over from the point where I knew things were working. By using the YYYYMMDD date format in the file name, it also means I can easily sort my files by name and find the most recent version.

Take risks. Try new things. Remember, you can always undo it or go back to an earlier version if it doesn't work. Best of luck.

* * *

Also, if you want to test your knowledge of this material check out *The Intermediate Excel Quiz Book* which contains quizzes for each section of this book as well as five exercises that will allow you to apply what you've learned here in real-world scenarios.

100 Excel Functions

EXCEL ESSENTIALS BOOKS 3 and 4

M.L. HUMPHREY

CONTENTS

50 MORE EXCEL FUNCTIONS

INTRODUCTION

In *Excel for Beginners* and *Intermediate Excel* I focused on how to use Excel to perform the tasks a user would need to know on a daily basis. In *Excel for Beginners* the focus was on entering information into Excel, formatting it properly, performing some basic analysis, and then printing the results. In *Intermediate Excel* it was on taking the analysis you can do in Excel to the next level using pivot tables, charts, and conditional formatting as well as some other data manipulation tricks I've found useful over the years.

And while I did cover certain functions in those books. Specifically, SUM and PRODUCT in *Excel for Beginners* and CONCATENATE, IF, COUNTIF/COUNTIFS, SUMIF/SUMIFS, and TEXT in *Intermediate Excel*, I didn't spend a large amount of time on functions in those books because the type of functions users will need are different.

I, for example, love to use SUMIFS and build nested IF functions. But it's possible another user would never use either one of those but might find a function like UPPER, which puts text into upper case letters, incredibly useful.

I didn't want to bog down either of those books with a discussion of functions that most users wouldn't use. However, as I was making the video course versions of those books it occurred to me that there was room to explore functions in more detail.

That's what this book will do. It covers a hundred useful Excel functions. (In my opinion. Others would probably have a different list.) There are functions related to text, statistics, math, dates, information, and logic, so it's a little bit of everything.

For those of you who've already read *Excel for Beginners* and *Intermediate Excel*, there will be some duplication both in terms of the functions covered as well as some of the topics around functions, like how to copy formulas and keep cell references fixed. But I think there is enough new content in this book that you'll still find value in it.

Do you need to read a book about the top hundred functions in Excel to use it effectively? No. You could stop with *Excel for Beginners* and be fine for most day to day uses. But using formulas and functions in Excel will allow you to take your usage of Excel to the next level. And I believe this book is a great introduction to that topic.

As with the other books in the series, this book is written using Excel 2013. Anyone with a version of Excel prior to Excel 2007 is going to be working in a version of Excel that looks very different and may be limited in its list of available functions. For example, SUMIFS and COUNTIFS were not available in versions of Excel prior to Excel 2007.

So that's what this book covers. Let's get started with an overview of how formulas and functions work.

HOW FORMULAS AND FUNCTIONS WORK

If you are writing a basic mathematical formula in Excel you do so by starting your entry in a cell with a plus (+), a minus (-) or an equals (=) sign. Unless you have a good reason for doing so, like years of ingrained habit, I recommend just using the equals sign.

So if I want to add two values together in Excel, I would enter something like this into the cell:

$$=2+3$$

I could also do so using cell references if those values were already stored in cells in my worksheet:

$$=A1+B1$$

(If you aren't familiar with cell notation in Excel, see Appendix A.)

When I hit Enter or otherwise leave that cell, Excel will display the result of the formula in the cell. In the top example, that means it would display the value 5 in the cell. Excel will, however, retain the formula that was used to calculate that value. You can either double-click in the cell or click on the cell and look to the formula bar to see the formula.

$\times$ ✓ f_x	=2+3 ⟵——— Formula		
B	**C**	**D**	**E**
	Value ⟶	5	

Excel formulas can use basic mathematical notation or they can use functions to perform specified tasks.

To add two numbers together in Excel you use the plus (+) sign between the values like I did above. To subtract one number from another you use the minus (-) sign. To multiply two numbers you use the asterisk (*) sign. To divide two numbers you use the forward slash (/). So:

=3-2 would subtract 2 from 3

=3*2 would multiply 3 times 2

=3/2 would divide 3 by 2

As I mentioned above, your formulas can either use cell references or numbers. So:

=A1-B1 would subtract the value in Cell B1 from the value in Cell A1

=A1*B1 would multiply the value in Cell A1 by the value in Cell B1

=A1/B1 would divide the value in Cell A1 by the value in Cell B1

Excel can handle as complex a formula as you want to throw at it. You can combine in one cell a formula that adds multiple values, divides values, subtracts values, and multiplies values as well as any number of other mathematical tasks or functions.

If you're going to combine calculation steps within one cell, you need to be careful that you properly place your parens so that calculations are performed in the correct order. There is a help document on this titled "Calculation operators and precedence in Excel" that lists the order in which calculations are done by Excel and also lists a number of operators (such as > for greater than) that are useful to know when working with formulas and functions in Excel.

If you're building a really complex formula it's always a good idea to test it as you go to make sure that all of the components are working properly and that the end result is the expected result. So I will build each component separately before combining them all in one cell.

Formulas in Excel go beyond the basic mathematical formula you learned in school. They can handle date-based, text-based, and logic-based calculations as well as mathematical calculations. They do this through the use of Excel functions.

Functions are essentially programmed shortcuts that do specific tasks. For example, the SUM function will add all of the values in a range of cells that you identify. Or the CONCATENATE function will take a set of inputs (usually text) and combine them together in one cell.

There are hundreds of functions in Excel that you can use in your formulas.

To use a function, you start a formula with the equals sign, type in the name of the function, use an opening paren, provide the inputs required for that function, and then use a closing paren.

So to sum a range of cells from A1 through A3, which we'll cover more when we start working through the functions covered by this book, you would type

=SUM(A1:A3)

The equals sign tells Excel this is a formula, the SUM portion tells Excel that we're using the SUM function, the opening paren says we're going to list inputs for that function, the A1:A3 tell Excel which cells to apply the function to, and then the closing paren says that's the end of the function. It doesn't have to be the end of the formula.

(As we'll discuss at the end, you can combine functions within one formula.)

I could have

$$=SUM(A1:A3) + SUM(C1:C3)$$

That's sloppy notation. I could as easily have written =SUM(A1:A3,C1:C3) and had the same result. But the point here is that a formula starts with an equals sign and then you use functions as part of that formula by using their name followed by opening and closing parens and providing the required information for the particular function within the parens.

Don't worry. We're going to walk through lots and lots of examples of this. You'll get it if you don't now.

Just remember to think of a function, whether it handles text or is logical or performs a mathematical function, as part of a formula. In other words, as part of something that is being calculated based upon your inputs.

Garbage in, garbage out. If you give the function the wrong inputs, you will get the wrong results. So if you get an error message (which we'll discuss at the end) when using a function, check that the information you input into your formula is formatted properly and is of the right type. That's usually where things go wrong.

Alright. Next we'll talk about where to find functions in Excel. But remember, you need an equals sign (=) to start a formula and then you can use numbers, cell references, operators, or functions to build that formula.

WHERE TO FIND FUNCTIONS

In this guide we're going to cover the hundred Excel functions I thought were most useful for the largest number of people. But there are far, far more functions than that in Excel. And chances are at some point you'll need one I didn't cover here.

In newer versions of Excel, you can go to the Formulas tab to see what Excel functions are available to you. There is a section called Function Library that lists various categories of functions. Mine shows Recently Used, Financial, Logical, Text, Date & Time, Lookup & Reference, Math & Trig, and then there's a dropdown for More Functions that shows the categories Statistical, Engineering, Cube, Information, Compatibility, and Web.

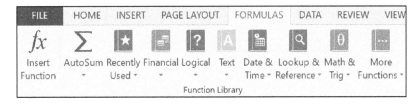

Click on the dropdown arrow next to any of the categories and you'll see a listing of functions that fall under that heading.

Now, unless you know what you're looking for, this listing probably won't help you much because the functions are named things like ACCRINT and IFNA. You can hold your cursor over each of the names and Excel will provide a brief description of the function for you, but for some of the lists that's a lot of functions to look through.

Each description also includes a Tell Me More at the end of the description. If you click on that option, the Excel Help screen will appear. You can then click on "Excel functions (alphabetical)" and choose your desired function from the list. This will show you additional information on the function and how it works.

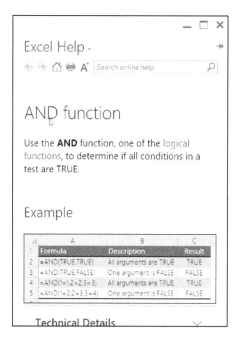

Instead of that, I would recommend that you use the Insert Function option which is also available in the Formulas tab on the far left-hand side.

Be sure you're clicked into an empty cell on your worksheet and then click on Insert Function. This will bring up the Insert Function dialogue box.

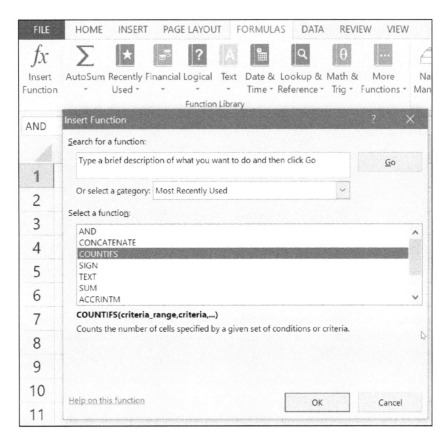

In the top section under where it says "Search for a function" you can type what you're looking to do and then click on Go. (Be sure that the category dropdown right below the search box is set to All unless you know for certain what category your function falls under.)

Excel will provide a list of functions that it thinks meet your search criteria. (Sometimes this list is very far off, so don't just accept the first choice blindly.) You can left-click on each of the listed functions to see a brief description of the function. This appears below the box where the functions are listed.

You will also see for each function a list of the required inputs for that function.

For COUNTIFS you can see in the screenshot above that the first input required is the criteria range and that the second input required is the criteria and that the description of the function is "Counts the number of cells specified by a given set of conditions or criteria."

(In this guide I have listed this information for each function at the top of the function's page.)

If you need more information on a function, you can click on the "Help on this function" link in the bottom left corner of the dialogue box. This will bring up the Excel Help box for that particular function.

Otherwise, you can just click on the function you want and choose OK.

This will insert the function into whichever cell you'd been clicked into before you chose Insert Function. You will also see a Function Arguments dialogue box that lists the inputs your function needs and provides a location for you to input those values.

You can either input numeric values in those boxes or use cell references by clicking on the cells in your worksheet or typing the cell references in.

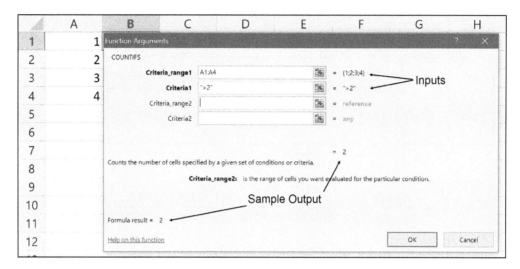

At the bottom of the list of inputs Excel will show you a sample value based upon the inputs you've chosen. The sample also appears in the bottom left corner of the dialogue box.

When you're done, click OK.

* * *

If you already know the function you want to use but aren't sure about the inputs, you can start typing your formula into a cell. After you type equals and the function name you will see a definition for the function.

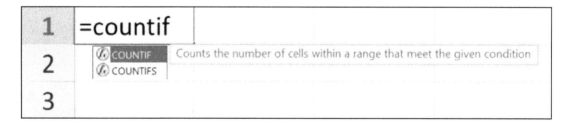

After you type the opening paren for the function you will see a description of the inputs needed for the function listed directly below the cell.

1	=countif(
2	COUNTIF(**range**, criteria)
3	

If you click on the function name after you've typed the opening paren, Excel will open the Excel Help dialogue box specific to that function.

* * *

If none of that works to help you find the function you need, then an Internet search is probably your best option.

A quick search for something like "How do I get Excel to identify the day of the week from a date?" will usually get you the answer you need. You can then use the Excel help for that formula either from within Excel or from the Microsoft website to guide you. (Or watch a free video on how to do it.)

* * *

One final note.

In older versions of Excel the Formulas tab didn't exist, so what I would do to bring up that Insert Function dialogue box is I would type equals into a cell and then go to the white dropdown box to the left of the formula bar, click on that dropdown arrow, and choose More Function from the bottom of the list.

This would bring up the Insert Function dialogue box and then I could follow the steps above.

So that's how you find the functions you need, what they do, and what inputs they require.

FORMULA AND FUNCTION BEST PRACTICES

Now let's discuss a few best practices when it comes to using formulas and functions.

Make Your Assumptions Visible

You're going to see as we move forward that you can build a formula that uses a function where all of the information to make the calculation is contained within that one cell.

So if I want to add the values 10, 20, and 30 together I can do that in one cell using the SUM function, =SUM(10,20,30), and all anyone will see in the worksheet is the result of that calculation, 60.

You may be tempted to do this because it's clean. All that people see is what you want them to, the result of your calculation.

And maybe you don't expect to have to adjust those values so you don't see an issue in having your formula built that way.

I would encourage you not to do this. In my experience, a best practice in terms of building formulas is to have any fixed values or assumptions visible in the worksheet. The reason to do this is so that someone looking at the sheet can see what assumptions fed the calculation.

Here's an example:

Let's say you're calculating how much you'll make if you sell your house. You figure you'll have to spend $2,500 to clean the place up a bit, pay a commission of 5%, and that the house is worth $500,000.

Now, if you sat down to discuss this with your spouse you could just show them the results of that calculation (the value on the left) or you could show them the results of the calculation and the assumptions you made (the value on the right).

	A	B	C	D	E
1		Option 1			Option 2
2				Home Price	$500,000.00
3	Net	$ 472,500.00		Commission	5%
4				Fix Up Cost	$2,500.00
5					
6				Net	$472,500.00
7					

Option 2 is more useful, because you can both see what assumptions were made and acknowledge and validate each one. Maybe your spouse knows that houses in the area have been selling for $400,000 instead of $500,000 or that the neighbors up the street worked with a great broker who only charges 4% commission. Without showing them your assumptions, they aren't given a chance to provide their input.

If you bury your assumptions in your calculation field they're easy to forget about. And that can be dangerous if they're wrong.

So I strongly urge you to always have your assumptions present and visible in your worksheet rather than buried in your formulas.

Use Paste Special - Values

The other thing I do that you may or may not want to do depending on why you're using Excel is that I frequently use Paste Special – Values when I'm done with performing a set of calculations.

Do not do this if the calculations you performed need to be updated on an ongoing basis.

But I do a lot of calculations where I want to keep the results for reference but will not be recalculating any values. In this case I want to lock those values down so that I don't lose them or inadvertently recalculate them by changing a value in an input cell or deleting data that fed those calculations.

The simple way to do this is to select the cells, Ctrl + C to copy, and then right-click and under Paste Special choose the Values option (the one with the 123 on the clipboard). This will replace any calculated cells in that range with just the values of the calculation.

After you do that, instead of a formula that says "add Cells A1 and B1 together" you'll have a cell that just contains the result of having added Cells A1 and B1 together. Now if you delete Cells A1 and B1 or change their values, your result field won't change.

Don't Mess With Your Raw Data

I mentioned this in the other books, but am going to mention it again here.

To the extent possible, you should always store your raw data in one location and do all of your calculations and manipulations on that data elsewhere. (Ideally you would also record all of the steps you followed to take that raw data and turn it into your final product, but it's not as easy to do in something like Excel as it is in a program like R.)

If you don't do this, all it takes is one bad sort or one bad function and your data can be irreparably changed if you don't catch it right away.

If you keep your raw data separate there is nothing you can't come back from. You might have to redo a lot of work, but you won't be left with a dataset that's useless.

I also save versions of my worksheets when I'm working on something particularly complicated. That way I can go back to a stage where everything was working without having to start over from scratch. Just be sure to label your files clearly so that you know which is the most recent version. (File V1, File V2, etc.)

Test Your Formulas

If I'm going to apply a formula to a large range of data I will usually test that formula on a much smaller sample of my data where I can visually evaluate the results. So if I'm writing a formula to sum customer transactions for customers from Alaska who bought Widgets (using SUMIFS), I'll run that formula against just ten rows of data to make sure that it's doing what I think it should before I apply it to ten thousand rows of data.

As much as possible you should always either check you formulas on a subset of data or "gut check" your results. Don't just accept the value Excel gives you without questioning whether it actually makes sense. (Because garbage in, garbage out. Excel's ability to perform calculations is limited by your ability to write those calculations properly. And we all make mistakes. One missing $ sign or one > instead of >= and the result you get will not be the result you wanted.)

Test, test, test. And then check, check, check.

COPYING FORMULAS

Before we move into discussing specific functions, I want to cover how to copy formulas and keep cell references fixed.

One of the most powerful aspects of Excel, for me, is in the fact that I can write a formula once, copy it, and paste it to thousands of cells, and it will automatically adjust to its new location

It's fantastic.

When that's what you want.

When copying a formula always check the formula first to be sure that it's going to copy well.

The biggest issue I run into with copying formulas is failing to lock down cells that need to be fixed references.

So if I've put interest rate in Cell A1 and I need every single calculation no matter the row to reference Cell A1, then I need to lock down that cell reference before I copy the formula. You do this by using $ signs in your formula.

To lock an entire cell reference use dollar signs in front of both the column and the row identifier. So $A$1 will always reference the cell in Column A and Row 1 no matter where I copy that formula to.

To lock just the column reference, put a dollar sign in front of the column identifier. So $A1. This will ensure that no matter where the formulas is copied to, that cell will always reference Column A. The row number, however, will be able to adjust. (I use this in my two-variable analysis grid.)

To lock the row reference, put a dollar sign in front of the row identifier. So A$1. This will ensure that no matter where the formula is copied to, the cell will always reference Row 1. The column reference, however, will change.

I find that when I'm copying formulas I need to check for not only fixed values, like the interest rate example above, but also for cell ranges.

For example, if I want to know what percent of my overall sales each product was and I have a list of sales by product I can calculate that by taking the sales for each product divided by the total sales for all products. If I take that total sales by referencing a cell range, such as A1:A25, then before I copy that formula down my row of values I need to lock in that range by writing it as $A$1:$A$25.

If I don't do that, in the next row down that cell range will change to be A2:A26 instead of A1:A25.

So always check before copying.

And if you just need to move a formula to a new location but don't want any of the cell references to adjust then you need to cut and move the formula instead of copying it.

OK. That's it for the preliminaries. Time to start talking about specific functions. We'll start with some basic Math & Trig ones first.

50 Useful Excel Functions

THE SUM FUNCTION

Notation: SUM(number1, [number2],…)
Excel Definition: Adds all the numbers in a range of cells.

The SUM function is probably the most basic function in Excel and I'd suspect the most widely used. What the SUM function does is add numbers together. These can be numbers that you type directly into the function (not recommended as discussed above under best practices) or they can be values that are stored in other cells. Cells do not need to be touching for their values to be added together, although it's much easier to write your SUM function if they are.

To use the function you use SUM and must include at least one number (or cell range) within the parens.

Some examples of formulas that use the SUM function are:

=SUM(2,3,4)

Adds the numbers 2, 3, and 4 together. So it's the same as using =2+3+4 as your formula.

=SUM(A1,A2,A3)

This formula does the exact same thing as the first formula except it's using cell references to add the values in Cells A1, A2, and A3 together. You could also type =A1+A2+A3 in a cell and get the same result.

=SUM(A1:A3)

This is where the SUM function becomes necessary. It's a cleaner way to write the second example since we've replaced A1, A2, A3 with A1:A3. Because of that cell notation it requires use of the SUM function to work.

=SUM(A1:A3,B2:B6)

This one is saying to add all the values in the range from Cell A1 to Cell A3 (so Cells A1, A2, and A3) as well as all the values in the range from Cell B2 to Cell B6 (so Cells B2, B3, B4, B5, and B6). Because of the use of the cell ranges, this one also requires use of the SUM function. The alternative would be to write =A1+A2+A3+B2+B3+B4+B5+B6 which no one wants to do.

$$=SUM(A:A)$$

This example is saying to sum all of the values in Column A.

$$=SUM(5:5)$$

This example is saying to sum all of the values in Row 5.

* * *

Neither of those last two can be easily replaced with a formula that uses the plus sign. They demonstrate how powerful such a simple function can be.

So, pretty simple, right? An equals sign, SUM, opening paren, whatever you want to add together using cell notation, closing paren. Done.

And as I mentioned above, you can also combine functions in a larger formula. So, for example, if I had a value in Cell A1 and I wanted to subtract all of the values in Column C, I could write that as:

$$=A1-SUM(C:C)$$

Or if I wanted to subtract the values in Column C from A1 but then also add the values in Column E, I could do that as well:

$$=A1-SUM(C:C)+SUM(E:E)$$

Note that when a function doesn't start a formula that you don't need to put the equals sign in front of it.

Alright.

Let's move on to PRODUCT which is another simple one, although I would expect much less popular.

THE PRODUCT FUNCTION

Notation: PRODUCT(number1, [number2],…)
Excel Definition: Multiplies all the numbers given as arguments.

The PRODUCT function does for multiplication what the SUM function does for addition. It will multiply all of the values that you include in the parens by one another.

A few examples:

$$=PRODUCT(2,3,4)$$

Multiplies 2 times 3 times 4.

$$=PRODUCT(A1:A3)$$

Multiplies the value in Cell A1 times the value in Cell A2 times the value in Cell A3.

$$=PRODUCT(A:A)$$

Multiplies all of the values in Column A times one another. So Cell A1 times Cell A2 times Cell A3, etc.

You could also just multiply values times one another using an asterisk (*). The top two examples above could be written as the following:

$$=2*3*4$$

$$=A1*A2*A3$$

But the value of PRODUCT comes in when you have a large range of values that you need to multiply times one another, like the last example which has 65,536 potential values.

Of course there aren't many circumstances where you'll want to multiply that many numbers times one another, which is why I suspect the function is rarely used.

The reason I've included it here is because of the next function we're going to discuss, SUMPRODUCT, which combines summing and multiplying values.

THE SUMPRODUCT FUNCTION

Notation: SUMPRODUCT(array1, [array2], [array3],…)
Excel Definition: Returns the sum of the products of corresponding ranges or arrays.

You use SUMPRODUCT when you have a range of cells that need to be multiplied times one another, like number of units and price to get total cost per product, and then summed, to get total cost, for example.

SUMPRODUCT is incredibly useful when you need it. You could get the same result using a combination of SUM and PRODUCT, but why do that when one little function will do it for you.

Now, that definition and the use of "array" in the Excel notation for the function probably seem a little intimidating. Don't worry, they're not.

Let's walk through an example:

	A	B	C	D	E
1	**Product**	**Units Bought**	**Price Per Unit**	**Income**	**Formulas in Column D**
2	Widget	3	$ 2.50	$ 7.50	=B2*C2
3	Whatsit	4	$ 3.20	$12.80	=B3*C3
4	Whatchamacallit	6	$ 4.40	$26.40	=B4*C4
5	Whatnot	2	$ 5.50	$11.00	=B5*C5
6					
7			**Total Earned**	$57.70	=SUM(D2:D5)
8			**Total Earned**	$57.70	=SUMPRODUCT(B2:B5,C2:C5)
9					

What we have here is a list of products bought by a customer. We have product name, number of units bought, and price paid per unit.

To calculate the total amount spent you could multiply units times price paid for each product and then sum those values. That's what happens in Cells D2 through D7. In Cells D2 through D5 we have the amount spent on each product (the formulas used are shown in Column E), and then in D7 we have the sum of those values. (That formula is also shown in Column E.)

Your other option is to use the SUMPRODUCT function. That's what happens in Cell D8. The formula, =SUMPRODUCT(B2:B5,C2:C5) is shown in Cell E8.

As you can see above in the Excel notation, SUMPRODUCT requires that you tell it the ranges of the cells that need to be multiplied by one another. In this case, our first range of values was number of units which is in Cells B2 through B5 and our second range of values was price per unit which is in Cells C2 through C5.

What SUMPRODUCT does is it takes the value from the first cell in each provided range, in this case Cells B2 and C2, and multiplies those values. It then does the same with the values in the second cell in each range, in this case the values in Cells B3 and C3. It continues to do this for the entire range. Once it has those multiplied values it then sums them together to get the final result.

It does everything we did in Cells D2 though D7, but in one step. Like I said, very useful when you need it.

A few things to be aware of. The ranges you input into the function need to be the same size for this to work. If they aren't you will get a #VALUE! result instead.

Also, be sure that the ranges you choose have numbers in them and not text. Excel will treat non-numeric values as zeros and any number times zero is…zero.

And, while the example I used above had values in two columns you are not limited to just two columns of values. (Just be sure the cells you select should be multiplied by one another and then added. So I could've had another column in there for sales tax, for example.) And you can also use SUMPRODUCT with values that are in rows instead or in a combination of rows and columns. The key is that the ranges you specify have to be the same dimension, so the same number of columns and rows.

THE AVERAGE FUNCTION

Notation: AVERAGE(number1, [number2],...)
Excel Definition: Returns the average (arithmetic mean) of its arguments, which can be numbers or names, arrays, or references that contain numbers.

The three functions we just discussed are all listed by Excel under the Math & Trig category. This next one, AVERAGE, is listed as a Statistical function, but when I think about taking an average I generally think of it along with addition and division so I'm including it here.

The definition above is slightly confusing when you read it, so let's rewrite it to clarify. Let's write it as this: The AVERAGE function returns the average (arithmetic mean) of its arguments. The arguments can be numbers like 1, 2, 3, or 4. Or the arguments can be a named range, an array, or a cell reference as long as the cells or range referenced include numbers.

What the AVERAGE function does is it takes the sum of a range of numbers and then divides that sum by the number of entries in the range that had a value.

For example, if I have the values 1, 2, 3, 4, and 5 in a range of 5 cells from A1 through A5 and I write =AVERAGE(A1:A5), Excel will add those values to get 15, divide that total by 5, and return a value of 3.

If I include Cell A6, a blank cell, in that range and write it as =AVERAGE(A1:A6), I get the same result even though I now have six cells in my range, because AVERAGE only looks at those cells that have values in them.

This is very important. And may not be what you wanted.

If you have a cell in your range that should be included but where the value is blank instead of zero, you need to put a zero in that cell or it will not be included in your calculation.

In our example above, putting a zero in Cell A6 changes our average to 2.5 from 3 because we're now dividing 15 by 6 instead of 5.

Here's are all three scenarios side-by-side with the formula used shown above each result.

	A	B	C
1	**Value Range**	**Value Range**	**Value Range**
2	1	1	1
3	2	2	2
4	3	3	3
5	4	4	4
6	5	5	5
7			0
8	=AVERAGE(A1:A5)	=AVERAGE(B1:B6)	=AVERAGE(C1:C6)
9	**3**	**3**	**2.5**

AVERAGE will, of course, also work on values that you enter directly in the formula. So =AVERAGE(1,2,3,4,5) would return a value of 3. (But doing this is not recommended, as discussed in the best practices chapter.)

If you use AVERAGE on a range of cells that include text in some of the cells, those cells that contain text will be ignored and treated the same as a blank cell, so not counted for the divisor.

For example, in the sample below even though there are five cells referenced by =AVERAGE(H2:H6) Excel is summing the numeric values in Cells H3 through H5 and dividing them by 3. It ignores Cell H2 which has text and Cell H6 which is blank.

	H
1	**Value Range**
2	Alpha
3	1
4	2
5	3
6	=AVERAGE(H2:H6)
7	2

So if you have a range that you are going to take an average from and you use AVERAGE be sure that the range only contains numbers and that all cells in the range that you want included in your calculation have a zero or a number in them.

THE AVERAGEA FUNCTION

Notation: AVERAGEA(value1, [value2],…)
Excel Definition: Returns the average (arithmetic mean) of its arguments, evaluating text and FALSE in arguments as 0; TRUE evaluates as 1. Arguments can be numbers, names, arrays, or references.

If you need to take an average from a range that has non-numeric values in it and you need those cells included when calculating the average, you can use AVERAGEA to do so.

As it says in the definition, AVERAGEA treats text entries and FALSE values as having a value of 0 and TRUE values as having a value of 1 when calculating the arithmetic mean.

For example, if I have a range of cells and they have the numeric values 10 and 6 and then the text values "This" and "That" in them, like this:

	A	B
1	10	
2	6	
3	This	
4	That	
5	4	=AVERAGEA(A1:A4)
6	8	=AVERAGE(A1:A4)

If I use AVERAGEA to take the average of those four cells, the value it returns is 4 because it takes 10+6 and then divides that by the number of cells with values in it, 4. 16 divided by 4 is 4.

If I use AVERAGE on that same range of cells, the value Excel returns is 8 because it takes 10+6 but then only divides by the number of cells that have numbers in them, 2. 16 divided by 2 is 8.

You will need to decide based on your data which function, AVERAGE or AVERAGEA, is the appropriate choice. With both of them, however, know that a completely blank cell will be skipped over in calculating the average, so you still need a zero value or something in each cell if you want that cell included in the calculation.

As noted in the definition, AVERAGEA also counts TRUE values as 1 when taking an average. So if you want to know the average outcome of a scenario, you could use an IF function to generate TRUE and FALSE values and then use AVERAGEA to calculate the average number of times the outcome occurred.

Here I've done so with a scenario to determine if the entries in Column G were greater than 11. The IF function (which we cover later) returns a value of TRUE if the value is over 11 and FALSE if it is not. I then used AVERAGEA to calculate the average outcome.

	H	I
1	FALSE	
2	FALSE	
3	TRUE	
4	TRUE	
5	0.5	=AVERAGEA(H1:H4)
6	#DIV/0!	=AVERAGE(H1:H4)

AVERAGEA returns a result of .5 since half of the time the result was TRUE and half of the time the result was FALSE. As you can see, AVERAGE returns an error message, #DIV/0!, because there were no values to include in the average calculation so Excel tried to divide by zero which it can't do.

THE MEDIAN FUNCTION

Notation: MEDIAN(number1, [number2],…)
Excel Definition: Returns the median, or the number in the middle of the set of given numbers.

The average calculation is very useful and very commonly used. But it can sometimes give very misleading results. That's where MEDIAN and MODE come in. They provide a better picture when your data is skewed in some way.

For example, writing income is highly skewed. (As is acting income.) There's someone out there making $100,000 a month and a lot of other someones out there making $10 a month.

If you average those incomes you'll see an average of $10,000 a month, which looks really good. But the reality is that it's either be that one person making $100,000 a month or everyone else making $10 a month. (Not really, but close.)

The average doesn't show this, but the median will.

So if you don't know the nature of your data, it's always a good idea to take both the average and the median and compare them.

If the data is evenly distributed (spread out nicely) then they'll give you similar results. But if it's skewed, like in my example above, you'll have vastly different outcomes.

To get the median, just give Excel your range.

In the example below I've used

=MEDIAN(A1:A9)

to calculate the median of the values in Cells A1 through A9:

	A	B
1	1	
2	1	
3	1	
4	1	
5	1	
6	1	
7	1	
8	1	
9	100	
10	1	=MEDIAN(A1:A9)
11	12	=AVERAGE(A1:A9)

It's that simple. (And, as you can see, because of the 100 value in that range compared to the 1s in all the other cells, MEDIAN and AVERAGE return very different results.)

If you give Excel a range that has an even number of values, so there isn't just one middle value, Excel will average the two middle values and return their average. So =MEDIAN(1,2,3,4) will return 2.5 which is the average of the middle two values, 2 and 3.

(Be careful with this. Because =MEDIAN(1,100) would return a value of 50.5 which is very misleading. In general, it's a good idea to chart or visually inspect a dataset so you can see when situations like this exist.)

Median also works on logical values (TRUE, FALSE) that are typed directly into the argument. So

=MEDIAN(TRUE,TRUE,FALSE)

will return a value of 1 and

=MEDIAN(FALSE,FALSE,TRUE)

will return a value of 0.

But if you reference a range with TRUEs and FALSEs in it you'll get a #NUM! error.

I'm not sure how much good it does you that you can type it into the function directly, but that's the way it works. If you do ever have a set of TRUE/FALSE results, you can always convert them to ones and zeros using an IF function and then take the median of the ones and zeros.

THE MODE FUNCTION

Notation: MODE(number1, [number2],…)
Excel Definition: Returns the most frequently occurring, or repetitive, value in an array or range of data.

Excel has a note on the MODE function that it only exists for compatibility with Excel 2007 or earlier. For those of you using Excel 2013 or later, you should look to MODE.SNGL and MODE.MULT instead.

MODE goes along with AVERAGE and MEDIAN as a possible way to look at your data and to figure out the result that most people will see.

As we discussed above, AVERAGE doesn't work well if your data has a high skew to it. So if most people score really low and there are just a few people who score really high then looking at an average is going to mislead you about how the average person will do. MEDIAN can sometimes be a better measure because it looks at the result in the exact middle.

But MEDIAN also has a flaw. And that's that it's not very good with data that has spikes that aren't near the median. Look at the following example:

	A	B	C	D	E
1	1				
2	1				
3	3				
4	3				
5	4		AVERAGE	94.67	=AVERAGE(A1:A12)
6	4		MEDIAN	17.00	=MEDIAN(A1:A12)
7	30		MODE	30.00	=MODE(A1:A12)
8	30				
9	30				
10	30				
11	500				
12	500				

There are twelve values to analyze. I've taken those values and used the COUNTIF function to figure out how many times each value occurs. You can see that 1, 3, 4, and 500 each occur two times and that 30 occurs four times.

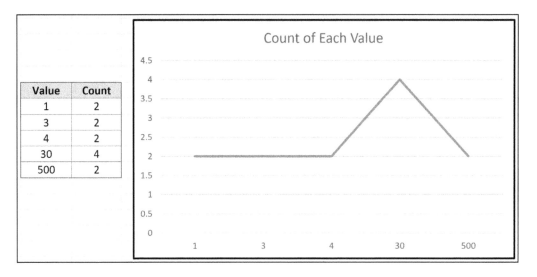

Value	Count
1	2
3	2
4	2
30	4
500	2

So if you were placing a bet on which number was most likely to occur, you'd want to bet on the 30. Right? If you had to choose just one of the five values, 30 would be the most likely outcome.

But the average of these numbers is approximately 95 and the median is 17. (The median is 17 because since there are an even number of values Excel takes the two closest to the center, in this case a 4 and a 30, and averages them.)

Neither of those functions comes close to providing the right answer.

But MODE, which returns the most frequently occurring outcome, will return a value of 30.

What it does is basically build a count table like I just did and then return the outcome with the highest number of occurrences.

Because in this case the most common outcome is not around the center, looking for the mode is the only way to predict the most likely outcome with any sort of accuracy.

(This is also why if you're dealing with a dataset that you're not familiar with it's good to visualize the data. The spike at 30 is very clear when we plot the count of each value. If you don't have discrete values, you can put a range of values in groups and plot the count of how many values fall in each group instead.)

MODE works just like AVERAGE and MEDIAN. Just give it a range of cells to evaluate:

=MODE(A1:A12)

In Excel 2013 and later versions of Excel the basic MODE function has been replaced with two new functions, MODE.SNGL and MODE.MULT, so let's talk about those next.

THE MODE.SNGL FUNCTION

Notation: MODE.SNGL(number1, [number2],…)
Excel Definition: Returns the most frequently occurring, or repetitive, value in an array or range of data.

MODE.SNGL is the exact same as MODE. See above for how that works. The big change that occurred with Excel 2013 was the introduction of MODE.MULT. So let's talk about that next.

THE MODE.MULT FUNCTION

Notation: MODE.MULT(number1, [number2],…)
Excel Definition: Returns a vertical array of the most frequently occurring,
or repetitive, values in an array or range of data.

The MODE.MULT function allows you to have Excel return more than one value when it calculates the mode for a range of values. So if you have multi-modal data (meaning there are multiple bumps in your data), using MODE.MULT will return those multiple values.

Now, there's a trick to using it.

And that's that it's considered an array formula. (Yeah, I'd never heard of it before either. There's a reason I've never written a book called *Advanced Excel*. But we'll cover it here in this one limited example so that we've fully discussed calculating the mode of a range of numbers.)

To use MODE.MULT you need a range of values that you're going to use for your mode calculation and a range of cells where you're going to put the result of that calculation.

Highlight the range of cells where you want your *results* to be displayed. You need to highlight enough cells to allow Excel to provide all possible values. (This is why plotting your data is a good idea. If you've plotted your data and seen that it has two equal-sized bumps in it, then you would know to highlight two cells. Otherwise you can guess and Excel will just return an #N/A value for the cells it doesn't use.)

In the example below, I highlighted Cells D5 through D8.

Once you have your cells highlighted where you want your results to display, *then* you type your formula into the formula bar.

In the example below I typed:

=MODE.MULT(A1:A10)

Then, and this is crucial because it won't work otherwise, instead of typing Enter, you need to type Ctrl + Shift + Enter all at the same time.

You'll know you've done it right, because when you click back into the cell the formula will have little brackets around it. Like this:

$$\{=MODE.MULT(A1:A10)\}$$

That exact same formula will appear in all of the cells you highlighted, not just the top one. And it will calculate the multiple modes in your data. Like this:

	A	B	C	D	E
1	1				
2	3		AVERAGE	63.3	=AVERAGE(A1:A10)
3	3		MEDIAN	16.5	=MEDIAN(A1:A10)
4	3		MODE	3	=MODE(A1:A10)
5	3			3	{=MODE.MULT(A1:A10)}
6	30		MODE.MULT	30	{=MODE.MULT(A1:A10)}
7	30			#N/A	{=MODE.MULT(A1:A10)}
8	30			#N/A	{=MODE.MULT(A1:A10)}
9	30				
10	500				

Here we have a dataset where 1 and 500 occur once and 3 and 30 occur four times. When I plot this data you can see that it's multi-modal, meaning it has more than one peak value. The likely outcome is either 3 or 30.

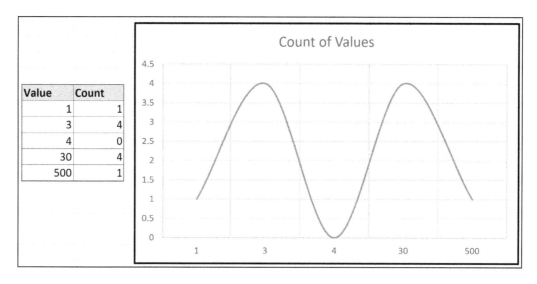

If I take just the average of these values, though, I get 63.3. And if I take the median I get 16.5. And if I take the basic mode which existed in earlier versions of Excel I get 3, because it returns the first most frequent value in my data.

But with MODE.MULT, Excel returns both 3 and 30.

Isn't that great?

And if you wanted your results to display in a single row instead of a single column, you just write the formula as =TRANSPOSE(MODE.MULT(A1:A10)) instead.

Very useful. But also only available in Excel 2013 or later.

(But you still need to be careful when you use this. It's not perfect. Because it only returns the most frequently occurring value(s). So if one value occurs 12 times and another occurs 11 it will only return the one that occurs 12 times. But it's better than nothing.)

THE MIN FUNCTION

Notation: MIN(number1, [number2],…)
Excel Definition: Returns the smallest number in a set of values. Ignores logical values and text.

Another useful Statistical function is the MIN function. This one takes a range of values or list of numbers and returns the smallest value.

You could say =MIN(1,2,3) and it would return a value of 1 or =MIN(-1,0,1) and it would return a value of -1, but the real power of this function is when you use it on a range of cells.

So, for example, let's say you want to know the lowest test score from a class that had 125 students in it and where all of the test scores were recorded in Column C. You would simply write the function as =MIN(C:C) and it would return for you the lowest test score in the range.

According to Excel, if you reference a range and ask Excel to return the minimum value and there are no numbers in the range it will return a value of zero.

Also, if the range contains an error value such as #DIV/0! the function will return that error value. In this case, #DIV/0!.

THE MINA FUNCTION

Notation: MINA(value1, [value2],…)
Excel Definition: Returns the smallest value in a set of values. Does not ignore logical values and text.

MINA is much like MIN except that it *will* consider logical values and text in determining the minimum value.

If you have a range that has TRUE and FALSE values in it, TRUE will be treated as a 1 and FALSE will be treated as a zero. Basic text entries such as "try" are also treated as zeros.

If there are no values in the range, the result will be a zero.

MINA on a range of numbers works just like MIN. So =MIN(1,2,3) and =MINA(1,2,3) both return the value of 1.

On a range that includes text entries and positive numbers only, since MINA treats those text entries as zeros, your result will be a zero. So =MINA(A1:A3) where the value of A1 is "test", the value of A2 is 1, and the value of A3 is 2 will return a value of 0. If there's a negative number included, MINA will return that negative number.

The only place I can see MINA adding value is for data that includes TRUE and FALSE entries.

THE MAX FUNCTION

Notation: MAX(number1, [number2],…)
Excel Definition: Returns the largest value in a set of values. Ignores logical values and text.

MAX is the counterpart to MIN. Where MIN looks for the smallest value in the range, MAX looks for the largest value in the range.

So =MAX(1,2,3) will return a value of 3 because that's the largest number in the list of provided values. Once again, though, the optimal use of MAX is by applying it to a cell range, such as an entire column or row.

=MAX(4:4) would return the maximum value in Row 4 of your worksheet.

If there are no numbers in the specified range MAX will return a value of 0.

If there is a cell that has an error message within the range, MAX will return that error message.

MAX ignores text entries and does not include logical values like TRUE or FALSE in its determination.

You could use the MAX function to find the largest transaction in a series of transactions or the highest test score, for example.

THE MAXA FUNCTION

Notation: MAXA(value1, [value2],…)
Excel Definition: Returns the largest value in a set of values. Does not ignore logical values and text.

MAXA is much like MINA except it calculates a maximum value instead of a minimum value. And, just as MINA did compared to MIN, MAXA incorporates logical values into its determination.

So if you have a range that has TRUE and FALSE values in it, those will be considered. TRUE will be treated as a 1 and FALSE will be treated as a 0. Also, text entries are treated as zeros.

As with MINA I think the use of MAXA is very limited. The only place I can see it adding value is if you have TRUE and FALSE in your range of cells and need those incorporated into your calculation. (The reason I've included both functions here is for thoroughness since we covered AVERAGEA and will be covering COUNTA later.)

THE ROUND FUNCTION

Notation: ROUND(number, num_digits)
Excel Definition: Rounds a number to a specified number of digits.

ROUND is a simple but potentially useful function. It takes a value and rounds that value to a specified number of digits.

(You can use the formatting options in Excel to give the appearance of having rounded a number. So Number or Currency or Accounting will all format a number to show two decimal places, but using the ROUND function actually transforms the number so that it now only has that number of decimal places.)

The inputs into the ROUND function are the value you want to round and then the number of digits to round that number to.

If you use 0 for num_digits, the number will be rounded to the nearest integer. So =ROUND(111.2345,0) will return 111 as the value.

If you use a number, such as 2, for num_digits the number will be rounded to that many decimal places. So =ROUND(111.2345,2) will return 111.23 as the value.

If you use a negative number for num_digits, such as -2, the number will be rounded to that number of 10's, 100's, 1000's places, etc.

So =ROUND(111.2345,-2) will return 100 as the value.

ROUND will not force a specific number of decimal places on a number, however. For example, if I use =ROUND(1.23,4) which means to round the number 1.23 to the fourth decimal place, ROUND will return a value of 1.23 not 1.2300. (You would need to use TEXT to enforce that type of formatting or you would need to format your cells that way using one of the number formatting options.)

The way Excel decides whether to round up or round down is by looking at the digit one past the one you're going to keep. If that digit is a 0 through a 4, Excel will round down. (Thus keeping the rest of the number unchanged.) If that digit is a 5 through a 9, Excel will round up and the final digit that you're keeping will go up by one.

This is easier to understand if we look at some examples:

=ROUND(1.234,2) says to change the number 1.234 to a number with just two decimal places. So the question is does that become 1.23 or 1.24? The answer is 1.23 because the digit one past the 3, which is the last digit we're keeping, is a 4. Since that value is in the lower range, 0 through 4, we round down.

=ROUND(1.235,2) says the same thing and we have the same two choices, 1.23 or 1.24. But now our last digit after the one we're keeping is a 5 so we round up and our final value becomes 1.24.

Where it gets interesting, for me, is when you have multiple numbers that you're not keeping. So =ROUND(1.2347,2) says to convert 1.2347 to a number with two decimal places as well. If you started at the end and rounded each number at a time you would go from 1.2347 to 1.235 to 1.24. But that's not how Excel works. (And not how rounding in general works either. I looked it up.)

As I explained above, Excel takes the 1.23 that we want to keep and ONLY looks at the next digit in the number. In this case that's a 4 so Excel would round down and return a value of 1.23.

So there you have it. That's how ROUND works. Now on to the two variations on ROUND, ROUNDUP and ROUNDDOWN.

THE ROUNDUP FUNCTION

Notation: ROUNDUP(number, num_digits)
Excel Definition: Rounds a number up, away from zero.

ROUNDUP works much like ROUND except that all numbers are rounded in one direction rather than being split between rounding up and rounding down. In the case of ROUNDUP, all numbers round away from zero. For example,

$$=ROUNDUP(12.31,1)$$

and

$$=ROUNDUP(12.37,1)$$

will both return a value of 12.4, because that is the value that is away from zero when choosing between 12.3 and 12.4.

If you use ROUNDUP with negative numbers you get the same result except as a negative value. So

$$=ROUNDUP(-12.31,1)$$

and

$$=ROUNDUP(-12.37,1)$$

both return -12.4 because you still round away from zero.

Be careful when using ROUNDUP (or its counterpart ROUNDDOWN), because there's bias when you only round in one direction. The reason people usually round half of the values up and half of them down is to balance things out over time. If you round up by 2 cents and then down by 3 cents and then up by 4 cents, etc. eventually you come pretty close to zero when you add all the amounts you shaved off together.

But ROUNDUP and ROUNDDOWN can have a purpose.

For example, when I'm estimating numbers for my budget I like to always round what I owe upward and what I'm going to get paid downward. This means I always err in my favor because I always think I have to pay more than I do and that I'm going to earn less than I am. By doing this I guarantee that actual results will always be better than I'd expected. (In college this trick was the only reason I had $40 to pay for groceries at the end of some months…)

So this can have its uses. But generally you'll want to stick with using the ROUND function instead. (Especially if you're a company collecting something like sales tax and don't want to get sued for taking people's money. Those fractions of pennies add up.)

THE ROUNDDOWN FUNCTION

Notation: ROUNDDOWN(number, num_digits)
Excel Definition: Rounds a number down, towards zero.

ROUNDDOWN is the counterpart to ROUNDUP. Where ROUNDUP rounds away from zero, ROUNDDOWN will always round towards zero. So, for example,

=ROUNDDOWN(12.31,1)

and

=ROUNDDOWN(12.37,1)

will both round to 12.3 because that is the number closest to zero between the two available choices of 12.3 and 12.4.

And the negatives of those examples,

=ROUNDDOWN(-12.31,1)

and

=ROUNDDOWN(-12.37,1)

will both round to -12.3.

As with ROUNDUP, using ROUNDDOWN can introduce bias into your numbers because when you always round in one direction you tend to skew your numbers. But there are times when that can be to your advantage.

Just be sure if you're using either ROUNDUP or ROUNDDOWN that you know why you're doing it and that it makes sense for you to do so in that circumstance. (And that it won't lead you to doing something illegal or fraudulent.)

Your default should be to use ROUND unless you have a good reason not to.

THE COUNT FUNCTION

Notation: COUNT(value1, [value2],…)
Excel Definition: Counts the number of cells in a range that contain numbers.

The COUNT function is a very basic function. Its derivatives, COUNTIF and COUNTIFS are much more useful and we'll discuss those in a moment, but I wanted to first cover COUNT and its extension, COUNTA, which we'll cover in the next section.

What COUNT does is it allows you to count how many cells within your specified range contain a number or a date.

So a range of cells that contain the values 1, 12/31/10, and "one" will be counted as 2 because the first two entries (1 and 12/13/10) are considered numbers, but the last entry ("one") is not. If you have a cell that shows a numeric value due to a formula, so the cell contents are actually =SUM(2,3) but the cell displays 5, that will be counted as well.

Excel says that it will also count an entry such as "1" as a number, but when I tried that it didn't work. So if you're going to use this function on a range, I would test it to make sure that it's counting your numeric entries properly.

Also, a cell can only contain a number or date. For example, "1 day" would not be counted since it includes the number 1 but also the text "day".

The COUNT function itself is very simple to use. For example, =COUNT(A1:A5) will count the number of cells in the range from Cell A1 through Cell A5 that contain a number or date.

You could also write a function such as =COUNT(1,2,3) and it would count the number of numbers or dates in the list within the parens. In this case, three.

If you don't want to limit your count to just numbers and dates, then you need to use COUNTA.

THE COUNTA FUNCTION

Notation: COUNTA(value1, [value2],…)
Excel Definition: Counts the number of cells in a range that are not empty

The COUNTA function allows you to count how many cells within your specified range are not empty. So not just those that contain dates and numbers, but those that contain anything.

So, for example, COUNTA will count the cell that has "1 day" in it as well as the cell that has a date or a number or the text "one". Anything in a cell will result in that cell being counted.

Be careful, however, because it will also count any cell that has a function in it even if that function is not currently displaying a value. (And using copy and then paste special – values to replace that function may not clear the cell enough for COUNTA to ignore it. You have to make sure that a cell is truly blank for it to not be counted.)

Once again, if you're going to use this test it on a small range to make sure that it works as expected.

To write a COUNTA function just include the cell range(s) you want to count within the parens. So =COUNTA(A1:B30) will count how many cells between Cell A1 and Cell B30 are not empty.

THE COUNTBLANK FUNCTION

Notation: COUNTBLANK(range)
Excel Definition: Counts the number of empty cells in a specified range of cells.

Since we covered COUNTA which counts the number of cells in a range that have are not empty, we might as well cover its counterpart, COUNTBLANK, which counts the number of cells that are empty.

According to Excel, formulas that return empty text ("") are counted as blank, but cells with zero values are not. I tested this with an IF function that returned a value of "", a value of " ", and a value of 0. The one that returned a value of "" was counted as blank, the other two were not.

This is important to know because a cell with a formula that returns a value of "" and one with a formula that returns a value of " " will look the same, but they perform differently when functions like this one are applied to them.

As always, be sure to check a sample of your data to see that the result you are getting is the result you expect and want. If it isn't, with COUNTBLANK you should look to the nature of your data.

THE COUNTIF FUNCTION

Notation: COUNTIF(range, criteria)
Excel Definition: Counts the number of cells within a range that meet the given condition.

For users of Excel 2007 or later, you can use the COUNTIFS function as a substitute for the COUNTIF function.

COUNTIF looks at a range of cells and it counts whether or not the specified condition is met. The first information you provide for the function is the range of cells you want evaluated. Then you specify what criteria must be met.

The criteria can be a cell reference, text, or numeric.

For example:

=COUNTIF(A1:A5,B2) says to count how many times the values in Cells A1 through A5 are the same as the value in Cell B2.

=COUNTIF(A1:A5,"YES") says to count how many times the values in Cells A1 through A5 are the text YES. It will only count those instances where the full value in the cell matches the value given in the quotes. So a cell that says YES, PLEASE would not be counted. Or one that has YES followed by an extra space would not be counted. It has to be an exact match.

=COUNTIF(A1:A5,">20") says to count how many cells between Cell A1 and Cell A5 have a numeric value greater than 20. Note that even though the criteria is related to a number value that it's still shown in quotes because it's an expression. (If you had =COUNTIF(A1:A5,20), which looks for any cells with a value equal to 20, you wouldn't need the quotes but you could still use them.)

If you want to reference a cell for your criteria but you also want to use a greater than or less than symbol, you need to combine the two using an ampersand (&).

For example =COUNTIF(A1:A5,">="&G2) would count how many times the cells in the range from Cell A1 to Cell A5 contain a value that is greater than or equal to the value in Cell G2.

You can also use wildcards with the COUNTIF function if your condition relates to a text value.

The asterisk (*) can be used to count any cell that contains text. You would write that as =COUNTIF(A1:A5,"*").

It can also be used in combination with other letters to, for example, count any entry where there is an e. You would write that as =COUNTIF(A1:A5,"*e*"). The asterisk on either side of the e says to look for any cells where there is an e anywhere.

If you want to count entries of a certain text length you can use the question mark (?) as a wildcard. It represents one single character. So =COUNTIF(A1:A5,"???") would count all cells in the range from Cell A1 through A5 where the entry is three letters or spaces long. (It doesn't work with numbers.)

You can also combine COUNTIF functions if you want to count two criteria within a range. So you can have =COUNTIF(A1:A5,"YES") + COUNTIF(A1:A5,"MAYBE") to count how many cells within the range contained either the value YES or the value MAYBE.

But be careful with this.

If you use something like this: =COUNTIF(A1:A5,"*a*") + COUNTIF(A1:A5,"*e*") where you're counting all entries in the range that contain an a and all entries in the range that contain an e, you can end up double counting.

And if you actually need to find an asterisk or question mark you can do so by using the tilde (~) before the mark you need. So ~? or ~* will look for an actual question mark or an actual asterisk

Always test different scenarios to make sure the count is counting everything you want it to but also not more than you want it to. (And be sure you've covered all possible scenarios in your testing, a mistake I know I've made at least once.)

THE COUNTIFS FUNCTION

Notation: COUNTIFS(criteria_range1, criteria1, [criteria_range2, criteria2],…)
Excel Definition: Counts the number of cells specified by a given set of conditions or criteria.

The COUNTIFS function takes the COUNTIF function to the next level by allowing you to specify multiple ranges and multiple criteria that must be met within each of those ranges for an entry to be counted. It is available to users of Excel 2007 or later.

So where COUNTIF would have allowed you to count all customers located in Alabama, for example, COUNTIFS allows you to count all customers located in Alabama, who spent more than $500, and did so in the last six months.

COUNTIFS can substitute for the COUNTIF function. Simply provide only one criteria range and one criteria. (Which means the only difference between the two when the range is a singular range is the use of the S at the end of COUNTIFS.)

To count based upon multiple criteria, simply include additional ranges and criteria for each of those ranges in the function.

The criteria range for all of your criteria must be the same size. So if your first cell range is A1:B25, then your other cell ranges must also be two columns wide and 25 rows long.

Ranges do not have to be adjacent, but they do have to be the same size.

Your criteria, just like with COUNTIF, can be a cell reference (B2), a number (25 or "25"), an expression (">25"), or a text value ("TRUE").

The way the count is performed is it looks at all first cells in each of the criteria ranges and sees if the criteria for each of those ranges are met. If so, that entry is counted. If not, it isn't. It then moves on to the second cell in each of the criteria ranges and checks to see if all of the second cells meet the specified criteria. And so on and so on.

Each time all of the criteria are met, Excel counts that as 1.

Let's walk through an example to see this in action.

Here is a table of six customer transactions that includes the state the customer is from and the total amount they spent.

If we want to know how many customers are from Alabama (AL) who spent $250 or more, we can write a COUNTIFS function to calculate this.

	A	B	C	D
1	State	Total Purchases		Customers From AL Who Spent At Least $250
2	AL	$ 250.00		2
3	AL	$ 125.00		Cell D2: =COUNTIFS(A2:A7,"AL",B2:B7,">=250")
4	AZ	$ 110.00		
5	AK	$ 95.00		
6	AR	$ 250.00		
7	AL	$ 300.00		

The function we need is

=COUNTIFS(A2:A7,"AL",B2:B7,">=250")

And the answer is 2.

Let's break that down.

The first criteria range is A2 through A7. Those are the entries with our State values in them. And we tell Excel we want to count any entry where the state is "AL". That's the first half of our COUNTIFS function.

The second criteria range is B2 through B7. That's our Total Purchases. And we tell Excel that we want to count any time when a value in that range is greater than or equal to $250. That's written as ">=250".

Excel takes the function =COUNTIFS(A2:A7,"AL",B2:B7,">=250") and it starts with Cells A2 and B2 and it says are both criteria met? In this case, yes, so that's counted. Then it moves to A3 and B3 and does the same thing. And on and on through to A7 and B7.

Now if you look at the data, there are three entries where the state is AL and three entries where the customer spent $250 or more. But Excel only counts those entries where both criteria are met. That occurs in Rows 2 and 7.

The entry in Row 3 is for a customer from AL who only spent $125. And the entry in Row 6 is for a customer who did spend $250 but is from AR.

For it to work, when you write a COUNTIFS function you need to make sure that your cell ranges are properly lined up.

And, as you can see above, you can use a different type of criteria for each criteria range. So here I had a text criteria for the first range ("AL") and an expression for the second range (">=250").

Also, as with COUNTIF, you can also use the wildcard symbols for text. So the asterisk (*) and the question mark (?) both work. The asterisk (*) represents any sequence of characters, the question mark (?) represents one single character. And if you want to search for either mark rather than using it as a wildcard, be sure to put a tilde(~) in front of it.

Now on to SUMIF and SUMIFS.

THE SUMIF FUNCTION

Notation: SUMIF(range, criteria, [sum_range])
Excel Definition: Adds the cells specified by a given condition or criteria.

For users of Excel 2007 or later, you can use SUMIFS instead of SUMIF, but be careful of the order of your arguments because they are different.

SUMIF allows you to tell Excel to only sum the values within a range of cells when they meet a specific criteria. For example, you can tell Excel to only sum the values in Cells A1 through A5 that are greater than zero using =SUMIF(A1:A5,">0")

That all occurs within one range of cells. Excel evaluates each cell and only includes the values that meet your specific criteria.

What's more powerful, in my opinion, is that you can use one range to specify your criteria and another to specify the values to sum. For example, using the below data, let's say I wanted to sum the total value of customer transactions (in Column B) that are related to customers from Alabama (in Column A).

	A	B	C	D
1	**State**	**Total Purchases**		**Sum Orders For Customers From AL**
2	AL	$ 250.00		$675.00
3	AL	$ 125.00		**Cell D2: =SUMIF(A2:A7,"AL",B2:B7)**
4	AZ	$ 110.00		
5	AK	$ 95.00		
6	AR	$ 250.00		
7	AL	$ 300.00		

I could do this with the following formula: =SUMIF(A2:A7,"AL",B2:B7)

The first value, A2:A7, is the range of values that contain my criteria, in this case the state the customer lives in. The next value, "AL", is the criteria that must be met for Excel to include the value in the next range in its calculation. The final value is the sum range, B2:B7. This is where the values I want to add together are stored.

As with COUNTIF and COUNTIFS, you can use criteria that are numeric (23 or "23"), expressions (">25"), or text-based ("AL"). You can also reference a cell (A1) as the criteria.

So you could have =SUMIF(A2:A7,G2,B2:B7) where the value in Cell G2 is what must match the values in Column A in order to sum the values in Column B.

And note that you must use quotation marks around the criteria except for when cell references (G2) or single numbers (23) are involved. (With a single number you can write it with or without the quotes.)

If the criteria used is a text-based criteria, you can also use the wildcards just like you could with COUNTIF and COUNTIFS. So an asterisk (*) stands for any number of characters and a question mark (?) stands for a single character. Because of this, if you're looking to use a criteria that references an actual asterisk or question mark, you need to include a tilde (~) before the mark. So ~* will look for an asterisk, but just * will look for any number of characters.

For example, if I wanted to sum the values in Cells A1 through A6 every time one of the entries in Cells C1 through C6 included a question mark at the end, I could write:

=SUMIF(C1:C6,"*~?",A1:A6)

The asterisk means any text, the tilde means the actual symbol that follows next, and then the question mark there is an actual question mark that we're searching for because of the tilde before it. And, of course, since it's a text-based search term the entirety is surrounded by quotation marks.

Also, you should know that if the match string is too long—in this case 255 or more characters—that SUMIF will return incorrect results.

SUMIF also has a weird quirk in that the sum range does not have to be the same dimensions as the criteria range. Excel will extend the sum range to the size needed if you don't specify the full range or a correctly-sized range.

So, for example, if your criteria range is A1:B25 but you just list C1:C3 as your sum_range Excel will use C1:D25 for its sum_range. It takes the first cell in the range you provide and creates its own range from that.

(I wouldn't rely on this, though. And it doesn't work with SUMIFS so it's a bad habit to get into to let Excel set your sum range for you.)

Alright. That's SUMIF. Those of you with later versions of Excel have a much more powerful option available to you: SUMIFS. Let's discuss that next.

THE SUMIFS FUNCTION

Notation: SUMIFS(sum_range, criteria_range1, criteria1, [criteria_range2, criteria2],…)
Excel Definition: Adds the cells specified by a given set of conditions or criteria.

SUMIFS allows you to sum the values in a range when multiple criteria are met. It can also work just like SUMIF if you only provide one criteria and one criteria range. But be careful, because the inputs into the SUMIFS function are provided in a different order than they're provided for the SUMIF function.

Which is why for those who have access to both (users of Excel 2007 or later) it's probably a good idea to get into the habit of using SUMIFS for everything.

Also, unlike with SUMIF, when using SUMIFS your sum range and the criteria ranges you use need to be the same size. They do not need to be next to one other, but they do need to cover the same number of rows and columns.

Like SUMIF, SUMIFS can use a number (22 or "22"), an expression ("<13"), a text-based criteria ("YES"), or a cell reference (H1) for the sum criteria. For anything except a single number or a cell reference, be sure to use quotation marks around your criteria.

With SUMIFS, just like with COUNTIFS, you don't have to use the same type of criteria for each range. So you can have an expression for one criteria, a cell reference for another, and a text-based criteria for a third.

So I could have

=SUMIFS(A1:A25,B1:B25,"USD",C1:C25,">10")

That would sum the values in Cells A1 through A25 if the value in the corresponding cells in Cells B1 through B25 contain "USD" and the values in Cells C1 through C25 are greater than 10.

For text-based criteria, you can use the wildcards. So the asterisk (*) to represent any number of characters, the question mark (?) to represent a single character, and the tilde(~) to distinguish when you're actually searching for an asterisk or question mark.

You can have up to 127 criteria. (Why you would want to do that, I don't know. But you can.)

SUMIFS is one of the functions that I use the most.

I use it in my budget worksheet to sum the amount I still owe on my bills each month. So I'll list all of my bills due for the month, whether I pay them with cash or with a credit card (when I was living overseas I would list which currency the bill had to be paid in since I had bills due in both USD and NZD), the amount due, and in a third column I'll put an X when the bill is paid.

The SUMIFS formula I use is =SUMIFS(C1:C10,B1:B10,"CASH",D1:D10,""). So that says sum the values in Column C if the values in Column B are "CASH" and Column D is blank. That lets me know how much cash I need in my bank account before those bills hit.

The other place I use this is with my payables from self-publishing. I am usually owed money at any given time in about five different currencies and from about ten different sources. I have a worksheet where I sum the amount owed in each currency that I haven't yet been paid using a formula similar to the one above. In this case: =SUMIFS(B$3:B$91,D$3:D$91,"USD",E$3:E$91,"")

This says to sum the values in Cells B3 through B91 if the values in Cells D3 through D91 are USD and the values in those cells in Column E are blank. I have a formula like this for each of the currencies I'm owed money in (CAD, AUD, INR, EUR, GBP, etc.) which is what the $ signs help with. This way I can just copy the formula to however many rows I need and all I have to update is the currency abbreviation.

That's just two examples of the power of SUMIFS. If you start to think about it, there are any number of places you can use it. (For me it would be worth upgrading to a current version of Excel if I didn't have it already. You can use multiple SUMIF functions to get the same result, but it's very messy.)

THE AVERAGEIF FUNCTION

Notation: AVERAGEIF(range, criteria, [average_range])
Excel Definition: Finds average (arithmetic mean) for the cells specified by a given condition or criteria.

If you have Excel 2007 or later, AVERAGEIFS can be used in place of AVERAGEIF.

The AVERAGEIF function works just like COUNTIF and SUMIF except it takes an *average* of the values when a specified criteria is met.

An example of when you might use this is if you wanted to know the average customer order amount for customers in different states.

So you could write =AVERAGEIF(F1:F11,"CO",G1:G11) to take the average of the values in Cells G1 through G11 but only when the value in Cells F1 through F11 are CO.

Your criteria can be a cell reference instead which is where this can be really powerful. So in the example above I could've used A1 as the cell reference and had CO in Cell A1 and then all the other states in subsequent cells in Column A.

To calculate the average for all of the states I'd just need to change my cell references to reference the entire column, or if that wasn't possible use $ signs to lock my cell references, and then copy that formula down the number of cells I needed.

The first entry would look like this:

=AVERAGEIF(F:F,A1,G:G)

Or if referencing the columns wasn't possible, it would look like this:

=AVERAGEIF($F$1:$F$11,A1,$G$1:$G$11)

When either of those formulas is copied down the A1 cell reference will change but the other values will not. Meaning I can write that formula once and have it do fifty separate calculations for me just by copying the formula and using a column with all of the states listed.

With AVERAGEIF you can also just average a range of numbers that meet certain criteria without referencing any other column of data.

So if I want to average all values in a column that are over 10, I could say =AVERAGEIF(F:F,">10") and Excel would average the values of all entries in Column F that have a value over 10 and ignore the rest.

Other things to know:

If you have a cell in the range portion that has a value of TRUE or FALSE, Excel will ignore it.

If you have a cell in the average_range portion that is empty, Excel will ignore it.

If a cell in the criteria portion is empty, Excel will treat it as a zero.

If Excel returns a #DIV/0! error, that likely means that there was nothing for it to average, which means the criteria you set weren't met or the range you provided is a blank or text value.

And as with COUNTIF and SUMIF, if your criteria is text-related, you can use the question mark (?) and asterisk (*) as wildcard characters. A question mark stands in for a single character, an asterisk for a sequence of characters. And to search for an actual question mark or asterisk, use the tilde (~) before the character. So ~? and ~* to search for those actual symbols.

Finally, your ranges do not have to be the same size. Excel will start in the top left cell of the average range you tell it and define a range that matches the size and shape of the range you specified for the criteria.

I would recommend, however, that you define the appropriate range yourself rather than rely on Excel to do it for you.

THE AVERAGEIFS FUNCTION

Notation: AVERAGEIFS(average_range, criteria_range1, criteria1, [criteria_range2, criteria2],…)
Excel Definition: Finds average (arithmetic mean) for the cells specified by a given set of conditions or criteria.

AVERAGEIFS extends the functionality of AVERAGEIF to incorporate more than one criteria just like COUNTIFS and SUMIFS do for COUNTIF and SUMIF. It is available to users of Excel 2007 and later.

With AVERAGEIFS and AVERAGEIF you need to know which one you're going to use because the information for each function is provided in a different order. So for those of you who have access to AVERAGEIFS, I would recommend always using AVERAGEIFS since it can serve the same function as AVERAGEIF if you just limit it to one criteria.

The inputs for the function are the range of cells that contain the values you want to average followed by the range of cells for your first criteria and then the first criteria. If you have more than one criteria you then list the next range of cells and the next criteria and so on and so on.

Your criteria do not have to be of the same type and can reference numeric values (24 or "24"), cells (A1), expressions (">42"), or text ("how"). Cell references and numbers do not need to be in quotation marks, expressions and text references do.

With AVERAGEIFS your ranges must all be the same size and shape. (Unlike AVERAGEIF where Excel will figure out the average_range given a starting location.)

For a value to be included in the average calculation, all of the criteria you specify must be met.

Be careful with empty cells, blanks, or text values where numbers are expected as these may generate an error message rather than a calculation or may impact the calculation. (See the Excel help screen for the function for a full listing of the errors and adjustments that Excel makes. Always check a formula against a small sample of data to make sure you're getting the result you want.)

As with AVERAGEIF, you can use wildcards for text-based criteria.

An example of using AVERAGEIFS might be if you were looking at student grades and wanted to see average score across teacher name and student gender. Here's our data:

	A	B	C	D	E	F	G	H	I	J	K
1	**Score**	**Teacher**	**Gender**								
2	50	Smith	F								
3	49	Barker	M			**Female**		**Male**			
4	68	Vasquez	F			80.25	**Smith**	84.50			
5	75	Smith	M			90.00	**Barker**	68.67			
6	90	Barker	F			68.00	**Vasquez**	76.00			
7	94	Smith	M								
8	93	Barker	M			Cell F4:	=AVERAGEIFS($A$2:$A$13,$B$2:$B$13,G4,$C$2:$C$13,"F")				
9	91	Smith	F			Cell H4:	=AVERAGEIFS($A$2:$A$13,$B$2:$B$13,G4,$C$2:$C$13,"M")				
10	76	Vasquez	M								
11	82	Smith	F								
12	64	Barker	M								
13	98	Smith	F								

Test score is in Column A, teacher name is in Column B, student gender is in Column C. My full list of teacher names is in Column G. The formula I write in Cell F4 is:

=AVERAGEIFS($A$2:$A$13,$B$2:$B$13,G4,$C$2:$C$13,"F")

What that's saying is, average the values in Cells A2 through A13 where the values in Cells B2 through B13 are equal to the teacher name in Cell G4 and the gender of the student in Cells C2 through C13 is listed as F.

Because I used the $ signs there and a cell reference for teacher name, I can then just copy that formula to Cells F5 and F6 and it adjusts to calculate for each teacher.

I can then copy the formula to Cell H4, change the F at the end of the function to an M, and then copy that down to Cells H5 and H6.

Done. (Not statistically robust, but an interesting result.)

Okay. On to some Text functions now. These will be pretty simple and then we'll ramp back up with the Logical functions

THE UPPER FUNCTION

Notation: UPPER(text)
Excel Definition: Converts a text string to all uppercase letters.

The UPPER function has a very simple purpose, and that is to take a text entry and convert it to all uppercase letters.

So, for example, =UPPER("test") will return TEST. Or, if you had the word "test" in Cell B2 and you wrote =UPPER(B2) it would also return the value TEST.

You cannot reference more than once cell at a time using UPPER. However, you can combine the UPPER function with other functions to return a result that is in upper case letters.

For example,

=CONCATENATE(UPPER(B2)," ",UPPER(C2))

or

=UPPER(CONCATENATE(B2," ",C2))

would return the text in Cell B2 followed by a space and then by the text in Cell C2 all in upper case letters.

We'll talk about CONCATENATE later, don't worry. Just know for now that you can combine UPPER with it or any other function where that might make sense.

THE LOWER FUNCTION

Notation: LOWER(text)
Excel Definition: Converts all letters in a text string to lowercase.

In the same way that the UPPER function converts all letters in a text string to upper case, the LOWER function converts all letters in a text string to lower case.

So, for example, =LOWER("TEST") will return test. Or, if you had the word TEST in Cell B2 and you wrote =LOWER(B2) it would return the value test.

As with UPPER, with LOWER you cannot reference more than once cell at a time. However, LOWER can also be combined with other functions, which is probably the primary way you would use it. Either that or to convert imported data that's in the wrong format.

THE PROPER FUNCTION

Notation: PROPER(text)
Excel Definition: Converts a text string to proper case; the first letter in each word in uppercase, and all other letters to lowercase.

The PROPER function is much like the LOWER and the UPPER functions but in this case it converts text entries to Proper Case, which as you can see in the above definition means the first letter of each word will be capitalized but all other letters will not.

(Note that this is different from Title Case where most of the first letters are capitalized, but not all of them. Excel does not convert text to Title Case.)

For example, =PROPER("this is the entry to test") would return a value of This Is The Entry To Test. (Whereas with Title Case that would be This is the Entry to Test.)

As with UPPER and LOWER, you can either include the text to be converted in the formula itself like I did above or you can use a cell reference.

So =PROPER(B2) would convert the text in Cell B2 to proper case.

If you include the text within the formula, be sure to use quotation marks around the text.

Since there is not an option to convert text to Title Case within Excel, PROPER is as close as you can get. (If you were desperate, you could probably use PROPER to convert your text strings and then use a find/replace command for words like "the", "of", "in", "is", "and", etc. to replace the Proper Case versions with lower case versions to approximate Title Case.)

THE LEFT FUNCTION

Notation: LEFT(text, [num_chars])
Excel Definition: Returns the specified number of characters from the start of a text string.

The LEFT function allows you to extract the left-most portion of a text string. This can be a useful function if you only want a portion of a standardized entry. For example, for a driver's license number that starts with a two-digit year, then a dash, then the license number, to extract the year portion, you could use =LEFT(B2,2) assuming the value was in Cell B2. That would give you just the year portion of that license number.

Note that the definition says it works on a text string, but I was able to also get it to work on a number. So =LEFT(1234,2) returns 12.

You can accomplish the same thing with Text to Columns using Fixed Width, but LEFT is a better option when all you want is that one portion of the entry and you don't need the rest of it.

Other identifiers that might be similarly structured include customer identification numbers and social security numbers.

The number of characters specified must be greater than or equal to zero.

If the number of characters you specify is greater than the length of the text entry, Excel will return the full text entry.

If you omit the number of characters, Excel will extract the left-most character only. So =LEFT("test") will return a result of t.

For languages such as Chinese, Japanese, and Korean you may need to use LEFTB instead and specify the number of bytes rather than the number of characters.

THE RIGHT FUNCTION

Notation: RIGHT(text, [num_chars])
Excel Definition: Returns the specified number of characters from the end of a text string.

The RIGHT function allows you to extract the right-most portion of a text string. Just as with the LEFT function, this can be a useful function if you only want a portion of a standardized entry.

For example, =RIGHT(B2,4) would extract the last four digits of a social security number that had been entered in Cell B2.

Again, as with LEFT, you could accomplish the same thing with Text to Columns using Fixed Width, but this approach only extracts the portion that you need rather than breaking the existing entry into sections. Other identifiers that might be similarly structured include customer identification numbers or driver's license numbers.

The number of characters you specify must be greater than or equal to zero. If the number of characters you specify is greater than the number of characters in the entry, the function will return the entire text entry.

If you omit the number of characters, Excel will assume the value is 1 and return the last character in the entry. So =RIGHT("try") will return a value of y.

Entries that are in Chinese, Korean, or Japanese may require the use of RIGHTB instead. If so, you'd specify a number of bytes instead of a number of characters.

THE MID FUNCTION

Notation: MID(text, start_num, num_chars)
Excel Definition: Returns the characters from the middle of a text string, given a starting position and length.

The MID function works much like the LEFT and RIGHT functions except it extracts characters from the middle of an entry. Because of this, it requires one more input, the start number. So you have to tell Excel which character in your string should be the first character pulled and then how many characters you want after that.

For example, for a social security number if you want the middle two digits of the value stored in Cell B2 you would use =MID(B2,5,2) assuming the number was written as XXX-XX-XXXX.

Be sure to count each space, dash, etc. in your determination of the start number.

If your start number is greater than the number of characters in your referenced text, Excel will return an empty text entry.

If you ask for more characters to be returned than exist, Excel will return what there is. So =MID("advice",3,7) will returned vice even though that's only four characters.

Your start number must be equal to or greater than 1. Your number of characters must be equal to or greater than zero.

If you are working with entries in Chinese, Japanese, or Korean you may need to use MIDB instead and specify a number of bytes rather than a number of characters.

THE TRIM FUNCTION

Notation: TRIM(text)
Excel Definition: Removes all spaces from a text string except for single spaces between words.

The TRIM function can come in very handy if you're trying to clean up text entries that are messy.

For example, if I did some sort of merge of a list of names (perhaps using CONCATENATE) to create a list of entries that had first name followed by a space followed by middle name followed by a space followed by last name followed by a space and then followed by a suffix such as Esq. or Jr., I would very likely end up with a list of entries with extra spaces in it.

Because for every entry that didn't have a middle name or suffix there would be an unwanted space.

So I might have "Albert Jones " as one of my entries. There's an extra space there between Albert and Jones because there was no middle name and an extra space after Jones because there was no suffix.

To remove those extra spaces, you can use the TRIM function. If that entry was in Cell B2, I'd just write =TRIM(B2).

Done. My new entry would be "Albert Jones".

I could also combine this with CONCATENATE so that the trimming was done at the same time I created the entry, which saves the use of an extra column.

In that case I would list the TRIM function first and in the parens for the TRIM function I would write my CONCATENATE function. So

$$=TRIM(CONCATENATE(\ldots))$$

Where the ... represents the values for the CONCATENATE function.

TRIM also works with text pasted directly into the function as long as you use quotation marks around the text. For example, =TRIM("Albert Jones ") with the extra spaces would return Albert Jones without the extra spaces.

Also, remember that when you use TRIM it's still a formula. To get just the text entry and not keep the formula you need to copy your data and then paste special – values.

You probably won't need to use TRIM often, but it's very useful when you do need it. Also, if you're pulling information off a website and have issues, see the TRIM Excel Help text for more guidance.

THE CONCATENATE FUNCTION

Notation: CONCATENATE(text1, [text2],…)
Excel Definition: Joins several text strings into one text string.

I've referred to it a couple times now, so we better talk about it. The CONCATENATE function is one I use often. It lets me take separate elements, such as first and last name, and create one entry that combines those elements.

For example, on a recent work project I was given a list of employee names that was in first name and then last name order. (Mark Smith, Betsy Poole, etc.) But some of the first names were nicknames or shortened names so it was always hard to find someone on that list. I'd look for Bob and he'd be listed under Robert or Robert and he'd be listed under Bob.

So I decided to redo the list with last name comma first name instead.

I used Text to Columns to separate first name and last name and then CONCATENATE to recombine the entries in the order I wanted. (E.g., Smith, Mark) This made searching the list much, much easier.

That's just one way to use CONCATENATE.

You can use it to combine any combination of values you want. And, because it's a formula, you can do this for multiple rows of data very easily.

Now, a few things to know about CONCATENATE before you start:

The inputs into your CONCATENATE function can be a cell reference (B1), a number (32 or "32"), or a text value ("entry"). If it's text it must have quotes around it. If it's a number the quotes are optional. For a cell reference, do not use quotes.

You can have up to 255 elements in a CONCATENATE formula and a total of 8,192 characters. (At least in Excel 2013 you can. Why you'd do that, I'm not sure, but it is possible.)

If you want a space or any sort of punctuation in your final result you need to include that in the CONCATENATE formula.

So, with the example above where I wanted last name comma first name, I had to write that as:

=CONCATENATE(B1,", ",A1)

Let's break that down a bit because it's a little hard to see what's happening there.

The first text entry I wanted was the value in Cell B1. So that's what I wrote after the opening paren.

Then I used a comma to separate that entry from the next entry.

So far we have:

$$=CONCATENATE(B1,$$

After that first comma I needed to tell Excel to add a comma and a space between the last name and the first name. Because that wasn't a cell reference I had to put quotes around it. So we end up with an opening quote, followed by a comma and a space, followed by a closing quote. Which is how we get the ", " portion of that formula.

That's our second entry in the formula. Since we have a third entry we want to include, we follow it with a comma.

At that point we have:

$$=CONCATENATE(B1,", ",$$

The third entry in the formula is another cell reference, so we just add that and close it all out with a closing paren.

And we get:

$$=CONCATENATE(B1,", ",A1)$$

There is a way to get the same result as the CONCATENATE function that doesn't require a function by using ampersands (&) between elements.

So if I write

$$=B1 \& ", " \& A1$$

that gives the same result as

$$=CONCATENATE(B1,", ",A1)$$

If you get a NAME#? error this is usually because you failed to put quotation marks around a text element in your formula.

Also, I should note here that Excel in their infinite wisdom—not—has added a new function CONCAT to Excel 2016, Excel Mobile, and Excel Online to replace CONCATENATE. They now warn that CONCATENATE may not be available in future versions of Excel. (Because that'll make users happy, to have to write something in two formats to support users using old versions of Excel and then newer versions of Excel.)

So be aware of this and know that you may have to adjust at some point to using the CONCAT function instead of the CONCATENATE function. Also, if that ever does happen and you're working with users in an older version of Excel know that you may have compatibility issues as a result.

That's CONCATENATE. Let's move on to TEXT next.

THE TEXT FUNCTION

Notation: TEXT(value, format_text)
Excel Definition: Converts a value to text in a specific number format.

The TEXT function is an interesting one. Because it really has two completely different uses. (In my opinion.) So let's start with the usage that's a lot like using CONCATENATE.

Basically, you can use TEXT to combine numbers with text or to specify how those numbers are formatted. So if you have a column of numbers, 1, 2, 3, etc. and you want to turn those into a column of entries that say $1.00 per unit, $2.00 per unit, $3.00 per unit, etc., TEXT is the easiest way to do that.

In that example, you would write

=TEXT(A1,"$0.00") & " per unit"

where the value being transformed is in Cell A1. That tells Excel to format the number in Cell A1 with a dollar sign and two decimal places and then to add a space and the text "per unit" to the end of the entry.

Now, the part of TEXT that interests me is its ability to extract information from a date. Using TEXT you can take a date, like 4/4/2018, and you can have Excel return for you the name of the day of the week or the month associated with that date. So "Wednesday" or "April".

I find that very useful, and recently used it when I was trying to create a pivot table with day of the week across the top but only had dates to work with.

To extract the name of the day of the week, use =TEXT(A1,"dddd").

To extract the name of the month, use =TEXT(A1,"mmmm")

You can also extract the abbreviated month or day of the week as well as just the number of the day or month by using a different number of d's or m's in your formula.

If you're really really interested in using the TEXT function I suggest reading the help text for the function, because Excel provides a seventeen-tab worksheet on how to use it. Since covering that here would overwhelm the other content in this guide, I'm just going to cover some high points.

Be careful when using TEXT to create number formats, because it is possible to create entries that no one would want. You can end up with an entry like where there's a number followed by a period and then nothing after that period. (Who would want that? Not me.) Or you can get a format where you have a number followed by a period followed by a space and then followed by another number. Again, no one wants that.

But Excel will let you do it. So if you use this function you need to be very careful to check your results to make sure you got it right.

Also, remember that this is a text function. So once you use it, the entry you create is text not a number. If you intend to do any sort of calculations on your values, you should retain a version of those values somewhere that are still formatted as numbers or do all of your analysis first.

If you aren't really interested in the TEXT function, I'd suggest you stop here. But if you want to dig in a little further, we can continue.

* * *

First, if you're not sure how to write a format that you want to use on a number, you can click on a cell and then go to the Format Cells dialogue box (Ctrl + 1 or right-click Format Cells), and then go to the Number tab. If the type of number format you want already exists, like Percentage, click on it first and then go to Custom and that format will be the one that's selected under Custom.

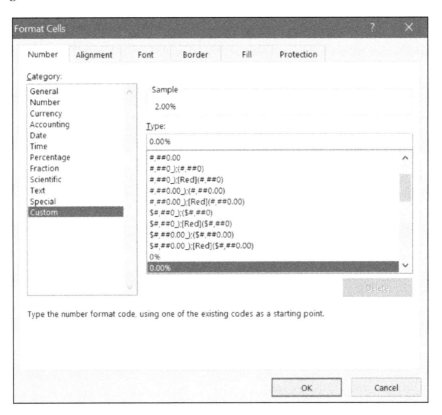

See above where the notation selected is now "0.00%" under Custom?

(Of course, if that's what you wanted, you could just format your cells as a percentage and be done. But I assume you're using TEXT because you want to combine that number formatting with text. So this approach allows you to pull that notation for inclusion in your TEXT formula and know that it will work.)

As an example:

$$=TEXT(A1,"0.00\%")$$

will format the value in Cell A1 as a percentage and including & " Completion" in that formula:

$$=TEXT(A1,"0.00\%") \& " Completion"$$

will return "50.00% Completion" as your result, for example, where the value in Cell A1 is .5.

Be sure to put quotes around the cell notation when you use it in your TEXT function.

Also, Excel may reject your format even if it's one you pulled from the Format Cells dialogue box, because Excel does not accept all of those formats as valid when used in the TEXT function.

If you want to build a cell notation from scratch, here are a few tips:

A comma between either pound signs (#) or zeros (0) will be treated as an indication that you should include a comma to separate out your thousands.

If you end your entry with a comma then Excel will round that number to the nearest 1000s. (In other countries, you may actually need to do this with a period instead of a comma.)

So =TEXT(12000000, "#,###") returns 12,000,000.

But =TEXT(12000000, "#,###,") returns 12,000 because the comma at the end says to round to the nearest thousand.

And =TEXT(12000000, "#,###,,") returns 12 because it has two commas at the end so you round to the nearest thousand twice.

If you use zeros (0) in your notation, Excel will force all entries to have that many numbers or zeros even if the number wouldn't otherwise.

So =TEXT(4,"0.0000") will return 4.0000 and =TEXT(4,"0000") will return 0004 with three zeros in front of the four.

(This is one way to fix a situation where Excel removed an initial 0 from a long number string. The other way to prevent that is to use the single quote mark before you enter the value.)

You can also use pound signs (#). In that case, Excel will round the number to that many places if the number is longer, but it won't force a number to have that many digits.

So =TEXT(4,"#.####") will return the number 4 followed by a period.

(Remember how I said you can get bad formatting with TEXT. This is how.)

Since it's a whole number no zeros are added. In this case, to have a "good" format you'd probably want something like =TEXT(4,"#.0###") so that you have 4.0 rather than that 4 with a period after it.

For comparison's sake, =TEXT(4,"####") returns 4 as the value. No added zeros before the number.

Bottom line here: TEXT can be useful for formatting existing numbers and combining those with text, but you need to be very, very careful how you do so and it's probably best to liberally borrow from Excel's existing number formatting for your notation.

It is also a very convenient and helpful way to extract the day of the week or month from a date. (It can also extracts hours, minutes, and seconds if needed.)

If you're going to work with it, use the Excel Help screen to find the notation you need.

Now on to a few Date & Time functions.

THE TODAY FUNCTION

Notation: TODAY()
Excel Definition: Returns the current date formatted as a date.

The TODAY function is very simple and basic. If you need today's date formatted as a date, you just enter =TODAY() into a cell and that's what you'll get.

Now, you might be asking yourself why you'd bother doing something like this. I mean, can't you just type in today's date? Yes, you can.

But the reason I use TODAY is because I'm usually using it in conjunction with a worksheet that's calculating days until something happens. So let's say you want to track which of your customer invoices are past thirty days. In other words, who should've paid you by now.

You can have a cell in your worksheet that uses TODAY so that you never have to re-enter today's date when making your calculations. It will update each time you open your worksheet. And then you can combine that with a calculation that looks at date billed to calculate how many days past due someone is on their payment. That, too, will automatically update each time you open your worksheet.

You can also use TODAY directly in a formula.

(But remember that best practice about having all of your assumptions visible. If you bury TODAY in a formula and someone doesn't realize it they may believe the values are static when in fact they will change each day as that value updates.)

So Option 1 is to put =TODAY() into Cell A1 and then have the formula =A1-C3 where A1 is today's date and C3 is the date the customer was invoiced.

Option 2 is to put

$$=TODAY()-C3$$

into a cell where C3 is the date the customer was invoiced. Both work.

As long as you format your cell as a number it should return the number of day's difference between the two dates.

Now you do have to be a little careful about dates in Excel.

Excel behind the scenes is storing each date as a number and that numbering starts with January 1, 1900. So if you ever find yourself dealing with dates prior to January 1, 1900 (which I did once when dealing with incorporation dates for companies), you will have some issues using Excel. I once imported data into Excel and it converted dates from the 1700s and 1800s into modern dates. Not something I wanted and not something that was obvious when the dates were formatted with just a two-digit year (1/1/18).

THE NOW FUNCTION

Notation: NOW()
Excel Definition: Returns the current date and time formatted as a date and time.

The NOW function is just like the TODAY function, except it also returns the current time of day. According to Excel the format the date displays in will be the format for your local date and time settings.

So if I use =TODAY() my computer displays 5/12/2018, and if I format that to show the time of day it displays as 5/12/18 0:00, so midnight of May 12th.

If I use =NOW() my computer displays 5/12/18 8:48 because it's currently eight forty-eight in the morning here as I type this. If I were to use NOW later in the day I might see 5/12/18 14:23 which would be two twenty-three in the afternoon.

You will not normally be able to tell the difference between the two entries unless you are using a date format in Excel that shows time of day. But if you are doing calculations on dates in Excel this could be an important difference.

Usually I just need to use TODAY for my purposes because I'm dealing with number of days between two dates, but if minutes and hours matter to your calculation, then you should use NOW instead.

Just keep in mind with NOW that just like with TODAY it will continue to update to the current time when your worksheet is recalculated. This happens when you press F9, do another calculation in the worksheet, or when you open the worksheet.

If you need an exact time to be preserved and used in the future, you need to take steps to lock that value in place. For example, by copying and using paste special – values.

(If you've ever used one of those memo templates in Word that autofill the date for you, you will understand why this can be an issue. You write the memo, save it, open it two weeks later, and suddenly it's dated for today instead of the date you wrote it. So think this through if you're using NOW or TODAY for documentation purposes.)

If you're interested in how to use NOW with addition and subtraction the Excel Help screen for the function gives a few examples.

Basically, with respect to time, Excel converts the hours in a day into decimals. So .5 is the equivalent of 12 hours, .25 is the equivalent of 6 hours, etc. You can say something like =NOW()-.5 to return a time 12 hours ago. Or =NOW()+7 to return a time that is exactly seven days from now. Be sure you include the () with the function name or it won't work.

THE IF FUNCTION

Notation: IF(logical_test, [value_if_true], [value_if_false])
Excel Definition: Checks whether a condition is met, and returns one value if TRUE, and another value if FALSE.

Now let's talk the IF function.

I love the IF function. It is probably the most valuable function to me. And it's not because of its most basic use which is to say, "If X happens return Y, otherwise return Z." That's pretty simple. Powerful but simple.

No, what I love the IF function for is the fact that I can nest them. So I can say, "If X happens, return Y. If X doesn't happen, but G does, then return H. And if neither X nor G happens, then return Z." And you can keep going and going and going with that until you have twenty possible outcomes.

(Maybe not for those of you in older versions of Excel. I used to run out of how many IF functions I could nest long before I was done and then I'd have to use an IF function that referenced another IF function to get what I wanted. But in newer versions of Excel that is no longer an issue. You can nest up to 64 IF functions in Excel 2013, although that would probably get highly unwieldy.)

So a basic IF function goes IF-THEN-ELSE or IF-THEN-OTHERWISE.

A nested IF function replaces that THEN or that ELSE with another IF Function.

Let's walk through some examples. First we'll build an IF function to give free shipping to any customer who spends at least $25. Any customer who spends less than $25 will pay 5% in shipping costs.

To calculate our shipping cost, we write that as

$$=IF(A1>=25,0,A1*.05)$$

Let's break that down.

The first part, our IF part, is A1>=25. We're saying that if the customer's purchase (in Cell A1) is greater than (>) OR equal to (=) 25 then we want the first outcome.

The second part, our THEN part or first outcome, is 0. If the customer's purchase is equal to or greater than 25, then don't charge for shipping.

That leaves us with the third part, our ELSE part. And that's A1*.05.

Notice that for the calculation A1*.05 we don't have to use quotation marks. (Unlike some other functions where you do.)

Also note here that we are calculating the *shipping charge*, not the customer's transaction cost. If we wanted the total customer cost we would use =IF(A1>=25,A1,A1*1.05)

So that was a basic IF function. One condition, two possible outcomes.

The complexity level ratchets up when you start to nest IF functions. Let's look at the basic format of an IF function again.

It's IF-THEN-ELSE, right? IF x, THEN y, ELSE z. Or IF-THEN-OTHERWISE. IF x, THEN y, OTHERWISE z.

When you nest IF Functions you're basically just replacing that y or that z with another IF function. So it becomes IF x, THEN other IF function, ELSE z.

And you can do that for layer after layer after layer.

The example I used in *Intermediate Excel* is a customer discount that escalates as customers spend more and more money. Spend $150, get $20 off. Spend $75, get $15 off. Etc. Let's look at a simplified version of that example that has just two tiers. If a customer spends at least $25 they get $5 off. If they spend $100, they get $10 off.

Here we go:

	A	B	C
1	**Customer Spend**	**Rebate**	
2	$25.00	$5.00	
3	$100.00	$10.00	
4			
5			
6	**Order Amount**	**Rebate Amount**	**Formula in Column B**
7	$10.00	$0.00	=IF(A7>=$A$3,$B$3,IF(A7>=$A$2,$B$2,0))
8	$25.00	$5.00	=IF(A8>=$A$3,$B$3,IF(A8>=$A$2,$B$2,0))
9	$50.00	$5.00	=IF(A9>=$A$3,$B$3,IF(A9>=$A$2,$B$2,0))
10	$100.00	$10.00	=IF(A10>=$A$3,$B$3,IF(A10>=$A$2,$B$2,0))
11	$125.00	$10.00	=IF(A11>=$A$3,$B$3,IF(A11>=$A$2,$B$2,0))

The formula for Row 7 is:

$$=IF(A7>=\$A\$3,\$B\$3,IF(A7>=\$A\$2,\$B\$2,0))$$

Let's walk through what that's saying.

First, if the value in Cell A7 (the customer order amount) is greater than or equal to the value in Cell A3 (the highest discount tier) then the customer gets the discount in Cell B3 (the $10 discount).

That's =IF(A7>=$A$3,$B$3,

Now, if this were a simple IF function, the next input to the function would be a value or cell reference. But because we're nesting IF functions, the next input is another IF function:

IF(A7>=$A$2,$B$2,0)

This one says that if the value in Cell A7 is greater than the value in Cell A2 (we already know it's not greater than the value in Cell A3 because Excel didn't return the value in Cell B3), then return the value in Cell B2. And if that's also not the case, then just return a value of zero.

If you had more levels that you wanted to consider you'd replace that zero with yet another IF function.

Now, note here that I started with the highest discount and worked my way downward. You could start at the bottom and work your way upward as well. Either direction will work. They'll just look different.

What I've found works best is to build a nested IF function so that I'm closing out all of my IF functions at once at the end. That means that if I build a nested IF function in the "correct" direction, that IF function will end with closing parens for however many IF functions I used. (See how up above there were two closing parens at the end?)

Now, I'll tell you. Most times I build a nested IF function it doesn't work on the first try. I always mess something up.

But that's okay. That's life.

When that happens, as it will, the first thing I check is that I have the right number of parens and that they're in the right spot. So after every single IF there should be an opening paren. And for every opening paren there should be one closing paren. They should all match up. That usually takes care of the "too many arguments" error message.

I also test the formula to make sure that I'm getting the results I expect at each threshold. So is it giving me "greater than" or is it giving me "greater than or equal to"? Are any of my conditions being skipped over or returning an incorrect response?

If that's the case, then the best way to address the issue is to replace everything else in your IF function with a placeholder and to test each section of the IF function in isolation.

So I don't try to decipher this all at once:

=IF(A22>$A$2,IF(A22>$A$3,IF(A22>$A$4,IF(A22>$A$5,
IF(A22>$A$5,$B$5),$B$4),$B$3),$B$2),0)

(This is an example written in what I find the harder format for nested IF functions because each new IF function is added in the middle of the formula rather than the end.)

What I do is remove everything except the first IF function. So I take that mess up there and I make it:

=IF(A22>$A$2,"THEN",0)

And I ask myself if that makes sense. If it does, then I check next part:

=IF(A22>$A$3,"THEN",$B$2)

Does that make sense?

I just keep going through one step at a time to make sure it's all working the way it should. And eventually I find where the error is.

Remember with nested IF functions: slow and steady wins the race. Take it one step at a time. Test your possible outcomes. Don't get frustrated. Draw a diagram if you have to.

Next we'll cover VLOOKUP which is what all my programmer/computer savvy friends swear by instead of using nested IF functions.

THE VLOOKUP FUNCTION

Notation: VLOOKUP(lookup_value, table_array, col_index_num, [range_lookup])
Excel Definition: Looks for a value in the leftmost column of a table, and then returns a value in the same row from a column you specify. By default, the table must be sorted in an ascending order.

Full disclosure here. I hate VLOOKUP. Every time I've wanted to use it it's caused me more problems than it's been worth. But I think if you were to set out to use VLOOKUP (as opposed to my trying to fit it into an existing scenario after the fact) that it could be very useful. And Excel (and my computer programmer friends) certainly thinks it's a better choice than using nested IF functions.

So if you're not like me, and you don't find it fun to nest six or seven levels of IF functions, this might be the better solution for you.

To effectively use VLOOKUP you need a data table that has values that can be looked up and values that are returned when there's a match. This data table needs to be sorted in ascending order. (That's the mistake I usually make. I want to look up values in a table of customer data that's in any old order and VLOOKUP can't do that.)

What VLOOKUP is good at is using a reference table, like our discounting example above. Something like this:

	I	J
1	**VLOOKUP TABLE**	
2	**Customer Spend**	**Rebate**
3	$0.00	$0.00
4	$25.00	$5.00
5	$50.00	$10.00
6	$75.00	$15.00
7	$150.00	$20.00

It can take each value you give it, compare it to the values in that reference table, and return a value for you based on where your data falls in the reference table.

The first input for VLOOKUP is the value from your data that you want to look up. So, in this example, the customer's transaction amount. I have a customer who paid $60. Do they get a discount? And, if so, how much?

The next input for VLOOKUP is a reference to the cell range where Excel needs to look for that value and where the value you want it to return is. So this isn't a single column. It's multiple columns.

In our example, just two. But it could be ten. Or twenty. Just not one. Because you need what you're looking up and then you need what value you're returning. That's two columns, minimum.

The left-most column of that range MUST be the value you're looking up. And then the value you're returning MUST be somewhere to the right of that. (These are the reasons VLOOKUP never works for me. Because my data isn't always built like they want it to be. Don't be me. Think about these things in advance.)

The third entry in a VLOOKUP is which column in the range of cells you gave in the second entry contains the value you want. Column 1 contains what you're using for your search. Count from there to find your column number for your result. In this table above, our number is 2 because it's the second column in our range.

Finally, you need to tell Excel whether it's looking for an exact match (0/FALSE) or an approximate match (1/TRUE). If it's an exact match, you'll only get a value returned when what you're looking up matches an entry in the table exactly. If it's an approximate match you'll get a result for all entries and your value will be determined based on the table sort and where that value falls in the range of values.

Let's look at the full table I used for discounting in *Intermediate Excel*.

It turns out we need to change our table to get this to work. When I tried using the table I'd used for the IF functions, I had an error for the lowest tier. So I had to put in a zero customer spend, zero discount row to make this work. Here we go:

	I	J
1	**VLOOKUP TABLE**	
2	**Customer Spend**	**Rebate**
3	$0.00	$0.00
4	$25.00	$5.00
5	$50.00	$10.00
6	$75.00	$15.00
7	$150.00	$20.00
8		
9	**Cell J11 =VLOOKUP(I11,$I$3:$J$7,2,TRUE)**	
10	**Order Amount**	**Rebate Amount**
11	$5.00	$0.00
12	$25.00	$5.00
13	$40.00	$5.00
14	$50.00	$10.00
15	$60.00	$10.00
16	$75.00	$15.00
17	$140.00	$15.00
18	$150.00	$20.00

Let's look at the sample for Row 11 that's shown in Row 9.

$$=VLOOKUP(I11,\$I\$3:\$J\$7,2,TRUE)$$

That first entry, I11 is where we have the customer transaction amount of $5.00.

The second entry $I$3:$J$7 is where we have our discount table. Note that the first column in the range, Column I is where we have the value we want to look up. And that the range contains the column, Column J, where the value we want to return is stored.

Note, too, that I did not include the header row in the provided range. (That returns an error message.)

Also, note that the table is sorted in ascending order. If it isn't VLOOKUP does not work correctly.

The third entry is where we tell Excel which column to look in for the results In this case that's 2, the second column in our range.

And finally, the fourth entry tells Excel whether we're looking for exact matches to the entries in the table or whether an approximate match is okay.

Since we have ranges we want to pull from ($0-$24.99 gets no discount, $25 to $49.99 gets $5, etc.) we say "TRUE" to allow for approximate results.

If I were to change that to FALSE, I would get a bunch of #N/A results except for rows where customer spend was $25, $50, $75, or $150.

Now, compare that to what we had to use to build a nested IF function that does the same thing:

$$=IF(A11>=\$A\$6,\$B\$6,IF(A11>=\$A\$5,\$B\$5,IF(A11>=\$A\$4,\$B\$4,IF(A11>=\$A\$3,\$B\$3,0))))$$

Clearly it's easier to write the VLOOKUP function to do this. But remember that I built that table so that VLOOKUP would work with it.

As I said above, I run into issues using VLOOKUP because I want to use it on unsorted data or on data that has the value I want to pull to the left of the lookup value in my lookup table. So for me it's easier to write a nested IF function than it is to rearrange my data so that it works with VLOOKUP. I suspect I am in the minority there.

Just think of nested IF functions as the way to do VLOOKUP without all the pesky rules. But because there are no rules, you have to do a lot more of the heavy lifting.

A few more points:

Excel cautions that numbers or dates stored as text may produce unexpected results and so may text entries that have inconsistent usage of spaces or quote marks.

If the data table you're using for your lookup values is large or complex, be very, very careful that the results you get are what you expect. And absolutely be sure to sort your data table in ascending order.

Also check, double-check, and check again.

And one final point.

With an IF function to change the IF formula to adjust for whether you want your criteria to be "a customer spent $25 or more" versus "a customer spent over $25" you adjust the formula from >= to >. With VLOOKUP, you'll need to adjust your lookup table not your formula. So instead of $25.00 in the table, we'd have $25.01 for a situation where customers get the discount if they spend over $25 as opposed to $25 or more.

OK. That's IF functions and VLOOKUP. Let's talk about some functions that on their surface are very basic, but when combined with other functions can be much more powerful. That's AND and OR.

THE AND FUNCTION

Notation: AND(logical1, [logical2],…)
Excel Definition: Checks whether all arguments are TRUE, and returns TRUE if all arguments are TRUE.

At its core, the AND function is very basic. You use it to determine whether more than one criteria is met. So, is that value greater than 10 AND less than 20? Is that customer from Alaska AND has he bought Widgets?

It doesn't have to be just two criteria either. You can use more than two with an AND function. (Although the help text for the function doesn't say exactly how many you can use.)

In my numeric example above, you would write that as

=AND(A1>10,A1<20)

If the value in Cell A1 was greater than 10 and less than 20 Excel would return a value of TRUE. Or in the second example I gave, you could write that as

=AND(A1="Alaska",B1="Widget")

(Assuming A1 contained the state information and B1 contained the product information). Again, if both criteria were met, Excel would return a value of TRUE.

In addition to working with numbers, like the first example above, and text references, like the second example above, AND works with cell references. So:

=AND(A1>D1,A1<D2)

looks to see if the value in Cell A1 is greater than the value in Cell D1 and also less than the value in Cell D2.

I rarely if ever use AND on a standalone basis. You could, like I showed in the examples above, but what I've used it for instead was if I had an IF function where I needed two criteria met.

For example, if I wanted all customers who bought Widgets and live in Alaska to qualify for 50% off their purchase amount. I could write an equation to calculate total cost as:

=IF(AND(A1="Alaska",B1="Widget"),C1*0.5,C1)

where A1 contains their state, B1 the product they've bought, and C1 contains the purchase amount.

In that example, I just replaced the first portion of the IF function with:

AND(A1="Alaska",B1="Widget")

I don't use AND often, but when I do it's very helpful. Same with OR which we'll discuss next.

THE OR FUNCTION

Notation: OR(logical1, [logical2],…)
Excel Definition: Checks whether any of the arguments are TRUE, and returns TRUE or FALSE. Returns FALSE only if all arguments are FALSE.

The OR function is similar to the AND function except it doesn't require that all of the conditions are met to return a TRUE value. With OR if one of the conditions in the list is met, then the value is TRUE.

Say, for example, I want to identify all of my customers who are in the states of Florida, Georgia, and North Carolina because I have a special promotion running in those states. I could write that as =OR(A1="Florida",A1="Georgia",A1="North Carolina") and if the value in Cell A1 was any of those (Florida, Georgia, or North Carolina), Excel would return a value of TRUE.

If none of the conditions were met, Excel would return a value of FALSE.

Once more, this is one I rarely use as a standalone, but it is nice to use it with an IF function. So say I was running a price promotion in those three states, I could write an IF function that says,

=IF(OR(A1="Florida",A1="Georgia",A1="North Carolina"),C1*.5,C1)

to give a 50% discount to any customer in one of those three states.

Like with AND, you can use text criteria (like above), numeric criteria, or cell references.

So =OR(A1=C1,A1=C3) would check to see if the value in Cell A1 was the same as the value in Cell C1 OR the value in Cell C3.

And =OR(A1=5,A1=10) would check to see if the value in Cell A1 was equal to 5 OR 10.

This is another one you probably won't use often, but will appreciate when you need it.

THE TRUE FUNCTION

Notation: TRUE()
Excel Definition: Returns the logical value TRUE.

When I was working on this guide I found myself occasionally needing a cell to return a value of TRUE or FALSE to test some of the different functions. Simply typing TRUE into the cell didn't always work, so I found myself using TRUE and its counterpart, FALSE.

If you use it, be sure to include the parens () or Excel may think you're trying to reference a named range.

You should also be able to just type TRUE and get the same result, but that didn't always seem to work for me.

I would likely use TRUE and FALSE in other functions, like IF functions rather than having the function return a value of 0 or " " if I were then going to apply a function such as AVERAGEA to the range.

According to Excel, TRUE exists primarily for compatibility with other spreadsheet programs.

THE FALSE FUNCTION

Notation: FALSE()
Excel Definition: Returns the logical value FALSE.

As I mentioned under the description for TRUE, when I was working on this guide I found myself occasionally needing a cell to return a value of TRUE or FALSE to test some of the different functions. Simply typing FALSE into the cell didn't always work even though it's supposed to, so I found myself using the FALSE function and its counterpart, TRUE.

Be sure if you're using the function that you include the parens, so write =FALSE() or if it's in the midst of another function write it as FALSE() with the parens after the text.

According to Excel FALSE exists primarily for compatibility with other spreadsheet programs.

THE NA FUNCTION

Notation: NA()
Excel Definition: Returns the error value #N/A (value not available)

You can use the NA function to mark empty cells. This avoids the issue of inadvertently including empty cells in your calculations.

A friend of mine suggested including it in this guide because he recently had a scenario where he was generating results using an IF function and then graphing those results. When his results generated an empty cell or a null value Excel tried to include those entries in the graph. He found that using NA fixed that problem, because Excel does not graph #N/A values.

To do this, you could write something like this:

$$=IF(A1>10,5,NA())$$

In this case, if A1 is greater than 10, Excel returns a value of 5 but if it isn't Excel returns a value of #N/A.

Be sure to use the empty parens as I did in the example above or Excel won't recognize it as the NA function.

THE RAND FUNCTION

Notation: RAND()
Excel Definition: Returns a random number greater than or equal to 0 and less than 1, evenly distributed. (Changes on recalculation.)

For some types of calculations, you need to have a random start.

For example, if I want to sample a series of transactions and be able to extrapolate my results to that entire population of transactions, I need to start at a random point and then take every nth transaction from that point forward until I've worked my way through the entire sample back to my starting point.

(The n is usually determined by taking your total population and dividing it by your sample size. Where I used to work we'd often take a sample of 60 transactions. So if my population was 10,000 transactions then I'd want every 167th transaction until I reached my sample of 60. You can use a function like RAND to make sure that you're starting at a random point, because starting at Transaction 1 each time isn't truly random.)

If I say =RAND()*10000, that gives me my starting point. Actually, for this example, it would be best to use =INT(RAND()*10000) to make sure that it gives me an integer instead of a decimal value.

Be careful with RAND, though. Because every time you press F9, make a new calculation in your worksheet, or reopen your worksheet it will calculate a new random value. And once it does that there's no way to go back to your prior value. Ctrl + Z will not work. That number is gone and it's not coming back.

So if you do this and you need to record the random number Excel generates, which you likely will, use copy and paste special – values to store the value as a number. (Or build a process that acts on that value as soon as it's generated.) Just know that as soon as you paste special – values the original value is going to change and will no longer match the number you just pasted.

THE RANDBETWEEN FUNCTION

Notation: RANDBETWEEN(bottom, top)
Excel Definition: Returns a random number between the numbers you specify.

RANDBETWEEN is much like RAND, except you can specify a range of numbers for it to choose between and the number returned will always be an integer (whole number).

As with RAND, every time the worksheet is opened or you hit F9 or choose recalculate, a new random value will be generated. So if you need to keep your number, generate the value and then convert it to just a number using paste special – values.

We could've used RANDBETWEEN for the example I gave above for RAND.

=RANDBETWEEN(1,10000)

would choose a random transaction to start with in our range of ten thousand transactions.

Another example of when you might use this is a jury duty selection. Say today's jurors have numbers assigned between 12345 and 23456, you could use

=RANDBETWEEN(12345,23456)

to randomly select the jurors who will serve on a jury.

If you need ten jurors, you can just copy and paste the formula until you have ten entries. (For small population sizes it is possible to repeat a value.) Your other option is to hit F9 to recalculate and record the values returned until you have the number of values you need for your sample. Just remember to write each one down or copy it over as a number before you calculate the next one.

THE RANK FUNCTION

Notation: RANK(number, ref, [order])
Excel Definition: Returns the rank of a number in a list of numbers: its size relative to other values in the list.

According to Excel this function only exists in current versions of Excel for compatibility with Excel 2007 or earlier. In Excel 2013 or later this function has been replaced with RANK.AVG and RANK.EQ.

As its definition says, RANK tells you the rank of a number within a range of numbers. Is it the 5th value in the list? The 10th? RANK will tell you.

The first input into the function is the number you're analyzing.

The next input is the overall range of numbers you want to compare it to. (The number can be pulled from the reference range and probably will be in most instances.)

The final input, order, tells Excel which way to rank things. If you omit it, which you can, or use a zero (0), then Excel will rank the value based on descending order. If you use a one (1) or any other number other than zero, Excel will rank the value based on ascending order.

I used a range of numbers from 1 through 15 and had Excel rank the 6 in that range.

=RANK(6,J1:J15,0) returned a value of 10 regardless of how the reference range was sorted.

=RANK(6,J1:J15) returned the same value.

So in those two instances, 15 was considered the best rank, 1 the worst.

=RANK(6,A1:A15,1) returned a value of 6 regardless of how the reference range was sorted.

In that instance, 1 was considered the best rank, 15 the worst.

I found this counterintuitive because my default is to always think of 1 as the best rank. So if you're like me you should test your data on an obvious sample to see if the rank you're getting makes sense before you apply it to a full range of data. If it's backwards from what you expected, then change the order input in your formula.

You also need to be careful when using RANK if you have duplicates in your reference range. RANK assigns the same rank to duplicate values but then does not assign the next rank(s) to any value until it has skipped past the number of duplicates.

So if I have the numbers 1, 2, 2, 3, 4 they would be ranked 1, 2, 2, 4, 5 or 5, 3, 3, 2, 1 depending on the rank order I specify. See how there are two ranks of 2 in that first example and two ranks of 3 in that second example? And how Excel skipped the rank of 3 in the first example and the rank of 4 in the second example?

(If you have a tie like this the help text for the function gives a correction factor you can use. Or if you have Excel 2013 RANK.AVG will average the ranks that would've been assigned to the tied values and return the average instead of the best rank.)

THE RANK.EQ FUNCTION

Notation: RANK.EQ(number, ref, [order])

Excel Definition: Returns the rank of a number in a list of numbers: its size relative to other values in the list; if more than one value has the same rank, the top rank of that set of values is returned.

RANK.EQ is one of the two functions that replaced RANK in Excel 2013. It works just like RANK.

Your first input is the number that needs ranked, the next input is the range to use as the reference range, and the final input tells Excel whether to evaluate rank based on ascending order or descending order.

If there's a tie and more than one value should have the same rank they will all be assigned the top rank and Excel will skip that number of ranks before assigning the next rank.

THE RANK.AVG FUNCTION

Notation: RANK.AVG(number, ref, [order])
Excel Definition: Returns the rank of a number in a list of numbers: its size relative to other values in the list; if more than one value has the same rank, the average rank is returned.

RANK.AVG is one of the two functions that replaced RANK in Excel 2013.

If there are no ties, it works just like RANK. If there are ties, RANK.AVG displays the average of the ranks that would have been assigned to those values.

Your first input is the number that needs ranked, the next input is the range to use as the reference range, and the final input tells Excel whether to evaluate rank based on ascending order or descending order.

With RANK.AVG if there is a tie in ranking, so two or more values have the same rank, Excel will return the average rank for that range of values.

So, for example:

If I have 1, 1, 1, 2, 2 in Cells A1:A5 and I want to know what the rank for a value of 1 is,

$$=RANK.AVG(1,A1:A5,1)$$

will return a value of 2.

That is because there are three values for 1 and they are ranked 1st, 2nd, and 3rd, respectively. The average of those ranks $(1+2+3)/3$ is 2.

If I have 0, 1, 1, 1, 2, 2 in Cells A1:A5 and I again use =RANK.AVG(1,A1:A5,1) this will return a value of 3 because the rank for the 1's is 2nd, 3rd, and 4th, and the average of those ranks $(2+3+4)/3$ is 3.

Compare this to RANK.EQ which would return a value of 1 in the first instance and a value of 2 in the second instance.

Here is an example of all three options side-by-side, showing the ascending and descending rank options for each using a reference range that contains 1, 2, 2, 3, and 4.

	A	B	C	D	E	F	G	H	I	J
1	REF RANGE		(0) RANK (1)			(0) RANK.EQ (1)			(0) RANK.AVG (1)	
2	1		5	1		5	1		5	1
3	2		3	2		3	2		3.5	2.5
4	2		3	2		3	2		3.5	2.5
5	3		2	4		2	4		2	4
6	4		1	5		1	5		1	5
7		Cell C2	=RANK($A2,$A$2:$A$6,0)		Cell F2	=RANK.EQ($A2,$A$2:$A$6,0)		Cell I2	=RANK.AVG($A2,$A$2:$A$6,0)	
8		Cell D2	=RANK($A2,$A$2:$A$6,1)		Cell G2	=RANK.EQ($A2,$A$2:$A$6,1)		Cell J2	=RANK.AVG($A2,$A$2:$A$6,1)	

THE SMALL FUNCTION

Notation: SMALL(array, k)
Excel Definition: Returns the k-th smallest value in a data set. For example, the fifth smallest number.

The SMALL function is pretty straight-forward. The first input is the cell range you want to use and the second input is a number representing the position in the range you're interested in.

So if you want the smallest value in a column (and didn't want to use MIN for some reason), you could use =SMALL(A:A,1) to return it.

You could also return the largest value in the range if you know the total size of the range (n) by using that value for your k value. (The ROWS function will let you count the number of rows in a range.)

THE LARGE FUNCTION

Notation: LARGE(array, k)
Excel Definition: Returns the k-th largest value in a data set. For example, the fifth largest number.

The LARGE function is the counterpart to the SMALL function. The first input is the cell range you want to use and the second input is a number representing the position in the range you're interested in.

So if you want the largest value in a column (and didn't want to use MAX for some reason), you could use =LARGE(A:A,1) to return it.

You could also return the smallest value in the range if you know the total size of the range (n) by using that value for your k value.

50 More Excel Functions

THE IFNA FUNCTION

Notation: IFNA(value,value_if_na)
Excel Definition: Returns the value you specify if the expression resolves to #N/A, otherwise returns the result of the expression.

The IFNA function is one that I didn't include in *50 Useful Excel Functions* even though I could have. The reason I didn't include it in the first fifty functions I covered is because I'm so comfortable with using IF functions that I just quickly write an IF function that does what IFNA does without looking to see if a function exists to do what I want, which is suppress that pesky #NA! result that sometimes occurs.

But I found myself using this the other day and it's very straight-forward and easy to use. The way it works is that you tell it a function to perform and if the result of that function is the #N/A! error then instead of returning that error you can specify what Excel returns instead.

(I say function here, but the Excel help text calls it an argument.)

The easiest way to show how this works is to walk you through an example.

Let's say I have a list of my books I've published and how much I've spent on ads for those books each month. I also have a list of how much I've earned for each book each month. And I decide I want to combine those two sets of information to calculate a profit/loss per month for each book.

I can use the CONCATENATE function to create an entry for both data sets that combines month-year-title into one column and then use VLOOKUP to look up the amount I spent on ads for each title in each month and bring that into the sales worksheet.

But when VLOOKUP can't find an entry—so in months where I had book sales but no ad spend, for example—Excel returns a value of #N/A! When that happens within a column of data you can no longer click on that column and see its summed value. This would prevent me from checking that I'd captured all of my ad costs.

But I can easily fix this issue using the IFNA function.

If my original formula was:

=VLOOKUP(D:D,'Advertising Spend By Series'!E:F,2,FALSE)

(That's saying look for the value in Column D of this worksheet in Column E of the Advertising Spend by Series tab and then pull the value from Column F, but only if the two values are an exact match.)

The revised formula using IFNA is:

=IFNA(VLOOKUP(D:D,'Advertising Spend By Series'!E:F,2,FALSE),0)

That looks complicated, but it's not. Replace the VLOOKUP portion with an X and you have:

=IFNA(X,0)

Basically, if there's a value for VLOOKUP to return then return that value, otherwise return a zero.

I chose to return a value of zero, but you could easily have it return a text statement instead. If you are going to have it return text, be sure to use quotation marks around the text you want returned. So if I wanted "No Match" returned instead of a zero, I'd use:

=IFNA(VLOOKUP(D:D,'Advertising Spend By Series'!E:F,2,FALSE),"No Match")

If you don't want anything returned, so you just want an apparently blank cell, then leave that second argument blank. You'll still need to use the comma, so it should look like this:

=IFNA(VLOOKUP(D:D,'Advertising Spend By Series'!E:F,2,FALSE),)

That will return a value of "" in that cell instead of the #N/A! error message.

That's it.

It looks a little complicated because we were working with a VLOOKUP function, but it's really very simple.

Take the formula you already have that's giving you the #N/A! results, type IFNA(between the equals sign and that first function, go to the end, add a comma, put in the result you want returned when there's an N/A result (if any), and then add a closing paren. Done.

Just keep in mind, of course, that you will not see an #N/A! result if you use this function, which could hide from you valuable information about your calculation or your data.

Also, it's particular to just that type of error. Other error messages, such as #DIV/0!, will still be displayed.

If you want to suppress all error messages, then you need to use IFERROR which we'll discuss next.

THE IFERROR FUNCTION

Notation: IFERROR(value,value_if_error)
Excel Definition: Returns value_if_error if expression is an error and the value of the expression itself otherwise.

The IFERROR function is just like the IFNA function except that it will return your specified value for any error message, not just the #N/A! error message. Error messages suppressed by the function include: #N/A!, #VALUE!, #REF!, #DIV/0!, #NUM!, #NAME?, and #NULL!

So be sure before you use it that you are okay with suppressing all of those error messages. For example, the #REF! error message usually will tell you when you've deleted a cell that was being referenced by a formula. That for me isn't something I would like to hide. If I've made that mistake, I want to know it.

But if you have a range of cells with a formula in them that's returning, for example, the #DIV/0! error because you're currently dividing by zero, which is an issue I've run into in some of my worksheets, this might be a good option.

Your other option is to use a simple IF function instead.

For example, I use

$$=IF(P1=0,"",J1/P1)$$

in one of my worksheets, because it returns a #DIV/0! error until P1 has a value and that annoys me. IFERROR would work the same in that situation. I could use

$$=IFERROR(J1/P1,)$$

instead. Note that I left the second argument, the value_if_error empty which will return a blank cell as long as dividing the value in Cell J1 by the value in Cell P1 produces an error message. To do that I still had to include the comma, though.

My temptation in using either IFNA or IFERROR is to have them return zeroes or empty cells, but I would recommend that if you're using IFERROR in a crucial situation that you have it return a text entry instead so that you always know when there's an error message that's being suppressed.

So

$$=IFERROR(J1/P1,"No Value")$$

is probably a better choice than

$$=IFERROR(J1/P1,)$$

because you will know for a fact that the formula generated an error message and won't think that the value in that cell was entered as zero.

Note above that I used quotes around the text I wanted to have Excel display in the place of my error message, just like I did with IFNA.

THE NOT FUNCTION

Notation: NOT(logical)
Excel Definition: Changes FALSE to TRUE, or TRUE to FALSE.

This next one, the NOT function, is one I'm including only because Microsoft themselves highlight it as useful. Also, it is related to the AND and OR functions, which I do think you should know, that I already covered in *50 Useful Excel Functions*.

But the fact of the matter is that my psychology background tells me that using a negative to build a function is a bad idea and I would encourage you to find another way to accomplish your goal if you're ever tempted to use the NOT function.

At its most basic, the NOT function returns the opposite result. So

$$=NOT(FALSE)$$

returns a value of TRUE. And

$$=NOT(TRUE)$$

returns a value of FALSE.

But you're never going to use it that way.

Where you might want to use it is to evaluate whether a criteria was met.

So let's say that I have two criteria that must be met for someone to be given a bonus. They have to have been employed for over 12 months and they have to have generated over $25,000 in sales.

I could use a NOT function to ask if that happened. So, was my employee's time with the company in Cell B5 greater than 12 months? To do this, I'd write

$$=NOT(B5<12)$$

to get a result of FALSE when the employee had not been there at least 12 months and a result of TRUE if they had.

See how I had to do less than 12 there to get the right result?

I could have just as easily used an IF function instead and written

$$=IF(B5>12,TRUE)$$

to get the same result without the mental gymnastics using the NOT function requires.

In the Excel help text for this function, they give a different bonus scenario and then write a really ugly looking formula to calculate the bonus. It looks like this:

$$=IF(AND(NOT(B14<\$B\$7),NOT(C14<\$B\$5)),B14*\$B\$8,0)$$

But let me flip that around for you by removing the NOT function and switching the less than signs to greater than signs. If I do that I get:

$$=IF(AND(B14>=\$B\$7,C14>=\$B\$5),B14*\$B\$8,0)$$

It returns the same result as using the NOT function but with a lot less headache. (Just be sure to test that border case of equals to B7 and B5 to make sure you get it exactly right…I had initially written it as > instead of >=, a common problem I have to watch out for.)

Bottom line with the NOT function: If you're ever tempted to use it ask yourself if there isn't a different and simpler way to do what you're trying to do. I'm not going to say that there's absolutely no possible use for this function, but I am pretty confident in saying that ninety-nine times out of a hundred you should be able to find an alternate way of doing your calculation that doesn't require you to use the NOT function.

But for that remaining one in a hundred scenario, now you know how to use it.

THE HLOOKUP FUNCTION

Notation: HLOOKUP(lookup_value, table_array, row_index_num, [range_lookup])
Excel Definition: Looks up a value in the top row of a table or array of values and returns the value in the same column from a row you specify.

While we're covering functions that relate to ones already covered in *50 Useful Excel Functions*, let's go over HLOOKUP. You'll notice that it has a very similar name to VLOOKUP, which is a function my friends swear by. (I'm coming around on it. It was recently very handy, but mostly because my data happened to be arranged in a way that I could use it without massive changes.)

Where VLOOKUP scans down a column to match your value and then pulls a result from another column in the row where the match was made, HLOOKUP scans across a row to match your value and then pulls a result from another row in that column where the match was made.

So it's a transposed version of VLOOKUP.

VLOOKUP is the much more popular of the two options because of how most people structure their data. But let's say I have a table of data with month across the top and vendor across the left-hand side and I want to extract how much was earned on a specific vendor in a specific month. I could do that using HLOOKUP.

Here's our example data table:

	A	B	C	D	E	F	G	H	I	J	K	L	M
1		January	February	March	April	May	June	July	August	September	October	November	December
2	Amazon	$100.00	$107.00	$114.49	$122.50	$131.08	$140.26	$150.07	$160.58	$171.82	$183.85	$196.72	$210.49
3	Createspace	$37.00	$39.59	$42.36	$45.33	$48.50	$51.89	$55.53	$59.41	$63.57	$68.02	$72.78	$77.88
4	ACX	$23.50	$25.15	$26.91	$28.79	$30.80	$32.96	$35.27	$37.74	$40.38	$43.20	$46.23	$49.46
5	Con Sales	$10.00			$25.00		$8.00		$100.00			$23.00	
6	Apple	$48.50	$37.00	$52.30	$131.08	$39.59	$42.36	$45.33	$43.97	$42.65	$41.37	$40.13	$38.92
7	Authors Republic	$51.89	$40.48	$31.57	$140.26	$116.41	$96.62	$80.20	$66.56	$55.25	$45.86	$38.06	$31.59
8	D2D	$55.53	$43.31	$33.78	$150.07	$124.56	$103.39	$85.81	$71.22	$59.11	$49.06	$40.72	$33.80
9	Google	$59.41	$46.34	$36.15	$160.58	$133.28	$110.62	$91.82	$76.21	$63.25	$52.50	$43.57	$36.17
10	Kobo	$25.15	$26.91	$28.79	$30.80	$25.57	$21.22	$17.61	$14.62	$12.13	$10.07	$8.36	$6.94
11	Nook	$37.74	$40.38	$43.20	$46.23	$38.37	$31.85	$26.43	$21.94	$18.21	$15.11	$12.54	$10.41
12	Pronoun	$25.15	$26.91	$28.79	$18.71	$12.16	$7.91	$5.14	$3.34	$2.17	$1.41	$0.92	$0.60

If I use the formula:

=HLOOKUP("April",B1:M12,4,FALSE)

that will look for a value for the month of April in the table contained in Cells B1 through M12 and will return the value from the fourth row of that table (ACX) for that month. A value will only be returned if there is an exact match to "April" in the first row of the table range I specified.

Let's break this down further.

The first entry in any HLOOKUP formula is going to be what you're looking up. This can be a numeric value, a text string, or a cell reference. In the example above, because I wanted to look up a specific text value, I had to use quotation marks.

With text entries, if you're looking for an exact match you can also use the wildcards that Excel has for text lookups. A question mark means any one character and an asterisk means any number of characters. So "*April" would search for any text string that has April at the end whereas "?April" would only search for any text string that has one character before ending in April.

(You can use a tilde sign (~) before a question mark or asterisk if you actually want to search for an asterisk or question mark and not use it as a wildcard.)

The second input into the HLOOKUP function is where you're going to search. That's the table array. The first row of that table array is where what you're searching for needs to be. The table array then has to have the row with the values you want to return somewhere below the search row. (This is where VLOOKUP always fails me. My data is rarely structured the way it needs to be to use VLOOKUP. But I suspect with HLOOKUP this would be less of a problem.)

With HLOOKUP (as with VLOOKUP), there are two options for what you're searching for. You can search for an exact match or you can search for an approximate match. If you choose to search for an approximate match, then your data in the lookup row needs to be sorted in ascending order for HLOOKUP to work properly. If you're looking for an exact match then the order of the entries doesn't matter.

When looking up values Excel treats uppercase and lower case entries as the same. It is not case sensitive.

(As a side note, you can sort the columns of a table using the Sort function in Excel. It's not something I covered in *Excel for Beginners* or *Intermediate Excel* because it's not something most people do, but it's there in the Sort dialogue box. You can change the Options choice to Sort Left to Right.)

The third value that you need to provide for any HLOOKUP function is which row to pull your results from. This is which row within the range of data you provided as the table array. So it is not the actual row number. It's which row within your specified data table that you want to pull from.

If you provide a negative number, you'll get an error message. If you provide a value that is larger than the size of the range you specified, you will also get an error message.

If you provide a value of 1 that will return either the value you were looking up (for an exact match) or the closest possible value (for an approximate match), which can be especially useful if you want the closest value to what you're looking up. (Although I suspect this is more likely to be useful with VLOOKUP than HLOOKUP.)

The final input into the function is optional. This is where you tell Excel whether you want an exact match or an approximate match. If you omit this input, Excel will look for an approximate match so will return a result for the value that's closest to what you were looking for. It defines closest by which value is the next largest without going over the value you were looking for.

If you use FALSE for this input, then Excel will look for an exact match only and return #N/A! if there is no match.

You will also get an #N/A! error if you ask for an approximate match but the lookup value you specify is smaller than the smallest value in the table.

If you do get an error message, check your spelling, that your table range is correct, and that your row references are correct. If that all looks good, then you can look at the help function for HLOOKUP to see which error message you received and what that might mean.

Where VLOOKUP to me seems to be best used for looking up values in a table, like a discount table, I see HLOOKUP as most useful when you want to extract data from an existing summary table like in the example I gave above. But the two do operate on the same principles, so if you understand how to use one you should be able to use the other as well.

THE TRANSPOSE FUNCTION

Notation: TRANSPOSE(array)
Excel Definition: Converts a vertical range of cells to a horizontal range, or vice versa.

The TRANSPOSE function is one that you probably won't use very often, but I wanted to cover it because it actually came up in *50 Useful Excel Functions*.

So let's walk through what TRANSPOSE does. It takes a series of entries that are in a column and displays them in a row instead or takes a series of entries that are in a row and displays them in a column. You can do this with a combination of rows and columns as well. It will basically flip those entries so that what was in columns is now in rows and what was in rows is now in columns.

TRANSPOSE is a special kind of function that Excel introduced called an array formula. There are two key things to remember when working with array formulas. First, you need to select a range of cells before you start typing your formula in or it won't work. Second, you need to use Ctrl + Shift + Enter when you're done entering your formula or it also won't work. These two steps are what, for me, distinguish array formulas from other formulas. (That and the fact that the values they return appear in a range of cells instead of a single cell, of course.)

Let's walk through an example:

In Cells A1 through A6 type the numbers 1 through 6.

Now, go to Cell E6 and highlight Cells E6 through J6. (These are the cells we want to paste that data into.)

Keeping those cells highlighted, start typing your formula which is

=TRANSPOSE(A1:A6)

Finish with Ctrl + Shift + Enter.

If you've done it right, you should now see the numbers 1 through 6 in Cells E6 through J6. If you click on one of those cells, the formula in the formula bar should look like this:

{=TRANSPOSE(A1:A6)}

Those squiggly brackets indicate an array formula.

Keep in mind, too, that for this to work the range of cells you select for your function have to be the same size as what you're transposing but in the opposite direction. So if you have a table that is four columns across and three rows down that you want to transpose, you need to select a range of cells that is four rows down and three columns across.

Now, the other option if you just want to change the orientation of your data is to copy and then use Paste Special-Transpose. To do this, select the cells you want to copy, click in the first cell where you want to paste that data (making sure enough cells are empty so you're not over-writing anything), and then right click, and under Paste Options choose the Transpose option. (The one with two little two-box grids with an arrow pointing between them in the bottom right corner of the clipboard image. For me, right now, that's the fourth image choice.)

(In older versions of Excel you can do this using the Paste Special dialogue box and clicking in the Transpose box at the bottom on the right-hand side.)

So if you can just copy and Paste Special-Values, why would you want to use this TRANSPOSE function instead? The key difference is that when you TRANSPOSE your data using the function it is still linked to the original source. So if you change the values in those original cells, the transposed data will update as well. If you use Paste Special – Transpose, that data is not linked anymore. You are just pasting in the values and if you update your original data it will do nothing to what you pasted.

Also, the use we saw in *50 Useful Excel Functions* was built into a formula that would have normally returned results in a column. By using TRANSPOSE as part of that formula we were able to have the results returned across a row. So if you're working with other array formulas, TRANSPOSE allows you to change whether results appear across a row or down a column.

Basically, which option (function or pasting) is the better choice will depend on why you needed to do that. If you just wanted to transform a row of data into a column or vice versa, which is my usually reason for doing this, then Paste Special – Transpose is the easiest choice. If you're wanting to change the orientation of data that's output from an array formula or you want to copy data from one source and paste it to another in a different orientation while keeping the two sources linked, then the TRANSPOSE function will be the better option.

Just remember that when you use it it's an array formula so has to be set up and completed in a different manner than a normal formula does, namely by highlighting your range of cells in advance and by finishing with Ctrl + Shift +Enter.

THE INDEX FUNCTION

Notation: INDEX(array,row_num,[column_num])
or
INDEX(reference,row_num,[column_num],[area_num])

Excel Definition: Returns a value or reference of the cell at the intersection of a particular row and column, in a given range.

The INDEX function can take two forms. It can be an array formula and return a range of values like we just saw TRANSPOSE do, or it can serve as a basic lookup formula and return a value in a specified column and row within a specified table.

I will note here that at least in Excel 2013 when you open the help box for this function that it links to a video which gives a very nice overview of both ways of using the INDEX function, so I'd encourage you to watch that. But I'm going to walk through it here, too, so you don't have to if you don't want to.

At its most basic, the reference version

=INDEX(reference,row_num,[column_num],[area_num])

looks for a specific value in a specified position in a table. (To me this is much like how VLOOKUP and HLOOKUP work except it's not looking for a match to a value but just a specific position.)

The first argument you provide in this version is the table you want to look in. Let's say you have student grades for a series of tests and the data table is in Cells A2 through E7 with the actual data in Cells B3 through E7. Like so:

	A	B	C	D	E
1		\multicolumn{4}{c}{Semester 1}			
2		Test 1	Test 2	Test 3	Test 4
3	**Student A**	82	87	94	92
4	**Student B**	88	81	84	83
5	**Student C**	65	68	64	63
6	**Student D**	98	98	98	99
7	**Student E**	86	88	84	83

If you want to extract from that table the grade on the third test for Student B, you could write either of the two following formulas using the INDEX function:

=INDEX(A2:E7,3,4)

or

=INDEX(B3:E7,2,3)

The difference between these two is the range of cells I told Excel to use for the reference data table. In the first one, I included the header row and column with the student names, Cells A2 through E7. In the second I just included the results, Cells B3 through E7. That's the first input into the INDEX function. The data range to use.

The second input is which row *in that range* to pull the data from. (This is where it's like VLOOKUP and HLOOKUP, because those work the same way.) This is not the actual row number in the worksheet. This is which row in your chosen range to pull from. So when I include the header row, Student B's data is in the third row of the data range. When I don't include the header row Student B's data is in the second row of the data range.

The third input is which column *in that range* to pull the data from. Same concept. Because in the first example I included the student names column, then to pull data for the third test we need to look at the fourth column in the data range. But in the second example where I only included the results, we pull from the third column.

There is a fourth input option that the INDEX function can use. It is very well demonstrated in that video that I referenced above, but I'll walk through it here as well.

The fourth input option works when you have more than one data table to look up values in. To use this option, the first input for the function has to include more than one data range. If you include more than one range in that first input then you can use the fourth input option for INDEX to tell Excel which of the multiple ranges you provided it should use.

(If you have not provided multiple ranges and specify a number for this fourth input you will get a #REF! error.)

The example they use is four tables where you have different sales values for different regions and different time periods for different products and want to pull the information for sales in the same region and time period for each of four products.

I'm going to use a different scenario here. Let's say that you teach the same group of students for two different semesters and so have test results for both of those semesters for the same students. Like this:

	A	B	C	D	E
1			Semester 1		
2		Test 1	Test 2	Test 3	Test 4
3	Student A	82	87	94	92
4	Student B	88	81	84	83
5	Student C	65	68	64	63
6	Student D	98	98	98	99
7	Student E	86	88	84	83
8					
9			Semester 2		
10		Test 1	Test 2	Test 3	Test 4
11	Student A	88	92	93	96
12	Student B	90	83	85	85
13	Student C	62	62	62	62
14	Student D	65	65	68	66
15	Student E	91	92	93	95

And now you want to pull the test score for the same student for the third test for each semester.

First, let's pull the same data we pulled above, but with the INDEX formula set up to pull from either table, and specifying which table to use.

We can rewrite both formulas to include both table ranges and to pull from the first table like so:

=INDEX((A2:E7,A10:E15),3,4,1)

or

=INDEX((B3:E7,A10:E15),2,3,1)

Now we can modify both of those formulas to pull a value from the second table instead by changing the value of the last input in the function:

$$=INDEX((A2:E7,A10:E15),3,4,2)$$

or

$$=INDEX((B3:E7,A10:E15),2,3,2)$$

Of course, the way I would actually use this is not by manually going in and changing that final number each time. I would instead build a table that pulls in values from each semester. Like this:

	I	J	K	L
8		**Test 3 Results**		
9				
10			**Semester**	
11			**1**	**2**
12	**Student A**	1	94	93
13	**Student B**	2	84	85

The formula I used here in Cell K12 is:

$$=INDEX((\$A\$2:\$E\$7,\$A\$10:\$E\$15),(\$J12+1),4,K\$11)$$

That says that there are two tables of data to pull from, that the row to use is equal to the number in Column J plus 1, that the column to use is the fourth one, and that the table to pull from is the table number in Row 11. I can then just copy that formula down to the other four cells and it will populate my table for me by looking in each of the semester grade tables for each student.

That to me has some potential value in extracting information from multiple tables to create a summary table.

The other potential value of the INDEX function is in its ability to pull an entire row or column of data out of a table. That is done by treating it as an array formula.

Remember from looking at the TRANSPOSE function that there are a few key things you need to do to treat a function as an array formula. You have to select a range of cells not just one cell and then you have to use Ctrl + Shift + Enter after you've created the formula.

So let's go back to our two tables of data and let's extract all of the test scores for Student A using INDEX as an array formula, one row per semester

In Columns I, J, and K and Rows 17 and 18 I've created a simple table with my semester number and my student row number so that I can use cell references to do this.

Once I've done that I can highlight Cells L17 through O17 and then in L17 put the formula:

$$=INDEX((\$B\$3:\$E\$7,\$B\$11:\$E\$15),J17,0,K17)$$

I finish by using Ctrl + Shift + Enter.

I can then repeat that with Cells L18 through O18 to pull grades for the same student for the second semester. What I end up with is something that looks like this:

	I	J	K	L	M	N	O
16			Semester				
17	Student A	1	1	82	87	94	92
18		1	2	88	92	93	96

Let's look at the formula again:

=INDEX(($B$3:$E$7,$B$11:$E$15),J17,0,K17)

What this is saying is that there are two tables to choose from, one in Cells B3 through E7 and one in Cells B11 through E15 and that I want to pull the data from the row specified in Cell J17. (Since we're just looking at the data and no header row, it can continue to reference the first row and not need to adjust.)

It then says that there is no column to pull from and that I want to do this from the data table specified in Cell K17.

I can then use that formula in Cell L18, adjusting for the row number with J17 and K17 becoming J18 and K18, to pull in the scores from the second data table for that student.

(I will note here that you can't just copy and paste that second formula down like you would with a normal formula. It took a little fiddling to get it to copy down properly for me.)

In the same way that we extracted a row from a data table, you can also extract a column. Just make the row value 0 and provide a column value instead. Also, make sure that you highlight the number of cells needed in a specific column instead of in a row.

And, to circle back to our TRANSPOSE function, if you wanted to return the column values as a row, you could pair the INDEX function with the TRANSPOSE function. So you could highlight five cells within a row and then use:

=TRANSPOSE(INDEX(($B$3:$E$7,$B$11:$E$15),0,3,1))

to pull the third column of data from the table of data contained in Cells B3 through E7.

Keep in mind that these are still formulas, so if you change your source data you will change the values that you've pulled from the table. To lock any values into place use Paste Special – Values.

THE MATCH FUNCTION

Notation: MATCH(lookup_value,lookup_array,[match_type])
Excel Definition: Returns the relative position of an item in an array that matches
a specified value in a specified order.

What MATCH is going to do for you is look in a range of cells, either a row or a column that you specify, and it is going to return for you the position of a specific value that you're looking for within that range. You can also have it return the position of the closest value to what you're looking for rather than an exact match.

Note that this is a position that you're getting back. It will tell you that that value you wanted is in the seventh row of the specified range. Or the third column of the specified range.

In and of itself, that's not going to do much for you. But where this becomes incredibly powerful is when you combine the MATCH function with other functions, like the INDEX function, to specify a row number or a column number.

So thinking back to what we did with INDEX, I can go back to that same table I had for student grades and I can use MATCH to look up the row number for each student and then combine that with the INDEX function to pull those student's grades on a specific test.

Here's our data table and result:

	A	B	C	D	E
1			Semester 1		
2		Test 1	Test 2	Test 3	Test 4
3	Student A	82	87	94	92
4	Student B	88	81	84	83
5	Student C	65	68	64	63
6	Student D	98	98	98	99
7	Student E	86	88	84	83
8					
9	Test 3 Results, Semester 1				
10					
11		Semester			
12	Student A	94			
13	Student B	84			
14	Student C	64			
15	Student D	98			
16	Student E	84			

331

I created a separate table that has each student name in it and then I used the formula

$$=INDEX((\$A\$2:\$E\$7),MATCH(\$A12,\$A\$2:\$A\$7,0),4)$$

to pull the test result from the fourth column of my data range for each and every student without having to know which row each student was in.

Let's break this down.

We start with the INDEX function. We're applying it to the range from Cell A2 through Cell E7. For the row component, which is the second component, I've used a MATCH function. And then for the column component I have the value of 4 which will pull test results on Test 3.

The MATCH portion of our formula is:

$$MATCH(\$A12,\$A\$2:\$A\$7,0)$$

That's saying to look at the value in Cell A12 and to compare that to the values in Cells A2 through A7 and return the row number within that range where there's an exact match to the value in Cell A12.

Pretty cool, huh? It requires a little twisting of your mind to get it to work, but this could be incredibly powerful if you can do that.

A few things to know:

MATCH will look for a numeric value, a text value, or a logical value. It can also work with cell references as we saw above. If you are looking for text and specify an exact match, you can use the wildcards (? or *) to look for approximate or partial matches.

There are three match types you can specify. Using a 0 means an exact match. Using a negative 1 means MATCH will find the smallest value that is greater than or equal to the specified lookup_value. Using a positive 1, so just 1, means MATCH will find the largest value that is less than or equal to the lookup_value.

If you use -1 or 1, you need to sort your data or it won't work properly; it will return a value of #N/A!. For -1, sort your data in descending order. For 1, sort your data in ascending order.

Excel's default is to treat MATCH as if you've specified 1 as your match type, so be very very careful using MATCH since the default match type requires a specific sort order. (I will note here that with all of these lookup functions I far prefer to use them for exact matches, because it's less likely I'll mess something up that way, but there are very good reasons to use them without wanting an exact match. You just have to be more careful.)

Keep in mind, too, that MATCH is not returning a row or column number. It is returning the *relative* row or column number *within your specified range of cells*.

For text, MATCH does not distinguish between upper and lowercase letters.

If there is no match, MATCH will return a result of #N/A!

One of the reasons I included this function was because I saw an interesting use of the INDEX function when paired with the MATCH function recently that used MATCH and INDEX to pull in rank order of 34 different variables for a list of individuals. I'm not going to walk through it here because parsing it out would take about two pages of text, but just suffice it to say that you can get very complex results by using two simple functions like these together.

(If anyone is really curious about what that looked like, you can always email me and I'll send the formula to you. I can't send the worksheet, though, because it's not mine to send.)

THE LEN FUNCTION

Notation: LEN(text)
Excel Definition: Returns the number of characters in a text string.

Those last few were pretty intense, so let's cover a simple one now. The LEN function. The LEN function returns a numeric value representing the number of characters in a text string. (Note that for some languages like Japanese, Chinese, or Korean that you may instead need the LENB function which returns the number of bytes in a text string.)

The count includes spaces as well as actual characters.

You can use LEN with text directly in the function or with a cell reference.

So

$$=LEN("Alpha")$$

will return a value of 5 for the a-l-p-h-a in Alpha.

I could also type Alpha in Cell A1 and then use =LEN(A1) to get the same result.

If there is a formula in a cell that is referenced by LEN, it will count the number of characters in the result of the formula.

If a cell is empty or has a "" value, LEN will return a value of zero.

You might be asking yourself when you would use this function. One possibility is when you want to remove standardized text from a longer text string. You could then pair that with a function like LEFT, RIGHT, or MID to extract the remainder of your text.

For example, let's say I have the following entries:

12,500 units
5,122 units
312 units

And I want just the numbers without the space or "units" included.

Assuming that first value is in Cell A1, I could use

$$=LEFT(A1,LEN(A1)-LEN(" units"))$$

I could then copy that formula down the next two rows and my results would be:

12,500
5,122
312

This works because all of the entries have the same text at the end, " units". Because the number of units isn't the same between each one, this is probably the only way to trim that off using a function. (You could also use the Text to Columns option on the Data tab as an alternative way to split the number from the units, but it would then require deleting the column of data you don't want to keep so one additional step.)

THE SEARCH FUNCTION

Notation: SEARCH(find_text,within_text,[start_num])
Excel Definition: Returns the number of the character at which a specific character or text string is first found, reading left to right (not case-sensitive).

Another function you could use for tasks similar to the one we talked about above for LEN is SEARCH. SEARCH will tell you the number of the character in a text string at which the text you care about first appears, moving from left to right.

So let's look at that example we used for LEN again. You have three entries:

12,500 units
5,122 units
312 units

And you want to return the numeric values without the " units" portion attached. If you wanted to do that with SEARCH instead of LEN, you could use the following for an entry in Cell A1.

=LEFT(A1,SEARCH(" units",A1)-1)

The SEARCH portion of that is saying to look at Cell A1 and take the number of characters starting on the left that's equal to the place at which the space in " units" occurs. Then you apply the LEFT function to the text in Cell A1 using that value from SEARCH minus 1. (You need that minus one or you end up pulling in the space as well.)

You can also just use the SEARCH function with text entries instead of cell references. So you can have

=SEARCH("mate","teammate")

for example, which returns a value of 5.

If for some reason you didn't want to start at the beginning of your text string, you can use the optional third input to specify where you do want to start.

Let's say I want the location of the first m in the word mamajama that comes after "mama". I could use

$$=SEARCH("m","mamajama",5)$$

and I'll get a result of 7.

Note that that last number in the function, the 5 in this case, is the *start* number. So if I had used 3 as that last input, it would have returned a result of 3 since there is an m in the third position in the word "mamajama".

Also, note that in the above examples that even though we had the search start later in the text string that the number SEARCH returns is still counting from the beginning of the text string.

I could also use

$$=SEARCH("m","mamajama",LEN("mama")+1)$$

if I didn't know how many characters there were in "mama" but knew I wanted to start after it was ended.

Finally, you can use wildcards (* or ?) in the find_text portion of your search. So if you want to find where "cozy" or "cozies" started, you could do so with "coz*", for example, which would capture both options.

If the value you're searching for does not exist in the text string you will get a #VALUE! error. You will also get a #VALUE! error if the start position you give is negative or a larger number than the length of the text you're searching.

SEARCH is not case-sensitive. If you need to do a case-sensitive search you need to use FIND which we'll discuss next.

Also, for languages that use bytes instead of characters you need to use SEARCHB instead of SEARCH.

THE FIND FUNCTION

Notation: FIND(find_text,within_text,[start_num])
Excel Definition: Returns the starting position of one text string within another
text string. FIND is case-sensitive.

FIND is just like SEARCH except it's case-sensitive and doesn't allow the use of wildcards.

Just like SEARCH, FIND requires that you start with the text you want to find and then enter what text string you want to find that text in. It also allows you to set a starting place for your search that is not at the beginning of the text string.

Like SEARCH, FIND also has a counterpart, FINDB, that you can use with languages that look at bytes instead of characters. And like SEARCH, FIND will return a #VALUE! error if the text string is not in the search string or if you specify a start number outside the feasible range.

Let's look at a couple examples that we used for SEARCH:

$$=LEFT(A1,FIND(" units",A1)-1)$$

returns the exact same result as using SEARCH did.
So does

$$=FIND("m","mamajama",LEN("mama")+1)$$

Where the two are going to differ is in the ability of the SEARCH function to work with wildcards, so

$$=SEARCH("coz*","teacozy")$$

will return a value of 4, but

$$=FIND("coz*","teacozy")$$

will return a #VALUE! error instead.

They also differ in the ability of FIND to work with upper case versus lowercase letters. So

$$=SEARCH("m","Mamajama")$$

will return a value of 1 but

$$=FIND("m","Mamajama")$$

will return a value of 3, because with SEARCH "M" and "m" are treated the same but with FIND they are not.

Okay? Pretty straight-forward I think.

In and of themselves the SEARCH and FIND functions aren't terribly useful, in my opinion, but they can pair nicely with other functions to do things like trim text, for example.

THE EXACT FUNCTION

Notation: EXACT(text1,text2)
Excel Definition: Checks whether two text strings are exactly the same, and returns
TRUE or FALSE. EXACT is case-sensitive.

The EXACT function compares two text strings to see if they're exactly the same or not. This is a function I never really knew existed, but that I've needed before. In the cases where I needed to compare two text strings I was able to write an IF function to do the same thing, but this would've been easier to use.

So I'll walk you through where I've needed this.

As part of my publishing I run advertisements on my books. And there are reports that I can download to see how my ads are doing, but because Amazon is annoying they don't let me run reports for a specified period of time. So if I want to know how my ads did for the last 30 days I need to have a report that I downloaded at the beginning of the period and one that I downloaded at the end of the period. I can then drop those two sets of information into one worksheet and take the difference between them to see how much I've spent and earned on those ads for that period.

But as part of that process I need to be sure that I'm matching up the right entries with one another. When I launch a new ad during a specific month Amazon in all their wisdom will sometimes insert that new ad into the middle of my data instead of at the end. To check if this happened, I usually drop an IF function into my worksheet to make sure all my ads match up. Something like this:

=IF(B2=P2,"","ERROR")

That's saying, do the text values in Cell B2 and Cell P2 match? If so, good. If not, tell me there's an error.

But I could have used this EXACT function instead and written:

=EXACT(B2,P2)

If the two values match it returns a value of TRUE. If they don't it returns a value of FALSE. EXACT is case-sensitive, but will ignore any differences in formatting.

339

Now, there's one challenge here, which is what to do with the results. They're not easy to visually scan because every cell will have a value of TRUE or FALSE.

And let's say that you have 10,000 entries that you were testing. How can you quickly see if there were any FALSE values in that range?

You could filter the entries. Or you could sort them. You could even use a pivot table to count the number of TRUE and FALSE entries.

You could also use the MINA function to take the minimum value of the range. If all of your values are TRUE, MINA will return a value of 1. If any of them are FALSE, it will return a value of 0.

So if you had this EXACT formula in Column N, you could just use =MINA(N:N) to see if you have any results where the two values were not exactly equal. But that doesn't tell you how many there are that aren't equal. To calculate that you could also use 1 minus AVERAGEA for the range times the number of entries in the range.

So, for example, for a series of entries in Column N you'd have:

$$=(1-AVERAGEA(N:N))*COUNTA(N:N)$$

where COUNTA pulls the number of entries in the range, AVERAGEA pulls the ratio of the entries in that range that have a value of TRUE, and the 1 minus portion then calculates the ratio of the entries in the range that are FALSE. By multiplying count by ratio we get the actual number of entries that are FALSE.

THE CONVERT FUNCTION

Notation: CONVERT(number,from_unit,to_unit)
Excel Definition: Converts a number from one measurement system to another.

CONVERT is an incredibly useful function that will allow you to easily convert from one measurement to another. (Let me note here that if the conversion you need is just a one-off you can easily use an internet browser to do this. Just type in "20 degree celsius to fahrenheit" in the search bar and hit enter, for example, and the top result or one of the top results will be the answer. But if you have a range of values you need to convert, then this function is the way to do it)

In the help text for the function there is a very long list of options for what you can convert spread across the following categories: weight and mass, distance, time, pressure, force, energy, power, magnetism, temperature, volume (or liquid measure), area, information (bits to bytes), speed, prefix, or binary prefix.

The function itself is very easy to use. The hardest part of using it is knowing what abbreviation to use for your from_unit and to_unit options. You can find all of the available abbreviations in the Help text dialogue box for the function or you can just start entering your function and look at the options provided when you reach that input field.

For example, when you reach the from_unit option you'll see a dropdown menu of the available measurements and you can just scroll down and double-click on the one you need. Same with when you reach the to_unit portion of the function. If you do it this way, the to_unit portion will only display the available options that are in the same category as the from_unit option, saving you the potential of having an error due to type mismatch between your from units and to units.

Let's walk through a few straight-forward examples:

I have a number of friends who live overseas and are always talking about how hot it is there, because it's 40 degrees out. Now, being from Colorado you tell me that it's 40 degrees out I'm bundling up before I head outside. This is because my friends are talking about Celsius temperatures and I'm talking about Fahrenheit temperatures.

So to find what 40 degrees Celsius is in Fahrenheit temperature, you could use:

=CONVERT(40,"C","F")

(That's 104 degrees Fahrenheit and, yes, I'd agree that's pretty darned hot.)

It's as simple as that. The first part of the function is the value you need to convert, the next part is its current units, and the final part is the unit of measurement you need to convert to.

Note that the abbreviation for the measurement has to be in quotes and is case-sensitive.

What about if you know an event is occurring in 1,200 days but aren't sure how many years from now that will be?

You can just use:

$$=CONVERT(1200,"day","yr")$$

Result? 3.285

Those are just two very simple uses for CONVERT. I'll note here that it's listed as an Engineering function and you can see that it might be useful in a context like that if you scroll through the list of available conversion options.

Make sure your units to and from are in the same category or you'll get a #N/A error. Same with if you try to use a measurement abbreviation that doesn't exist. This includes if you input the value using the wrong case. So "day" is a valid unit value, but "Day" is not.

Let me add here, too, that even though it's not on the list of available options you can use "km" for kilometers and "mi" is the miles option you want if you're just trying to convert a good old standard mile to a different distance measurement. (The Help text refers to "mi" as a statute mile.)

Also, in the Help dialogue box they show how to handle squared units by doubling the CONVERT function. So to convert 100 square feet into square meters they say to use:

$$=CONVERT(CONVERT(100,"ft","m"),"ft","m")$$

By nesting the two CONVERT functions that way it appears to work to convert a squared unit to a squared unit.

(I tested it with squared inches to squared feet and it worked on that as well, I'm just using hedging language here because I haven't personally thought through *why* that works the way it does. I'm sure someone more mathematically inclined than I am could write up a little mathematical proof to show me why that works that way, but suffice it to say it does.)

THE ABS FUNCTION

Notation: ABS(number)
Excel Definition: Returns the absolute value of a number, a number without its sign.

Since we were talking math a moment ago, let's continue that with a few mathematical functions that could come in handy at some point in time.

The first of these is the ABS function, which essentially converts any number you have into a positive number. I could see this being useful if you are calculating, say, a ratio of two numbers and it doesn't matter whether one or both of those numbers is negative, you just want the ratio as a positive number.

So, for example, if I had -6 in Cell A1 and 2 in Cell A2 and wanted the ratio of those two numbers as a positive value, I could use:

$$=ABS(A1/A2)$$

And my result would be 3. If I had just divided those two numbers without using ABS the result would have been -3.

That's pretty much it.

(Interestingly enough, if you have numbers stored as text a function like SUM or PRODUCT will not work on them, but ABS still does. So does using the plus sign (+) to add the two numbers or the * sign to multiply them. Odd, but true.)

THE MOD FUNCTION

Notation: MOD(number,divisor)
Excel Definition: Returns the remainder after a number is divided by a divisor.

This next one is a little funky, but could come in handy in certain circumstances. (I suspect its counterpart will be more useful, but I'm covering this one first because there's another way to do the other one that I'll cover after this.)

Anyway.

Sometimes you divide a number and all you really want is the remainder not the integer portion. So it doesn't matter to you that Number A goes into Number B 522 times, you just care about what's left over after that happens.

Well, that's where the MOD function can come in handy. It will take those two numbers and return for you just the remainder.

So, for example, let's say I want to know what day of the week it will be 3,653 days from today and today is January 10, 2019.

I can first divide 3,653 by 7 and find the remainder to see how many days I have left over after however many weeks have passed from today using:

$$=MOD(3653,7)$$

What Excel returns for me is the number 6. So now I know that whatever day of the week it's going to be in 3,653 days it's going to be 6 days past today's day of the week.

I can then use the TEXT function (which we covered in *50 Useful Excel Functions*) to take today's date of January 10, 2019 and add six days to it and return a day of the week value using:

$$=TEXT(("1/10/19"+6),"dddd")$$

Excel returns a value of Wednesday, which is the day of the week for the date six days past January 10, 2019.

I could combine all of this into one calculation (assuming that the number 3,653 is stored in Cell L2) like this:

$$=\text{TEXT}((\text{"1/10/19"}+\text{MOD(L2,7)}),\text{"dddd"})$$

That's just one example of how you might use MOD. I'm sure if you need it you'll think of it.

The one quirk to the formula is that you don't do your division before you use it. It does the division for you. So your first input is the number that needs to be divided and your second input is what it needs to be divided by. As a result, you will not get the whole number of times A went into B, you will just get the remainder.

Also, you can't divide by zero. And if you're dealing with negative numbers, the sign of the result will always be the same as the sign of the divisor even if both of the numbers you provide are negative.

THE QUOTIENT FUNCTION

Notation: QUOTIENT(numerator,denominator)
Excel Definition: Returns the integer portion of a division.

Now to discuss the flip side of the MOD function, the QUOTIENT function. So where MOD provides the remainder, QUOTIENT provides the whole number portion of the result. Or in math-speak, the integer portion when you divide a numerator by a denominator.

(Don't we feel all smart and fancy now using math terms…)

So if I don't care what the remainder of a number is and just want the number of times X goes into Y, I'd use QUOTIENT.

Taking our example from above, let's say I have 3,653 days and want to know how many weeks that is but don't care if any days are left after that division. I could use:

=QUOTIENT(3653,7)

That returns a value of 521 instead of the 521.8571 I'd get if I divided 3653 by 7.

QUOTIENT does not have the same weird way of handling negative numbers as MOD does. If one of the numbers is negative, you'll get a negative result. If both are negative, you'll get a positive result.

Also, you still can't divide by zero and both inputs need to be numbers but it does seem to work with numbers stored as text.

THE TRUNC FUNCTION

Notation: TRUNC(number,[num_digits])
Excel Definition: Truncates a number to an integer by removing the decimal,
or fractional, part of the number.

The TRUNC function has an end result much like the QUOTIENT function—to just return the integer portion of a number—but it's a function that can work on any number. Meaning it's not limited to a situation where you're dividing two numbers.

Let's walk through this.

$$=TRUNC(3/2)$$

will return a result of 1 just like =QUOTIENT(3,2) will.
Both are returning the integer portion of 3 divided by 2.
But you can also use TRUNC with a cell reference. So if I have 2.34567 in Cell B1, I can write

$$=TRUNC(B1)$$

and it will return a value of 2.
I can also use TRUNC with any calculation within the function. For example:

$$=TRUNC(2.345^5)$$

returns a value of 70 which is the integer portion of the result when you take 2.345 to the fifth power. (We'll cover powers later in this guide, don't worry.)
The default for TRUNC is to round to the nearest integer, but there's an optional input for the function, num_digits, that will let you specify how precise you want your truncation to be. Remember, this is not rounding. This is just chopping the number off at the specified location.
Let's look at some examples.

	A	B	C	D
1	**Test Number**	**Num_Digit**	**Result**	**Comment**
2	**137,254.32451**	0	137254	No decimal places
3		1	137254.3	One decimal place
4		2	137254.32	Two decimal places
5		3	137254.324	Three decimal places
6		4	137254.3245	Four decimal places
7		-1	137250	Truncated without the 1s
8		-2	137200	Truncated without the 10s
9		-3	137000	Truncated without the 100s
10				
11	**132,798.79867**	0	132798	No decimal places
12		1	132798.7	One decimal place
13		2	132798.79	Two decimal places
14		3	132798.798	Three decimal places
15		4	132798.7986	Four decimal places
16		-1	132790	Truncated without the 1s
17		-2	132700	Truncated without the 10s
18		-3	132000	Truncated without the 100s

Here we have two numbers, 137254.32451 and 132798.79867 and I've applied the TRUNC function to each one using different values for the num_digits value.

See how you can cut the number off at any point you want by using varying num_digits values? I can keep the number up to two decimal places (using 2 for num_digit) or I can even have it return a value that's only showing numbers for the hundreds place (using -3 for num_digits).

Also note here that TRUNC does not round numbers. So

=TRUNC(132798.79867,-3)

returns a value of 132000, not a value of 133000 like you would get with

=ROUND(132798.79867,-3)

THE INT FUNCTION

Notation: INT(number)
Excel Definition: Rounds a number down to the nearest integer.

Just like TRUNC, the INT function also returns the nearest integer for a number you specify but it uses a different methodology. It's also not as flexible as TRUNC. It will only return the nearest integer. There is no num_digits option with this function.

The difference between the two is that TRUNC literally just chops off the last portion of a number whereas INT rounds down to the nearest integer. This means that when a number is positive the two functions will give the same result, but when the number is negative they will give different results.

ROUND is another function that returns a similar result to INT and TRUNC, but ROUND will round up or down depending on which number is closest, so sometimes it will return the same result as TRUNC for negative numbers and sometimes it will return the same result as INT. (For positive numbers ROUND will only return the same value as INT and TRUNC about half of the time.)

Let's look at some examples:

	A	B	C
1	**Test Number**	**Function**	**Result**
2	**70.3458**	INT	70
3		TRUNC	70
4		ROUND	70
5	**70.8974**	INT	70
6		TRUNC	70
7		ROUND	71
8	**-70.3458**	INT	-71
9		TRUNC	-70
10		ROUND	-70
11	**-70.8974**	INT	-71
12		TRUNC	-70
13		ROUND	-71

The formulas here for the value in A2 are:

$$=INT(A2)$$

$$=TRUNC(A2)$$

$$=ROUND(A2,0)$$

You can see that when a number is a positive number (the first and second examples), that both INT and TRUNC will return the same value. INT is rounding down and TRUNC is dropping anything after the decimal place, but for positive numbers the outcome is the same. ROUND, however, will round down if the value after the decimal is less than five and up if it's 5 or more. So you can see that for 70.3458 all three functions return the same value, but that for 70.8974 ROUND returns a value of 71 instead of 70.

When the number is a negative number things get even more interesting. INT is always going to round down, which means it will return the next integer away from zero. In our examples that's -71. But TRUNC continues to just chop off all of the numbers after the decimal, so it returns a value of -70 in both cases. ROUND is rounding towards the closest integer so for -70.3458 it returns a value of -70 and for -70.8974 it returns a value of -71.

Which function you use will depend on why you're doing what you're doing. If I was going to be performing ongoing calculations and precision mattered, I'd got with ROUND. But I can see using INT or TRUNC for displaying information. For example, due to the way that books are read in Kindle Unlimited, I sometimes have fractional reads of my titles and I don't want my reports to display 2.645 "sales" of a title. I could easily see using TRUNC or INT to just display 2 rather than rounding up to 3.

One more thing to add here. In the Help text they mention that if you want just the decimal portion of a number and you aren't doing division so can't use MOD that you can combine the INT function with subtraction to do that.

That's not actually true. At least not for negative numbers.

But you can do this with the TRUNC function and it will work for both positive and negative numbers. Simply take the number minus the TRUNC of the number to get the decimal portion. So for a value in Cell A2, you'd use:

$$=ABS(A2-TRUNC(A2))$$

Assuming that the value in Cell A2 is 3.4567 the result you'd get is .4567. Same with a value of -3.4567. I used the ABS function there because otherwise for a negative value in Cell A2 you'd have a negative value returned by the function.

THE POWER FUNCTION

Notation: POWER(number, power)
Excel Definition: Returns the result of a number raised to a power.

I promised we'd cover how to do powers, so let's do that one now.

First, you don't need a function to do powers, you can just use the little carat symbol (^) and input your power that way.

So

$$=3\text{^}2$$

returns the value of three squared which is 9.

And

$$=9\text{^}.5$$

returns the value for the square root of 9 which is 3.

You use whole numbers to take a number to a power and decimals to take the root of a number. You can also use negative powers to indicate that the number is part of the denominator. (So =3^-2 is the same as 1 divided by three squared or 1/9.)

But the POWER function is there for when you can't hand-write your formula. Say you're working with a table of 10,000 entries and need to perform a calculation that includes taking the values in Column A to a power that you specify. That's when you'd use this.

It's very simple. The first value is the number you want to take to a power, the second number is the power you want to use.

So three squared would be

$$=POWER(3,2)$$

And the square root of 9

$$=POWER(9,.5)$$

I've used squared and square root examples here, but you can use any number you want. So, two to the fourth power is

$$=POWER(2,4)$$

or 16.

The power can also be a negative number which, as mentioned above, will return a decimal value. So

$$=POWER(2,-4)$$

is the same as 1 divided by 2 to the fourth power or 1/16 or .0625.

If the power is 0 then the result is 1.

If you do

$$=POWER(0,0)$$

you will get a #NUM! error. Otherwise it should work with any numbers you give it.

THE SQRT FUNCTION

Notation: SQRT(number)
Excel Definition: Returns the square root of a number.

The SQRT function is a specialized version of the POWER function that only requires one input because it will always take the square root of the number provided.

So

$$=SQRT(9)$$

is equivalent to

$$=POWER(9,.5)$$

If you're writing a long complicated formula and aren't pulling the power to use from your data, it might make sense to use SQRT instead of POWER to simplify things. Otherwise, POWER is the more generic of the two functions and can be used in place of SQRT.

THE PI FUNCTION

Notation: PI()
Excel Definition: Returns the value of Pi, 3.14159265358979, accurate to 15 digits.

The PI function is another function that can make life simpler. If you need to do a calculation that involves the number pi, 3.14 etc. etc., using the PI function will return that value for you accurate up to the 15th digit.

So, for example, the area of a circle can be calculated using pi times the square of the radius. Let's assume radius is in Cell A1.

I could write

$$=PI()*(A1\char`\^2)$$

to make that calculation.

Note that when I use the function PI I need to include those opening and closing parens to let Excel know that's what I'm doing. You don't put anything in them, though.

If you just want the value of pi in a cell type

$$=PI()$$

in that cell and hit enter.

THE SQRTPI FUNCTION

Notation: SQRTPI(number)
Excel Definition: Returns the square root of (number * Pi).

I'm sure there's some specific mathematical use for this one, but it's not one I know off the top of my head. What SQRTPI does is returns the square root of the product of a number and pi.

So if you want the square root of pi you can get that with

$$=SQRTPI(1)$$

(You could also get it with =PI()^.5)
If you want to use a different number, let's say 3, then you'd write:

$$=SQRTPI(3)$$

That would give you the square root of the value of 3 times pi, or the square root of 9.424778. which is approximately 3.07.

Note that this is not the same value as the square root of 3 multiplied times pi. Nor is it the same value as the square root of pi multiplied times 3.

This function takes the value that you enter, multiplies that times pi, and then takes the square root of the resulting product.

(This is why I'm sure it's part of some common mathematical computation I just can't think of right now. Because why else would you have a function dedicated to something that specific?)

Anyway. If you need it, it's there. But know that you can also just recreate it with something like:

$$=SQRT(X*PI())$$

where X is the number that you want to use.

THE EXP FUNCTION

Notation: EXP(number)
Excel Definition: Returns e raised to the power of a given number.

Since we talked about how to have Excel tell you the value of pi, let's talk about another common mathematical value that you may need, *e*, which is often used in connection with natural logarithms. According to the Wikipedia entry I looked at today, e is an irrational and transcendental number. It has a value approximately equal to 2.718281828.

This value is then used in connection with natural logarithms which are defined as the power to which e would have to be raised to derive a value, x. But don't take my word for it. If you need to use natural logarithms talk to someone who actually uses them.

I'm just here to tell you how to use EXP to derive that value so you don't have to memorize it or input it each time.

If you want the value of *e* for use in an equation, simply use

=EXP(1)

and Excel will return for you a value of 2.718281828.

You can also, of course, use EXP to get any value of *e* raised to a power, but I wanted to point out that specific use because of the function we're going to look at next, LOG.

THE LOG FUNCTION

Notation: LOG(number,[base])
Excel Definition: Returns the logarithm of a number to the base you specify.

Many years ago when I was still in school we didn't have fancy computer programs that could solve problems for us so we had to learn all about logarithms and how to solve them by hand. I have, thankfully, pushed all those memories into a dark hole. But I still have flashes of base 2 calculations or natural logs. And a vague memory that it had something to do with my math and physics classes.

If you need it, hopefully you have a much better understanding of how and when to use logs than I obviously do, because let me assure you that the Wikipedia entry for logarithms is not friendly to novices or those of us who've forgotten what they learned in high school.

Enough of that digression, let's look at what the LOG function does for you.

The default is to assume that you're working with base 10. So if you don't provide a second value in the function and just write

$$=LOG(10)$$

it will assume that the base you meant it to use is base 10.

That means the answer you'll get is 1.

Because 10 to the what power gives you 10? 1

That's why

$$=LOG(1000)$$

is 3. Because 10 to the what power gives you 1000?

If you want to work with a different base than 10, say 2, you just put that into the function as your second argument.

So

$$=LOG(32,2)$$

is asking what power you have to take 2 to to get 32. (That's a mouthful of 2's isn't it?)

Answer, 5.

And if you ever need to use base e and aren't sure how to get the value of e (2.7183), you can always use =EXP(1).

So

$$=LOG(86,EXP(1))$$

will return for you the power to which you have to take e to get a value of 86, which is approximately 4.45.

THE LN FUNCTION

Notation: LN(number)
Excel Definition: Returns the natural logarithm of a number.

If you don't want to use my little workaround with LOG and base e, you can instead just use the LN function. The LN function is essentially the LOG function with a base of e.

So

$$=LOG(86,EXP(1))$$

and

$$=LN(86)$$

will give you the exact same result. If you're going to do a lot of work with natural logs then using LN is probably the better option.

THE LOG10 FUNCTION

Notation: LOG10(number)
Excel Definition: Returns the base-10 logarithm of a number.

LOG10 is the base-10 version of the LOG function, but in this case it's not worth learning in addition to LOG like LN is, because you get the exact same result from

$$=LOG10(100)$$

and

$$=LOG(100)$$

since the default of the LOG function is base 10.
I just mention it here for the sake of thoroughness.

THE FACT FUNCTION

Notation: FACT(number)
Excel Definition: Returns the factorial of a number, equal to1*2*3*…*Number.

Let's continue our exploration of how to use Excel to perform mathematical calculations I learned in school and then promptly forgot but that others might care about, this time with factorials.

Factorials are used when calculating permutations and combinations. Permutations are ordered combinations. So with permutations 123 is different from 321. Combinations view 123 and 321 the same.

Let me give you a scenario. You have three people in a room and you want to know how many ways you could put those three people into order. How many permutations of 123 can you come up with? There's 123, 132, 231, 213, 312, and 321. In total, you have six options.

It's easy enough to calculate manually when you have three people. But what happens when you have fifty people? How many ways can you order those 50 people that are unique?

Fortunately, there's a mathematical shortcut for how to do this called a factorial. Don't ask me how the math works (there's an excellent discussion of permutations and combinations at www.mathisfun.com if you're really interested), but suffice it to say that if you have a group of x values and you want to know how many unique permutations you can make from those x values that you use a factorial.

A factorial starts with x and then multiplies that by x-1 and then by x-2 and so on until it reaches 1. That value is the total number of unique permutations for those x values.

So in our three-person scenario we have 3 times 2 times 1 which is equal to 6 and can be written as 3! where the exclamation mark indicates this is a factorial.

For our fifty-person scenario it would be 50! or 50 times 49 times 48 all the way to 1.

Excel can do this calculation for you using the FACT function. So

=FACT(3)

will give you a value of 6 which is equal to 3 times 2 times 1.

And

$$=FACT(4)$$

will give you a value of 24 which is equal to 4 times 3 times 2 times 1.

If you try to use a number that is not a whole number with the FACT function Excel will truncate it to a whole number. So

$$=FACT(4.567)$$

returns the same value as

$$=FACT(4)$$

(Note that's a truncation not rounding. 4.567 became a 4 not a 5.)

Also, keep in mind that you can't have a factorial of a negative number and that the factorial of zero is returned as a value of 1 since that's standard practice when working with factorials.

If you want to use a factorial to calculate the number of permutations of a subset of that pool, you can combine two factorials to do so.

So, for example, if my true interest is in how many three-person permutations I can make out of a pool of fifty participants—let's say for assigning 1st, 2nd, and 3rd place prizes—I would take the factorial of 50 (the total number of permutations) and divide that by the factorial of 50 minus 3, or 47. (In mathematical notation that would be 50!/47!)

Doing that would leave me with 50*49*48 which is the total number of unique three-person permutations that I can create from a pool of fifty participants.

This is often written as n!/(n-r)! where n is the pool of things to choose and r is the number of them we want to choose each time. This assumes that there are no possible repetitions—once someone is chosen they can't be chosen again, they are out of the pool.

So you can have #50, #48, and #46 as one choice and #48, #46, and #50 as another but you can't have #50, #50, #50.

So that's using factorials with permutations and without repetition.

You can also use factorials to calculate the number of combinations possible. However, lucky for us, Excel has built-in functions that do all the work for you—COMBIN and COMBINA. Let's talk about those next.

THE COMBIN FUNCTION

Notation: COMBIN(number,number_chosen)
Excel Definition: Returns the number of combinations for a given number of items.

Combinations differ from permutations because with a combination the order doesn't matter. Let's look at our three-person scenario from above. We had the following permutations: 123, 132, 231, 213, 312, and 321, but really all six of those permutations are the same if order doesn't matter. They include 1, 2, and 3 so there's only the one *combination*.

If you were assigning medals, order would matter, you'd use permutations. Did person 1 get the gold, the silver, or the bronze? There are six different ways in which those medals could be assigned.

But if you're building three-person work groups then order doesn't matter and you need combinations. Whether I list Mary, John, or Doug first, I still have a group that consists of Mary, John, and Doug.

So while the permutation of three people is six, the combination of those three people is 1. In fact, if the pool you're choosing from and the group size you want to choose are equal, the combination will always be 1.

Let's say instead that we want to build two-person teams out of those three potential participants.

We have the following six possible permutations: 12, 13, 23, 21, 31, 32

But if order doesn't matter then 12 and 21 are the same, 13 and 31 are the same, and 23 and 32 are the same. So in terms of unique combinations, we only have 3.

To do this mathematically, we have to take the number of possible permutations and reduce that number to account for repetition. As we noted above, to calculate the number of permutations for a population of size n and a sample of size r, you can use $n!/(n-r)!$. To reduce that number so that 123 and 321 are treated the same you then multiply that value by $1/r!$.

Which gives you:

$$n!/r!(n-r)!$$

This is also sometimes referred to as n choose r. In our example here, 3 choose 2.

Note that this is how it works when you can only choose each participant once per combination. So this does not have 11 as an option or 22.

Let's see if it works.

Our n! part of the formula is =FACT(3) or 6. That's the total number of permutations for the population.

Our (n-r)! part of the formula is =FACT(3-2) or =FACT(1) which is 1.

Which means our total number of permutations for two-person teams out of a group of three is =FACT(3)/FACT(1) or 6.

We then multiply that by 1/r! or 1/FACT(2). Since 1/(2!) is .5 that gives a final result of 3, which matches what we determined above.

That's the total number of combinations in a pool of three possible choices where we want to choose two at a time and not have repetition.

Good news is you never have to go through that mess again. (Unless it's for a math test.) You can just use the COMBIN function.

You tell COMBIN your population size and then your sample size, like so:

=COMBIN(3,2)

And it returns your value of 3.

Now, remember, this was a scenario where you can't repeat which one you choose. But if you do want to allow for that sort of repetition then there's a function for that, too, COMBINA.

THE COMBINA FUNCTION

Notation: COMBINA(number,number_chosen)
Excel Definition: Returns the number of combinations with repetitions
for a given number of items.

COMBINA works much like COMBIN but in this scenario you throw everyone back into the pool each time you make a choice. So if you're pulling 2-person permutations from a pool of 3 you not only have 12, 13, 23, 21, 31, 32 you also have 11, 22, and 33 as options.

That gives nine possible permutations. (You calculate the number of permutations with replacement by taking the number of choices in the pool (3) and raising it to the power of the number of items you want to choose (2).)

But for unique combinations there are only six: 12 or 21, 13 or 31, 23 or 32, 11, 22, and 33.

The COMBINA function will calculate this value for you. Simply use

$$=COMBINA(3,2)$$

(You could also reach it using FACT, but that one's pretty complex so I'm not going to walk through it here.)

So. To sum it up.

COMBIN and COMBINA work in situations where the order of your values doesn't matter. In other words, where 12 is the same as 21.

COMBIN is the option to use when you can only choose each value once per grouping.

COMBINA is the option to use when you can choose a value more than once per grouping.

FACT can also be used for combinations but you don't need it for that because of the existence of the COMBIN and COMBINA functions.

What FACT can be used for is calculating permutations. You use permutations when the order of your values *does* matter. In other words where 12 is not the same as 21.

Having said all of this, let me give my disclaimer:

I am not a math teacher. I have not used factorials since high school. If this really matters to you find a better source of instruction than me. The actual use of the Excel functions is very straight-forward.

For COMBIN or COMBINA the first input is the size of the pool you're choosing from. The second input is the number of values you want to choose.

For FACT there is only one input, the number you need the factorial of. What that number will be depends on the calculation you're making and where you're using it.

All other discussion provided here has just been to provide context on why you should care about learning these functions, but do not trust me for your math instruction.

THE PV FUNCTION

Notation: PV(rate,nper,pmt,[fv],[type])
Excel Definition: Returns the present value of an investment: the total amount that a series of future payments is worth now.

Excel also has a large number of finance-related functions. One calculation that we performed frequently in my MBA program was present value. It's a key component to figuring out how much a company is worth. If this company is expected to earn $100,000 a year for the next five years, what is that worth in today's dollars? Hint: It's not $500,000.

Or another way to use the formula is to calculate what the present value of that loan you're about to take out is. If you're going to pay $2,000 a month at a rate of 8% a year, what is that loan worth today? Would you be better off paying cash if you can?

Luckily, there's an equation for this. And it's available to you through Excel using the PV function.

The function has five possible inputs. Let's walk through each one.

Rate, the first input, is the rate you're paying *for the period*. So if the rate is 8% per year, then that's .08 if all your inputs are annualized. Or it's .0066667 if your inputs are based on monthly payments.

If you were using this to look at valuing a company, then you'd want to use the expected interest rate for the period or the expected return you could get on an alternative investment. Basically, you're asking does it make more sense for me to invest this money at an annual rate of 8% or to invest in this company?

The next input, nper, is the number of periods in your calculation. If we're looking at a 30 year mortgage that you pay once a month, then that's 360 periods. If we're looking at five years of annual payments then that's 5 time periods.

Make sure that for all of your inputs the time periods line up. Don't use an annual rate and then list the number of months and the monthly payment amounts. Or don't list a monthly rate then list the number of years. All of it has to align.

Pmt is actually an optional input. You can choose not to list an amount for pmt and instead list an amount for fv. Pmt is the amount that will be paid for each of the periods just specified. If you do list it, the value you list has to be the same value for each period. This function cannot handle variable payment amounts.

So, in a loan example, you might have 2000 here representing your monthly mortgage payment. For a corporate valuation you might list 100000 here for an annual cash flow from the business of a hundred thousand dollars.

(According to the help text, you'd list any value you're paying out as a negative number and any value you're receiving as a positive number. But I'd recommend doing whatever makes you comfortable and being sure it works with whatever else you're going to do with that number. Just be sure that if you have values for both pmt and fv and that if one is incoming money and one is outgoing money that they have opposite signs.)

Fv is an optional input which represents a value you'll receive or pay out at the very end.

Type, the final input, can be either 0 or 1 and represents when payments are made. If you use 0 or omit this argument then the assumption is the payments are made at the end of each period. If you use 1 then the assumption is that payments are made at the beginning of each period.

So let's put this into practice.

Let's say your buddy owes you $1,000 and he gives you three options.

One, he'll pay you $750 right now.

Two, he'll pay you $100 a month for the next 8 months.

Three, if you can wait three years he'll pay you $1,000 at the end of that period but nothing until then.

(He's not a very good friend. Don't loan him money again.)

Let's assume he'll make good on whatever you choose and that you could invest any funds you have at a rate of 10%.

Which of those payment plans has the highest present value?

The first one has a present value of $750. Cash in hand is cash in hand.

The second one has a present value of $770.81. Not the $800 it sounds like, but more than the $750 you'd get if he paid you today.

We can calculate that using

$$=ABS(PV((0.1/12),8,100))$$

(I used ABS value there because otherwise it returns a negative number and for my purposes that's not what I wanted.)

The third one has a present value of $741.74. You get your $1,000 back but because you could have been investing your money at a rate of 10% per year for those three years it's not worth $1,000 to you today.

That we calculate using:

$$=ABS(PV((0.1/12),36,0,1000))$$

In this one there are not interim payments, just the final lump sum which we put in for the fv variable.

So, between the three options, the best one to choose is option 2, the eight monthly payments of a hundred dollars. But if you play with the assumptions about interest rate or alternative investment, that could change. If you had an opportunity to invest that money today at a rate of 20% then you'd want to choose option 1 because changing the rate from 10% to 20% makes $750 cash in hand worth more to you than $800 paid out over the next eight months.

Note that this is a pretty simple version of a present value calculation since it requires keeping the payment rate and the payment amounts constant for all periods, but it is effective for looking at loans or annuities where that may be the case.

THE NPV FUNCTION

Notation: NPV(rate,value1,[value2],…)
Excel Definition: Returns the net present value of an investment based on a discount rate and a series of future payments (negative values) and income (positive values).

Closely related to the PV function is the NPV function. The PV function takes a standard set of payments and a rate and gives you a present value. The NPV function lets you take a series of payments that can be of different amounts, both positive and negative, and tells you their present value given a specified rate. So NPV gives you more flexibility than PV, but it also requires more inputs because it works with a range of values not just one payment amount or one future lump sum payment.

You could use multiple PV calculations to get the same results as NPV, but using NPV will save you time.

One trick with NPV is that your incoming and outgoing funds have to occur on a regular basis. So, for example, annually. Or monthly. If you have one payment that occurs in January and another in April and another in October, then you're going to want to structure your rate and values to be monthly values with zeros for the months where no payment is made.

Also, any initial inflow or outflow of cash that's made on Day 0 has to be treated separately from the NPV calculation.

So, let's say I have the following scenario:

I am going to pay $15,000 to start a company today. I expect that I will lose $2,500 in my first year of operations and then make $3,500 in the second year, $5,000 in the third year, and $12,500 in the fourth year. Beyond that I'm expecting $0 in earnings.

If I could instead invest that $15,000 at a rate of 8%, should I make the investment?

You can use NPV to figure this out. Put your cash flows in Cells A1 through A4. So -2500, 3500, 5000, 12500. Added up they total to $18,500, more than my investment, but with that 8% that I could earn instead, it might not be enough to justify making the investment.

So I use

=NPV(0.08,A1:A4)

379

to calculate what those future cash flows are worth today and I get $13,842.91. I also paid $15,000 to start the business. So net, I'm out $1,157. I could've made more by just investing that money at a rate of 8% for those four years.

But what if that $12,500 came in the first time period? And I didn't lose the $2,500 until year four? So I have 12500, 3500, 5000, and -2500 in Cells A1 through A4? Then

$$=NPV(0.08,A1:A4)-15000$$

gives me $1,706 so I'd be more profitable if I started that company than just invested the funds.

You could recreate these results using the PV function, but you'd have to do it with separate calculations for every single payment. (You could also just use payment divided by interest rate raised to the power of the time period for each one and then add all those values to get the same result.) But it's much simpler to just use NPV.

THE FORECAST FUNCTION

Notation: FORECAST(x,known_y's,known_x's)
Excel Definition: Calculates, or predicts, a future value along a linear trend
by using existing values.

An interesting statistical function that Excel provides is the FORECAST function.

Now, one thing to note right up front is that this only works with linear trends. So the plotting example I used in *Intermediate Excel* about calculating time to hit the ground when an object is dropped from different heights would not work with FORECAST since that's not a linear relationship.

Which means you should definitely plot your data before you apply FORECAST to it to see if it's following a general linear trend.

Also, if you have Excel 2016 or later this function still exists but it has technically been replaced with FORECAST.LINEAR since Excel 2016 added the ability to forecast using exponential triple smoothing as well. (Which we are not covering here since I'm working in Excel 2013.)

The way FORECAST works is you give Excel a table of known x and y combinations and Excel then uses those data points to create the best linear fit through the points.

You then tell Excel your x value that you want to predict y for.

Your x value must be a number otherwise you will get a #VALUE! error.

You also must provide an equal number of x's and y's that have values. If they don't match up or one is empty you will get a #N/A! error message.

If there is no variance in your x values you will get a #DIV/0! error message.

If you want to know the formula Excel uses to do this calculation, it's in the help documentation for the function.

Now let's walk through an example. Here's a data table where I've put monthly units sold. Column A is the actual month the sales occurred in, but I can't use that column for the function because the x values need to be a number. So in Column B we have a number that corresponds to each month. Column C has units sold.

	A	B	C
1	**Month**	**Month #**	**Units**
2	Jan-18	1	125
3	Feb-18	2	150
4	Mar-18	3	175
5	Apr-18	4	200
6	May-18	5	225
7	Jun-18	6	250
8	Jul-18	7	275
9	Aug-18	8	300
10			
11	**FORECAST EXAMPLES**		
12	Jan-19	13	425
13	Nov-17	-1	75

You can see the two FORECAST examples below the table.

The first is forecasting into the future. Given the data in the table, what do we predict units sold will be in January, month 13? The answer, 425.

The formula I used here was

=FORECAST(B12,C2:C9,B2:B9)

where B12 is the number 13, for the thirteenth month given our data table values, C2 through C9 contains our y values, and B2 through B9 contains our x values.

Now, one thing to point out here, because it tripped me up the first time I used the function, is that you list all of your y values before you list all of your x values. This was backwards to me since every point coordinate I ever remember seeing was written x, y.

If you look at the data you'll see that I have it structured so that every single month the number of units goes up by precisely 25 units. So if I want to know the number of units in January 2019 given this data I know that it should be 25 times the number of months between August 2018 and January 2019 plus the number of units for August 2018. So 300+(5*25) or 425.

And that's exactly what we get using FORECAST.

The second example I have there is for predicting a value in the past. In this case, November 2017.

This one also required me to make an adjustment I hadn't expected because Excel thinks it's dealing with numbers but I had converted from months to numbers. Meaning Excel was using the value of 0 as a legitimate point and I wasn't thinking that way.

Originally, because November 2017 is two months before January 2018 I used -2 for my x value. But that gave me a wrong answer. I wasn't thinking that December 2017 would have a value of 0 to Excel instead of a value of -1. Once I realized that, I was able to change the value for November 2017 to -1 and it worked just fine.

The function for November 2017 in this example is:

$$=FORECAST(B13,C2:C9,B2:B9)$$

If I'd been using two ranges of numeric values for my x's and y's this wouldn't have been an issue. But it does serve as a good reminder to always, always check your results.

Also, keep in mind that even though my example was custom-built to use exact changes of 25 every period, that FORECAST will work even when the change between periods is not exact. For example, look at the below data and chart of that data:

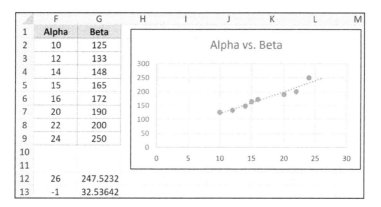

I've added a forecast trendline to the graph to show what Excel is doing mathematically with that data. You'll see that for that last data point, an alpha of 24 and a beta of 250, that the overall trendline actually comes in below the data point.

That means that when we ask Excel to predict a beta given an alpha value of 26 that it predicts a value for beta that is less than the value we have when alpha is 24. With the FORECAST function, Excel is basically moving along that trendline to find each value.

Lastly, I wanted to show you a non-linear scenario like in the example below.

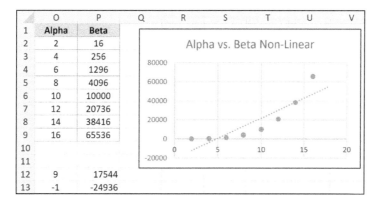

See how the linear trendline misses the actual beta values except for when the alpha is about 6 and 14? If I use FORECAST anywhere except those two points, like I did for 9, the prediction Excel returns will be inaccurate. It's trying to apply a linear relationship to something that is not linear.

This is why you should always, always plot your data first. (I used scatter plots in the two charts above.)

One final note. Even though in the examples above I had the data points sorted by x-value, you don't need to do that. Your data can be out of order and Excel will still be able to work with it effectively.

THE FREQUENCY FUNCTION

Notation: FREQUENCY(data_array,bins_array)
Excel Definition: Calculates how often values occur within a range of values
and then returns a vertical array of numbers having one more element than Bins_array.

In *50 Useful Excel Functions* I covered the functions for calculating average, median, and mode. And as part of doing so I pointed out that one of the drawbacks of even MODE.MULT is that it only cares about the most frequently occurring value or values. So if you have a value that appears 29 times and one that appears 28 times, MODE.MULT will only return the value that appears 29 times.

One way to get around this is by building a frequency table.

Or you can use the FREQUENCY function to pull your x-most-frequent values.

So let's look at that. Here's a data table of values.

	A
1	1
2	3
3	3
4	3
5	3
6	30
7	30
8	30
9	500
10	500

We have the values 1, 3, 30, and 500 with 3 being the most frequent of the values, but 30 coming in close behind that.

If I were to use MODE.MULT on this data range I would get the result of 3 back, but nothing else.

So we want a function that will give us more depth than that. We can use FREQUENCY, but it has its own quirks because it only works if you provide "bins" for it to use. If you don't provide these bins, you'll just get a count of all of your values.

What are bins? Bins are essentially value ranges. In this case I want each of my values in that table to be treated as a separate bin, so I'm going to use Remove Duplicates under the Data tab to copy the entire table and then generate a list of unique values from that table. That will give me my bins.

I can then use the FREQUENCY function to get the frequency of each value in that table.

FREQUENCY is an array function so you have to highlight all of the cells where you want your results to be displayed before you type the function.

In this example, we can highlight Cells D2 through D5 and then type

$$=FREQUENCY(A1:A10,C2:C5)$$

where A1 through A10 is the data and C2 through C5 contain the values for creating the bins. To finish, use Shift+Ctrl+Enter instead of simply using Enter.

This is what we get:

	C	D
1	**Bins**	**Count**
2	1	1
3	3	4
4	30	3
5	500	2

I have four 3's, 3 30's, 2 500's, and 1 1 in that data table.

Let's say we didn't use the values to create our bins. Instead I chose to arbitrarily assign ranges at 25, 50, 500, and 1000. Those values are in Cells G2 through G5. I then highlighted five cells and used the following function:

$$=FREQUENCY(A1:A10,G2:G5)$$

This is what we get:

	G	H
1	**Bins**	**Count**
2	25	5
3	50	3
4	500	2
5	1000	0
6		0

What's happening here is that Excel is giving a count of all values up to 25, so in this case the five 1s and 3s. Then it's giving a count of all values between 25 and 50, so in this case the three 30s. And then it's giving a count of all values between 50 and 500, in this case the two 500s. After that is a count of all values from 500 to 1000, or 0, and then finally a count of all values over 1000, again 0.

So you can use FREQUENCY for precise counts of each value, like we did in the first example, or for counts across a range of values, like in the second example. You just have to structure your bins correctly.

And remember to highlight enough cells when inputting the function to cover the less than and more than portions of the range. So I had four bin inputs but needed to highlight five cells when I built the second function.

Also, FREQUENCY will ignore blank cells and text, so if you want the FREQUENCY of text values, you can't use it. It only works with numbers.

And remember, this is an array function, so always highlight all of your cells where you want your answers before you input your function and use Shift+Ctrl+Enter when you're done or you won't get the right results.

HOW EXCEL HANDLES DATES

Before we dig into the various date-related functions that Excel has there are a few things it helps to know about dates and how Excel handles them.

By default Excel actually encodes each date as a number starting with the number 1 for the date January 1, 1900 and then moving forward one number at a time for each subsequent date. You can test this by typing the number 1 into a cell and then formatting that cell as a date. As soon as you format that cell as a date you will see January 1, 1900 in that cell. (Unless you're on a Mac, in which case continue reading.)

This is important for a few reasons.

First, it means that Excel does not do well with dates prior to 1900. I learned this the hard way on a work project that had dates back to the 1700s when I found that Excel had converted those 1700s and 1800s dates to 1900s dates after they were imported from a SQL database into Excel. So it's something to keep an eye on if you're working with older dates.

Dealing with future dates is not as much of a problem because Excel can work as far into the future as the year 9999.

Second, because Excel encodes dates as numbers this means that simple addition and subtraction works on dates in Excel. If you want a date fifteen days in the future, you just add 15 to the current date. So say that date is stored in Cell A1, then you'd write =A1+15 and Excel would return a date for you that is 15 days past the date in Cell A1. If you wanted a date that was 14 days prior to that date then you would write =A1-14.

As long as the dates remain in the range of January 1, 1900 to December 31, 9999 you're fine.

There are also functions that specifically exist to do this type of math. For example, the DAYS function which we'll cover in more detail momentarily returns the difference in the number of days between two dates.

Third, the fact that dates are encoded as numbers means that any date functions that mention a serial_number as the input are actually telling you to input the date that you want to use.

Now, to put a wrinkle in this, if you're using a Mac instead of a PC, what I said above about the date range covered by Excel is not accurate. For Macs Excel actually starts with the date January 2, 1904 and moves forward from there. This means that the two systems represent the same date as different numbers. There will be a difference of 1,462 days between how any date is represented by Excel for Windows versus Excel for Mac.

If you're moving files back and forth between the two platforms, Excel is set up to account for this. There's a checkbox for using the 1904 date system and when you open a file created using Excel for Mac that box will be checked already in Excel for Windows so that the dates aren't impacted. If you don't want that, you can uncheck the box under File->Options->Advanced->When Calculating this Workbook.

Another option if you're moving back and forth between the two platforms with the same dataset is to perhaps store your dates as text and then convert them once they're on the new platform. (This may also be a good time to point out that Excel is not necessarily the ideal option for handling large amounts of complex data. It's great for basic usage and calculations but when you really get into data it's probably time to use something else. For example, I've worked with R, Stata, and SQL databases when dealing with large amounts of data.)

This difference between the two systems means that if you try copying data from a file that was created in Excel for Windows to a file that was created in Excel for Mac or vice versa it's quite possible your dates will be off. Same with referencing a Cell in an Excel file that was created on the other platform.

(You can use the Paste Special-Values-Operation option in Excel to paste dates from one to the other. This will allow you to add or subtract 1462 to each date value as you copy and paste it to the other type of file. You can also update your formulas to add or subtract the required number of days if needed. Ridiculous, I know. This is why standardized approaches to data handling are a good idea, but that's what you get when you have competing platforms.)

Bottom line: Be aware of this and check to see if it's an issue when you're working with dates.

Also…

Best practice when dealing with dates in Excel is to enter the four-digit year. So if I want January 1, 2019 it is best to enter that date as 1/1/2019 so that Excel knows exactly what date I want. If you leave off the first two numbers of the year, so use 1/1/19 instead, Excel will convert that to a four-digit year using the following logic:

Numbers 00 through 29 are interpreted as the years 2000 through 2029. Numbers 30 through 99 are interpreted as the years 1930 through 1999.

(I'm not sure what they're going to do about that when we get to 2025 or so and people start expecting to enter 30 and see 2030, but I guess we'll cross that bridge when we come to it. There is a way to change your Microsoft Windows settings so that Excel (and all other Windows programs) uses a different conversion range than that, but the danger is in using files that were created on another computer that was still default range, so I'm not going to cover how to do that here.)

I'd say for now it's something to be aware of, and that you should make sure you enter your dates as four-digit years as much as humanly possible. (Keeping in mind, of course, that dates prior to 1900 won't work as dates in Excel.)

Good times.

Now that we have a basic understanding of how dates are handled by Excel, let's look at some date-related functions.

THE DATE FUNCTION

Notation: DATE(year,month,day)
Excel Definition: Returns the number that represents the date in
Microsoft Excel date-time code.

We're going to start our exploration of the date and time functions in Excel with the DATE function. This is one I don't regularly use but we need to discuss it first because in the help text for most of the date and time functions Excel has a caution that dates used in each function should be created using the DATE function or as results of other formulas or functions. The implication is that if you don't do this your results may not be fully accurate.

In general, I don't think you'll have an issue using a date you've typed in. For example, 1/1/11, 1-1-11, 1/1/2011, 1-1-2011, and January 1, 2011 all work as long as you keep in mind what we discussed above about how Excel handle dates.

But if it's vitally important that your date calculations be accurate then maybe use the DATE function.

So how does it work?

For the most basic usage, you input a value for year, month, and day and Excel turns it into a numeric value representing a date. For example:

=DATE(1900,1,1)

will return a value that displays as 1/1/1900 and is automatically formatted as a date. (At least in Excel 2013. If you get a number back instead, then change the cell formatting to Date.)

There are, however some definite quirks with this function. The worst one is that if you input a year value between 0 and 1899, Excel will add that value to 1900 to calculate your year.

It's the most ridiculous thing I've ever seen, but that's how it works. (An error message would've been better in my opinion.)

So

=DATE(1880,1,1)

which you would hope returns a date of January 1, 1880 will actually return a date of 1/1/3780.

A reminder that if you're going to work with dates in Excel you must drill into your head that they only work between the years of 1900 and 9999. Also, a good reason to always have your dates display with a four-digit year so you can see when this happens, because 1/1/80 looks like it could be 1/1/1880 even though it's actually 1/1/3780.

With the DATE function if you put in a year that's less than 0 or past 9999 you do get an error message, the #NUM! error.

DATE can do more than just create a date from your inputs. It can also take an existing date and by adding values to year, month, and day create a new date. For this reason, you can enter any value you want for month and for day.

If the value for month is greater than 12, Excel will add that number of months to the first month in the year specified. So

$$=DATE(1900,14,1)$$

returns a date of 2/1/1901, which is two months into the next year. And

$$=DATE(1900,38,1)$$

returns a date of 2/1/1903, which is two months into the year three years from 1900.

If you enter a negative value for month, Excel will subtract "the magnitude of that number of months, plus 1, from the first month in the year specified."

I find that wording horrible. (I promise, I won't be so critical of all of the functions we're going to discuss in this book, but the date functions can be some of the trickiest to deal with in my experience.)

What you have to keep in mind is that when you go backwards, Excel includes the value of zero as a legitimate value. So if I use

$$=DATE(1905,-2,1)$$

Excel returns a result of 10/1/1904 which is three months prior to January. To get a date of 12/1/1904, I have to use

$$=DATE(1905,0,1)$$

So technically that's not adding 1 to the number of months, it's subtracting 1.
Let's look at

$$=DATE(1905,0,1)$$

which gives us December. 0 plus 1 would be 1. That would give us February. What it's actually doing is subtracting an additional 1. So 0 minus 1 gives us -1 months, or December.

The same thing happens with days of the month. If you're going negative you have to adjust by 1 because of the fact that Excel will take a value of 0 as the value for one day prior and then work from there.

I'd be very careful using DATE to go backward for this very reason. It's far too easy to mess up if you're not paying attention, so check, double-check, triple-check your results.

And once again I will urge you to keep it simple and just use DATE, if you choose to use it, to create a date directly by inputting a year between 1900 and 9999, a month between 1 and 12, and a day of the month between 1 and 31.

Now let's walk through the more complex usage for DATE and the reason all the craziness exists.

The DATE function can be used in conjunction with other functions or basic math to create new dates.

So, for example, you can create a date five years from now by taking a date that's in Cell A1 and combining that with the DATE function as well as the YEAR, MONTH, and DAY functions to extract the values for year, month, and date, respectively. This is more precise than adding 365 times 5 days to that date because it won't be impacted by something like leap year.

What does that look like?

Assuming your date is stored in Cell A1 and you want a date five years from that date, you would write:

$$=DATE(YEAR(A1)+5,MONTH(A1),DAY(A1))$$

That's saying, take the year from the date in Cell A1 and add 5 to it. Then take the month from the date in Cell A1 and the day from the date in Cell A1, and build a date with those values.

If Cell A1 was 1/1/2015 you would now have a date of 1/1/2020 which gives us a date exactly five years from January 1, 2015.

If we had instead used five times 365 days and added that to the date in Cell A1, so =A1+1825, we would end up with a date in 2019, specifically December 31, 2019, because of the existence of a leap year in that date range.

So use DATE if you want to create a new date x number of years or months in the future. Use math if you want to create a date x number of days in the future.

Also, just to note that if I had wanted to use the date in the formula for =A1+1825, I would need to use quotation marks to do so, like this:

$$="1/1/2015"+(365*5)$$

Alright, now let's actually walk through the YEAR, MONTH, and DAY functions.

THE YEAR FUNCTION

Notation: YEAR(serial_number)
Excel Definition: Returns the year of a date, an integer in the range 1900-9999.

The YEAR function extracts the four-digit year from a date.

If this matters for you, the dates are treated as Gregorian dates. Even if they're displayed as some other date type, the year that YEAR will return is the Gregorian-equivalent year for that date.

It's very simple to use. You have a date in a cell and then you use YEAR to reference that cell. So

=YEAR(A1)

will return the year of the date in Cell A1.

If you reference a date stored as text or written in a text format and formatted as text, Excel will still be able to extract the year for you. Assuming, of course, that the date is a valid date to Excel, so has a year value between 1900 and 9999.

If Excel doesn't recognize the date as a valid date, then it will return a #VALUE! error.

You can also enter the date directly into the function, like so:

=YEAR("january 1, 2010")

=YEAR("1/1/2010")

=YEAR("1-1-2010")

Each of the above will return a value of 2010.

Just be sure to use the quotation marks or you'll get a #NUM! error message.

THE MONTH FUNCTION

Notation: MONTH(serial_number)
Excel Definition: Returns the month, a number from 1 (January) to 12 (December).

The MONTH function works much like the YEAR function except it extracts the number of the month from a date instead of the four-digit year. It will also work with a date written as text.
So,

=MONTH("December 21, 2010")

returns a value of 12.
As does

=MONTH("12/12/2010")

You can also, of course, use MONTH with a cell reference, so

=MONTH(A2)

will return the numeric value of the month for the date in Cell A2.
As with the YEAR function, Excel returns a value related to the Gregorian value for the date regardless of the display format for the date.

THE DAY FUNCTION

Notation: DAY(serial_number)
Excel Definition: Returns the day of the month, a number from 1 to 31.

The DAY function works like the MONTH and YEAR functions, except it returns the number of the day of the month for a given date.
So

$$=DAY("June\ 2,\ 2010")$$

will return a value of 2.
And

$$=DAY(A1)$$

will return the day portion of the date in Cell A1.

If the cell you reference has text that can't be recognized as a date you'll see the #VALUE! error message instead.

THE HOUR FUNCTION

Notation: HOUR(serial_number)
Excel Definition: Returns the hour as a number from 0 (12:00 A.M.) to 23 (11:00 P.M.).

Next we have the HOUR function which will return the hour number for any given date/time entry. Now, one thing to keep in mind is that if you enter a date without entering a time to go with it the date is going to default to a time of midnight, or 12:00 AM. If that happens using HOUR will return a value of zero.

Same with the MINUTE and SECOND functions which we'll discuss next.

But if you have entries that include a time of day, HOUR can extract the hour component from that time.

The easiest way to demonstrate this is to combine HOUR with the NOW function. (The NOW function was one we covered in *50 Useful Excel Functions* that returns the time right this minute, down to the second.)

So if it's 1:15 PM and I use

=HOUR(NOW())

I will get a value of 13.

That's because the hour value that Excel returns is written in military format. Military format assigns a value of 0 to midnight, a value of 1 to 11 for the hours in the morning up until noon, a value of 12 to noon, and a value of 12 + the hour for any time after noon and up to midnight. So 3 in the morning is 3, but 3 in the afternoon is 15. There is no AM or PM used to distinguish morning times from afternoon times.

Now, you already know that Excel assigns a number to each date starting with January 1, 1900. But what we hadn't covered yet is what Excel does with the hours between each day. It turns out that Excel converts those values to decimals. So if there are 24 hours in a day, then each hour is equivalent to .04166667.

The HOUR function can work with that. So

$$=HOUR(.083333)$$

will return a value of 2 since that's the decimal equivalent of two in the morning. HOUR will also work with a time rendered as text.

$$=HOUR("7:30")$$

will return a value of 7.

$$=HOUR("7:30\ PM")$$

will return a value of 19.

THE MINUTE FUNCTION

Notation: MINUTE(serial_number)
Excel Definition: Returns the minute, a number from 0 to 59.

The MINUTE function works like the HOUR function except it returns the minutes for the time instead of the hour.
So

=MINUTE("7:30")

will return a value of 30.
As will

=MINUTE("7:30 PM")

This one also works with decimals in the same way that HOUR did. So if each hour is represented by the decimal value of .0416667 then each minute is represented by the decimal value .000694.

That means that if we use the MINUTE function with 15*.000694, which is .010417, we should get a value of 15. And we do.

=MINUTE(.010417)

does in fact return a value of 15
As does

=MINUTE(.510417)

Do you understand why?
Because .5 is equal to half of a day and we're only extracting minutes from that number. So .510417 is equal to half a day plus fifteen minutes.

Sorry if that threw you. It was just my weird way of trying to make this one more interesting than it is…

MINUTE also works with cell references. So

=MINUTE(A1)

will return the number of minutes in the date/time in Cell A1. Which, as mentioned with the HOUR function, will be zero unless you intentionally added a time component to your date.

THE SECOND FUNCTION

Notation: SECOND(serial_number)
Excel Definition: Returns the second, a number from 0 to 59.

To round out this conversation we have the SECOND function that works just like the HOUR and MINUTE functions except it returns the second component of a date/time entry.

For example, I just used

=SECOND(NOW())

and Excel returned a value of 41 for me because at the time I hit enter we were 41 seconds into that minute. When I just hit F9 to refresh that calculation it returned a value of 15 because we were 15 seconds into the next minute.

You can write a time with seconds as 4:45:30. That last portion represents your seconds component. If you do that, you can then use the SECOND function to extract that.

So

=SECOND("4:45:30")

will return for you a value of 30.

As with hours and minutes, seconds can also be represented as a decimal. Each second is worth 0.000011574 so

=SECOND(0.000011574)

will return a value of 1 and

=SECOND(0.000683)

will return a value of 59.

Also, remember that a date entered as "1/2/2010" or "January 2, 2010" that isn't specifically entered with a time component will have a time assigned to it of midnight and using the SECOND function on a date like that will return a value of zero.

Basically, as with HOUR and MINUTE, the SECOND function will only return a value other than 0 when your date has been specifically set up to include a time component.

THE WEEKDAY FUNCTION

Notation: WEEKDAY(serial_number,[return_type])
Excel Definition: Returns a number from 1 to 7 identifying the day of the week of a date.

The WEEKDAY function is another one that's similar to what we just discussed. But this function identifies the day of the week for a specific date. So does it fall on a Monday? A Wednesday? A Sunday? The WEEKDAY function lets you figure that out.

By default the WEEKDAY function returns a number for the day of the week, so a number between 1 and 7, where 1 is equal to Sunday and 7 is equal to Saturday and each day in between is assigned a number value within that range.

So

$$=WEEKDAY(A1)$$

where A1 has January 1, 2019 in it and that date is a Tuesday, will return a value of 3.
You could also write that as

$$=WEEKDAY("1/1/2019")$$

or

$$=WEEKDAY("January 1, 2019")$$

If you don't like having Sunday be your first day, you can use the return_type input variable to define a different start point for numbering the days of the week.

Using a return_type value of 2 will assign a value of 1 to Monday instead of Sunday and will then number each day of the week from there ending with a value of 7 for Sunday.

So

$$=WEEKDAY("1/1/2019",2)$$

will return a value of 2 instead of the default value of 3.

Using a value of 3 for return_type assigns a value of 0 to Monday on through to a value of 6 for Sunday. So

$$=WEEKDAY("January 1, 2019",3)$$

would return a result of 1 since Monday is 0 which makes Tuesday 1.

Using a return_type value of 12 assigns a value of 1 to Tuesday on through to a value of 7 for Sunday.

And so on. If you look in the help text in the function you'll see that there's an option for every single day of the week to be your starting point using values from 11 through 17 for return_type.

You may be asking yourself, when would I use this function? (Like I did a minute ago.)

One option is to check what day of the week it is and then have different reactions based on that result.

So let's say you run an amusement park and you want to have one set of prices, $24.95, for weekday attendees and another price, $29.95, for weekend attendees.

You could write

$$=IF(WEEKDAY(A1,11)<6,24.95,29.95)$$

That's saying that using a numbering system where Monday is 1 and Sunday is 7 that if the number of the week is 1 through 5 (or Monday through Friday) then assign a cost of $24.95. If it's not, assign a cost of $29.95.

Done. Works.

That's just one way to use it. I'm sure there are more.

THE WEEKNUM FUNCTION

Notation: WEEKNUM(serial_number,[return_type])
Excel Definition: Returns the week number in the year.

The WEEKNUM function is much like the WEEKDAY function except it returns what week of the year a date falls in.

So

=WEEKNUM("January 1, 2019")

will return a value of 1 because that day is in the first week of the year, no matter how you slice or dice it. But, interestingly,

=WEEKNUM("December 31,2019")

returns a value of 53 even though there are only 52 weeks in a year.

This is driven by how Excel defines a week.

The default is for Excel to define a week as starting on a Sunday and only including dates for that year. So in 2019 the first week of that year is considered to be January 1st, a Tuesday, through to January 5th, a Saturday. Week 2 of 2019, if you're using the default return type, starts on January 6th, a Sunday. That means that the final days of the year, December 29th through December 31st, fall in the 53rd week of the year.

Under the default, dates in December will always be assigned to their year even if that means that the WEEKNUM result you get back is 53. However, you can use the return_type input option to change how Excel defines a week.

The values of 11 through 17 can be used to start a week on any day from Monday (11) through Sunday (17) but they still keep dates within their year meaning you can still have a week number 53.

There is, however, an option, return_type 21, which follows the ISO 8601 standard for week numbering which is used in Europe. The ISO approach keeps weeks together even if they cross years. It will start the first week of the new year on a Thursday, even if that Thursday falls into the prior year.

So

$$=WEEKNUM("12/31/2018",21)$$

will return a value of 1, since under the ISO methodology the first week of the year is from December 31, 2018 through January 2, 2019.

Using the return_value of 21 you will never have a week 53 in your results. But you will have end-of-December dates that are assigned to the first week of the next year.

So choose wisely if you use this one..

THE ISOWEEKNUM FUNCTION

Notation: ISOWEEKNUM(date)
Excel Definition: Returns number of the ISO week number of the year for a given date.

Of course, if you don't want to be bothered to include a return_value of 21 for the WEEKNUM function in order to use the ISO standard, you can just use the ISOWEEKNUM function instead. It gives you the exact same result.

So

=WEEKNUM(A1,21)

is the same as

=ISOWEEKNUM(A1)

This function was introduced with Excel 2013, so if you're using an earlier version of Excel it's not available. That also means that if you're designing a workbook for use by a group of users and you don't know that they have Excel 2013 or later, then you should not use this function.

THE DAYS FUNCTION

Notation: DAYS(end_date, start_date)
Excel Definition: Returns the number of days between two dates.

The DAYS function allows you to calculate how many days there are between two separate dates. So, for example, let's say it's June 1st and I want to know how many days it is until Christmas.

I can simply write

$$=DAYS("12/25/18","6/1/18")$$

and get my result. (Sorry for you non-U.S. users that think those dates look funny.)

Note here that when I include the dates within the formula itself that I have to use quotation marks around each date.

Another way to do this is to enter each date into its own Cell and then use cell references with the DAYS function.

For example, if I put December 25th into Cell A1 and June 1st into Cell A2, then I could use the formula

$$=DAYS(A1,A2)$$

and I'd get the same result.

Note that with DAYS you're using an end date and a start date. Your end date *can* be the earlier of the two dates if you want. If it is then the result you'll get will be a negative number. So I can have

$$=DAYS("6/1/18","12/25/18")$$

and my result will be -207.

This is one where you can get the same result without using a function. The minus sign will work just as well. So I can write:

$$="12/25/18"-"6/1/18"$$

and it will return a value of 207 just like writing

$$=DAYS("12/25/18","6/1/18")$$

did. I can also write =A1-A2 where A1 and A2 have my dates and it will return the same result as

$$=DAYS(A1,A2).$$

Because Excel stores dates as numbers, you can also just use those numbers in the DAYS function. So

$$=DAYS(5,3)$$

will return a value of 2.

This only works, however, if the numbers provided are in a legitimate range to be a date value, meaning that it will not work with a negative number or one outside Excel's range.

$$=DAYS(-5,3)$$

will result in a #NUM! error.

The DAYS function also works on dates stored as text. For example, if I have "December 25, 2018" in Cell A1 and "June 1, 2018" in Cell A2 and I've formatted both as text, I can still get a valid result from the formula =DAYS(A1,A2). This is because Excel will apply the function DATEVALUE to each entry first.

(As discussed a little later, the DATEVALUE function converts a text entry version of a date into its numeric value. So December 25, 2018 becomes 43459 which is the date 43,458 days after January 1, 1900.)

If you try to use the DAYS function on entries that Excel can't convert into a date, you will get a #VALUE! error. So, for example, if I misspell December in the cell that has "December 25, 2018", the formula can't convert that entry into a numeric value and therefore can't complete the calculation.

THE DAYS360 FUNCTION

Notation: DAYS360(start_date,end_date,[method])
Excel Definition: Returns the number of days between two dates based on a
360-day year (twelve 30-day months).

This next one is a more-specialized function, but it can come in handy in certain situations.

The DAYS function calculates the actual number of days between two dates, meaning that it accounts for the fact that there are 30 days in November but 31 in December and January. However, sometimes you don't want that level of precision. Sometimes uniformity is preferred.

For example, there are certain securities instruments that calculate their payouts using a 30-day month for all months of the year regardless of the actual number of days in that month. This allows interest payments to be the same each and every month.

If you find yourself in a situation like that, then what you'd need to do is calculate the number of days based on the assumption that every single month has 30 days in it. To do this you can use the DAYS360 function.

The DAYS360 function works just like the DAYS function in the sense that it takes the difference between two dates, except it assigns 30 days to every single month not the actual number of days.

Note, too, that it lists the dates in opposite order. So for DAYS360 you list the start date first and the end date second. Also, help text for the DAYS360 function has a caution that you should not use dates entered as text.

You can enter the dates into the formula directly. For example,

=DAYS360("6/1/18","7/1/18")

returns a value of 30.

So does putting 6/1/18 and 7/1/18 into Cells A1 and A2 respectively and then using

=DAYS360(A1,A2)

There is a third optional component to the DAYS360 function that allows you to specify how dates that fall on the 31st of a month are treated. The default method, which will be used if you don't specify a third variable, is what's referred to as the U.S. (NASD) method. Under this method, if the starting date is the last day of a month then it becomes equal to the 30th day of that month.

So, for February 2019, for example, if I put in February 28th and March 15th as my two dates that will return a value of 15 because it's treating February 28th as a fictional February 30th for purposes of the date calculation.

In addition, according to Excel, if the ending day is the last day of a month and the starting date is earlier than the 30th of the month, the ending date will become equal to the 1st of the next month. Otherwise the ending date becomes equal to the 30th of the month.

So

=DAYS360("5/29/19","5/31/19")

returns a value of 2, because it treats May 31st as equivalent to June 1st and then with a 30-day month that means two days between May 29th and the 1st of June.

And

=DAYS360("5/30/19","5/31/19")

returns a value of 0, because Excel treats May 31st as May 30th which means no difference between the two dates.

The other option is to use TRUE as your third variable. This will apply what's referred to as the European method of handling dates that fall on the 31st of a month. If you use this method, any dates that fall on the 31st of a month are treated as if they fall on the 30th of the month.

So

=DAYS360("5/29/19","5/31/19",TRUE)

will return a value of 1 since it treats May 31st as May 30th. And

=DAYS360("5/30/19","5/31/19",TRUE)

will return a value of 0 since, again, this method treats May 31st as May 30th.

(It's a little confusing, but if you need to know this, you'll learn it. And you'll know which method applies to your situation. I hope. My goal here is to just point it out to you so you're aware that the issue exists.)

THE EDATE FUNCTION

Notation: EDATE(start_date,months)
Excel Definition: Returns the serial number of the date that is the indicated
number of months before or after the start date.

The EDATE function takes any given date and gives the date x number of months from that date. It returns the same result as using DATE with YEAR, MONTH, DAY that we looked at above, but it's a lot easier to use.

So, for example, I could use

=DATE(YEAR(B1),MONTH(B1)+6,DAY(B1))

where the date in Cell B1 is June 15, 2018 and I'm telling it to add six to the month value. That will return a date of December 15, 2018, exactly six months past June 15, 2018.

Or I could just use

=EDATE(B1,6)

Now, one thing to keep in mind with EDATE is that it will initially return the serial number for the date, so you need to format that cell as a date or your result will be a number. 43449 in this example.

EDATE also works with negative numbers for the number of months. So =EDATE(B1,-6) will give the date six months before the date in Cell B1; in this example that's December 15, 2017.

Note that EDATE returns the exact same date of the month each time, regardless of how many days are in each of the months in between. If for some reason your date is February 29th and you move in a twelve-month increment it will return the 29th if that's available for that year or the 28th if it isn't.

Also, any month value you use that's not an integer will be truncated not rounded. (So 5.89 would be treated as 5 not 6.)

THE EOMONTH FUNCTION

Notation: EOMONTH(start_date,months)
Excel Definition: Returns the serial number of the last day of the month before or after a specified number of months.

The EOMONTH function is similar to the EDATE function except it provides the last day of the month x months from your specified date. So where EDATE would move from the 15th to the 15th, EOMONTH will move from the 15th to the end of the month, whatever that date happens to be.

Let's look at the example from above where we were working with June 15, 2018 as our start date

=EDATE(B1,6)

returned a date of December 15, 2018.

=EOMONTH(B1,6)

returns a date of December 31, 2018. So the end of that month six months in the future.

=EDATE(B1,-6)

returns a date of December 15, 2017.

=EOMONTH(B1,-6)

returns a date of December 31, 2017. So the end of the month that was six months in the past.

Just like EDATE, the initial value that EOMONTH returns is the number version of the date, so you'll need to format the cell as a date to convert it to a recognizable date format.

And any month value you use that's not an integer will be truncated not rounded. (So 5.89 would be treated as 5 not 6.)

THE NETWORKDAYS FUNCTION

Notation: NETWORKDAYS(start_date,end_date,[holidays])
Excel Definition: Returns the number of whole workdays between two dates.

The final four functions we're going to discuss are all related to one another. NETWORKDAYS has been around for a long time and allows you to calculate the number of whole workdays between two dates, something I needed in my prior career which is how I ran across it the first time.

Basically, it allows you to take a starting date and an ending date and calculate the number of whole workdays between them. But if you're dealing with holidays, too, then you need to tell Excel which days are holidays so it can treat those as non-workdays and exclude them from the count.

Let's walk through an example. (Apologies in advance to non-U.S. folks who'll think those dates look reversed.)

Today is December 21, 2018.

I want to know how many workdays there are between now and when I'm flying to Washington, DC on January 8, 2019.

Let's first just look at the calculation without holidays included:

=NETWORKDAYS("12/21/2018","1/8/2019")

The answer it gives me is 13.

If I look at my calendar I can see that it's including today, the 21st, as well as January 8th. Because there are five days in the next two weeks, that gives us ten days, as well as today, a Friday, and Monday and Tuesday of the week with the 8th in it.

Not exactly between those two dates. It's inclusive of the dates you include in your function. Good to know, right?

Let's test that on a much shorter example:

=NETWORKDAYS("1/7/2019","1/11/2019")

That looks for the number of workdays between January 7th (a Monday) and January 11th (a Friday). The result is 5. So once again, the NETWORKDAYS function calculates the number of workdays "between" two dates and includes those two dates in the calculation.

Now back to the original example:

=NETWORKDAYS("12/21/2018","1/8/2019")

I don't want to include Christmas or New Year's in that count, so I need to include a third argument that excludes them.

The easiest way to do this is to probably have a separate data table where I list all holidays and then I can just use a cell reference to reference the values in that table. In this case, I put the dates in Cells C1 and C2, which then gives me:

=NETWORKDAYS("12/21/2018","1/8/2019",C1:C2)

And the answer it comes back with is 11.

Now, if I don't want today and that last day included, because today is pretty much shot already and that last day I'm traveling and what I'm trying to figure out is how many days I have left to get this novel written, I can combine the NETWORKDAYS function with some basic math:

=NETWORKDAYS("12/21/2018","1/8/2019",C1:C2)-2

By adding a minus two to the end of the formula I take out the first and last day from the calculation. Simple as that to account for how the function works. The key is to remember that's how it works so you know if you need to make that kind of adjustment or not.

In the examples above I used a cell range for my holidays, but how do you include more than one date within the function itself? Hint: You can't just use parens like I thought.

You have to use curly brackets around your holiday date entries. Like so:

=NETWORKDAYS("12/21/2018","1/8/2019",{"12/25/2018","1/1/2019"})-2

See the { and the } around the holiday dates of 12/25/2018 and 1/1/2019? You have to use those if you're going to list more than one date for holiday within the function.

Also note that for every date I listed in the formula above that I had to put quotes around it for Excel to recognize it as a valid date.

So that's NETWORKDAYS, but it has one potentially significant limitation. And that's that it treats Saturday and Sunday as weekend days that don't get counted. Well, what do you do if you only want Saturdays excluded? Or if your weekends fall on Sundays and Mondays?

That's where NETWORKDAYS.INTL comes in. So let's talk about that one now.

THE NETWORKDAYS.INTL FUNCTION

Notation: NETWORKDAYS.INTL(start_date,end_date,[weekend],[holidays])
Excel Definition: Returns the number of whole workdays between two dates
with custom weekend parameters.

The NETWORKDAYS.INTL function is a more sophisticated version of NETWORKDAYS that was introduced with Excel 2010. So if you have an earlier version of Excel it's not available to you.

What NETWORKDAYS.INTL does is it allows you to specify what constitutes a weekend. Otherwise it works just like NETWORKDAYS.

So

=NETWORKDAYS("12/21/2018","1/8/2019")

and

=NETWORKDAYS.INTL("12/21/2018","1/8/2019")

will return the exact same result.

But note that the third value you input for NETWORKDAYS.INTL is an optional weekend variable. When you get to this point in inputting your values, you will see a dropdown menu of options you can use to specify what days Excel should consider weekends. Using numbers 11 through 17 allow a single-day weekend and numbers 1 through 7 allow two-day weekends of any consecutive two days in a week.

So let's say that I work in hospitality and that I work weekends because that's when all the customers are in town. I get off Monday and Tuesday of each week. Looking at that list of options, to set Monday-Tuesday as my weekend, I'd need to use a value of 3 for the weekend input variable. It looks like this:

=NETWORKDAYS.INTL("12/21/2018","1/8/2019",3)

Interestingly, the result is still 13, but it's using different dates to get there.

If I expand the function to include my two holidays (which both happen to fall on a Tuesday), I get this:

=NETWORKDAYS.INTL("12/21/2018","1/8/2019",3,{"12/25/2018","1/1/2019"})

and my result is *still 13*.

Remember with NETWORKDAYS it was 11 because the holidays fell on a workday, but because the holidays in this scenario fall on our "weekend" they've already been excluded from our count of workdays and don't need to be excluded again.

Let's walk through another example.

Remember how we used

=NETWORKDAYS("1/7/2019","1/11/2019")

which gave us a value of 5 for the days from Monday through Friday?

Let's write that using NETWORKDAYS.INTL and a weekend that falls on Monday/Tuesday:

=NETWORKDAYS.INTL("1/7/2019","1/11/2019",3)

Since the 7th and 8th are a Monday and Tuesday and therefore get excluded from the count of workdays, our result is 3.

So there you have it. NETWORKDAYS.INTL works just like NETWORKDAYS except it allows more flexibility in terms of determining what a weekend is. The two are not directly interchangeable because of the fact that they put the weekend variable as the third input variable for NETWORKDAYS.INTL which means the holidays are entered in a different order for the two functions. That means you need to know which one you're working with when you build your formula. And if you change from one to the other later, you need to adjust for that.

THE WORKDAY FUNCTION

Notation: WORKDAY(start_date,days,[holidays])
Excel Definition: Returns the serial number of the date before or after
a specified number of workdays.

The WORKDAY function is related to the NETWORKDAYS function. They basically solve for different parts of the same equation. So where NETWORKDAYS calculates the number of workdays between two dates, WORKDAY calculates what date it will be in x workdays.

So you have x-y=z and one function is solving for y and the others is solving for z. But be careful with that. Because they actually treat the dates differently, as you'll see in a second, so they don't actually fit together that neatly.

NETWORKDAYS includes the start date in its count, but WORKDAY does not.

Let's walk through an example.

Say we're on a project and I ask someone how long it will take for them to complete their portion of the project and they tell me ten days. It's currently December 21st. When can I expect that person to be done with their portion of the project, knowing that they are not going to work weekends or holidays?

I can use:

=WORKDAY("12/21/2018",10,{"December 25, 2018","January 1, 2019"})

So, starting today, moving ten workdays into the future, and excluding Christmas and New Year's, what day is that going to be?

According to the function, it will be January 8, 2019.

Let's see if that makes sense:

Between now and then we have December 21st, December 24th, December 26th through December 28th, December 31st, January 2nd through January 4th, and January 7th and 8th as workdays that are not holidays.

That's actually 11 days. But remember what I said before? Excel doesn't count your start date. That's unlike how NETWORKDAYS works, right?

Let's test that some more.

If we use

$$=WORKDAY("1/7/2019",5)$$

what do we get?

A date of 1/14/2019, which is the next Monday. Same issue. We end up going across six workdays.

How about

$$=WORKDAY("1/7/2019",1)$$

So just one day?

That gives us 1/8/2019, which makes it pretty clear that WORKDAY is adding that number of days onto the current date without including the current date in its count of available days.

So going back to our original example, what if it's first thing in the morning and you know that person will be working on that project today, so you want to adjust for that?

Then you'd basically have to do either:

$$=WORKDAY("12/21/2018",10,{"December 25, 2018","January 1, 2019"})-1$$

Or you'd have to use 10-1 days in your function, like so:

$$=WORKDAY("12/21/2018",9,{"December 25, 2018","January 1, 2019"})$$

Of course, there's nothing wrong with having a little wiggle room in a project timeline, so I might just leave it as is, but it's good to know that's how this function works in comparison to the NETWORKDAYS function. Because if for some reason you're using both of them on the same project and not adjusting for the difference, you may have these one-day discrepancies that can cause an unnecessary misunderstanding.

Alright. Just like NETWORKDAYS has a new and improved version that allows more flexibility, so does WORKDAY. Let's cover that one next.

THE WORKDAY.INTL FUNCTION

Notation: WORKDAY.INTL(start_date,days,[weekend],[holidays])
Excel Definition: Returns the serial number of the date before or after a specified number of workdays with custom weekend parameters.

WORKDAY.INTL works just like WORKDAY, except it allows for customized weekend parameters. So

=WORKDAY.INTL("12/21/2018",10,1,{"December 25, 2018","January 1, 2019"})

gives the same result as

=WORKDAY("12/21/2018",10,{"December 25, 2018","January 1, 2019"})

And just like with NETWORKDAYS.INTL, when you get to that third input variable you will see a list of available options for your weekend. Values of 1 through 7 let you set a two-day weekend using any two continuous days of the week. 11 through 17 let you set a single-day weekend.

You can also create a completely customized set of weekend days if you want using a binary string of numbers to represent workdays or weekend days where 1 is a non-workday and 0 is a workday and you start the string with Monday.

So in the below example I have Monday, Tuesday, Wednesday, Thursday as workdays, then an off day on Friday, then a workday on Saturday, then a non-workday on Sunday.

=WORKDAY.INTL("1/7/2019",1,"0000101")

That returns a value of January 10, 2019 because I have the Monday through Wednesday (the 7th, 8th, and 9th) designated as non-workdays.

Also, because weekend is the third variable and then holidays is the fourth for WORKDAY.INTL, you need to know if you're working with WORKDAY or WORKDAY.INTL when you build the function since holidays are in a different location in the two functions.

Finally, WORKDAY.INTL wasn't introduced until Excel 2010, so if you have an earlier version of Excel it won't be available to you. If you have a more recent version of Excel it probably makes the most sense to use WORKDAY.INTL all the time even when you don't need a customized weekend parameter. If you do that, just make sure to enter 1 as your weekend parameter to get a standard Saturday/Sunday weekend when you include holidays.

OTHER FUNCTIONS

That's it for this guide to functions. There are many, many more functions in Excel, and chances are there's at least one I didn't cover that you'll need at some point.

Hopefully, though, you now have enough understanding of Excel functions to feel comfortable with how they work and to be able to work with one that's new to you.

I also hope this has further demonstrated the potential power and breadth of Excel. Don't be afraid to explore the program and see if it has what you need, because chances are it does.

Next I'm going to talk briefly about how to combine functions within a formula as well as the various error messages and what they mean. I'll also cover what to do when your formula isn't working.

COMBINING FUNCTIONS

The functions we discussed in this guide are powerful in their own right, but where the real power of Excel can come into play is when you combine functions.

As I mentioned with INDEX and MATCH, each one seems somewhat limited by themselves, but I saw them combined to create a very powerful data table listing rank order for thirty-four different attributes for a group of individuals.

And if you look back at the examples we used in the DATE function, you can see how useful it can be to combine, in that case, four functions in one formula.

So if you find yourself using multiple columns to perform multiple steps maybe see if you can instead combine those steps into one.

The key to keep in mind when combining functions is that only the beginning of the formula requires an equals sign. After that first function or value you just list the function name followed by an opening paren when you need to use a different function within your formula.

And also, to be careful of your paren and comma placement when using multiple functions within a formula.

(And if you're doing calculations and facing a significant file size issue and are using Excel 2013 or later, you might want to explore array formulas a bit more. This is not my area of expertise, but from the little I read about them it appears they can save a lot of file space for repetitive calculations.)

WHEN THINGS GO WRONG

Chances are if you work with formulas enough that you will run into some error messages.

You might see a #DIV/0! or a #REF! or a #VALUE! or a #N/A or a #NUM! error. It happens. Sometimes you'll realize exactly what you did, but at other times it's going to be a puzzle.

So let's me see if I can help a bit.

#REF!

If you see #REF! in a cell it's probably because you just deleted a value that that cell was referencing. So if you had =A1+B1+C1+D1 in a cell (and I do have something similar to this in my budget worksheet), and then you deleted Column C that would create a #REF! error. Excel won't adjust the formula and drop the missing value, it will return this error message instead.

To see where the cell generating the error was in your formula, double-click in the cell with the #REF! message. This will show you the formula, including a #REF! where the missing cell used to be.

So you'll see something like =A1+B1+#REF!+D1 and you'll know that the cell you deleted was used as the third entry in that formula. If it's something like the example I just gave you where you just need to delete that cell reference, do so. Turn it into =A1+B1+D1. But you may also realize that your formula now needs to reference a different cell. If so, replace the #REF! with that cell reference. Hit enter when you've made your changes and you're done.

(This is also a good time for using Ctrl +Z if you thought you were deleting a blank cell and didn't realize it was being used in a formula and are okay with bringing that cell back.)

#VALUE!

According to Excel, a #VALUE! error means you typed your formula wrong or you're referencing a cell that's the wrong type of cell.

If you're using dates, see if the date is left-aligned. If it is, then chances are Excel is treating the date as a text entry not a date entry. That means subtraction won't work on it.

Same with numbers. If you use SUM and get this error on a range of numbers make sure that they're formatted as numbers and not text. (This shouldn't be a common problem, but could be if you've imported a data file from elsewhere.)

It can also mean that you have non-standard regional settings and that your minus sign is being used as a list separator (rather than the more standard, at least in the U.S., comma).

Or it can mean that you're referencing a data source that is no longer available like another workbook that was moved.

#DIV/0!

This is a common error to see if you've written a formula that requires division. If I input the formula =A1/B1 and there are no values in Cells A1 and B1, Excel will return #DIV/0!

You need a numeric value for your denominator to stop this from happening. (The numerator can be blank, but not the denominator.)

I usually use IF functions to suppress the #DIV/0! when I have a data table where values haven't been inputted yet. So I'll write something like =IF(B1>0,A1/B1,"").

Just be sure if you do that that the IF condition makes sense for your data. (In the example I just gave, any negative number would also result in a blank cell.)

#N/A

According to Excel, a #N/A error means that Excel isn't finding what it was asked to look for. In other words, there's no solution. This occurs most often with the VLOOKUP, HLOOKUP, LOOKUP, and MATCH functions. You tell it to look for a value in your table and that value isn't in your table.

This can be valuable information that perhaps points to a weakness in your data or your function. For example, it could indicate that the data in your lookup table is in a different format from the data in your analysis table. Or that there are extra spaces in the entries in one or the other table

But if you know this is going to happen and don't want to see the #N/A in your results, you can use the IFERROR function to suppress that result and replace it with a zero, a blank space, or even text. Just be careful, because IFERROR will replace all error messages and that may not be what you want.

#NUM!

According to Excel, you will see this error when there are numeric values in a formula or function that aren't valid. The example Excel gives involves using $1,000 in a formula instead of 1000, but when I just tried this to validate it Excel wouldn't even allow me to use that formula, it wanted to fix the formula for me as soon as I hit Enter. So this may be more of an issue in older versions of Excel.

Excel will also return this error message if an iterative function can't find a result or if the result that would be returned by the formula is too large or too small. (If you're running into this error for those reasons chances are you're doing some pretty advanced things, so we're not going to worry about that here.)

Circular References

Excel will also flag for you any time that you write a formula that references itself. (I do this on occasion without meaning to.) For example, if in Cell A5 you type =SUM(A1:A5), when you hit

Enter Excel will display a dialogue box that says "Careful, we found one or more circular references in your workbook that might cause your formulas to calculate incorrectly."

Say OK and then go back to the cell with the formula and fix the issue.

Keep in mind that sometimes a circular reference error can be generated by an indirect circular reference, so you're referencing a cell that's referencing another cell and it's that other cell that's the issue.

If you can't figure out the cause and Excel doesn't "helpfully" start drawing connections on your worksheet to show it to you, in newer versions of Excel you can go to the Formulas tab and under Formula Auditing click on Trace Precedents to see what values are feeding that cell.

(Usually when this happens I know exactly what I did and it's just a matter of getting Excel to stop trying to fix it for me so I can make the correction myself. YMMV.)

Too Few Arguments

I also on occasion will try to use a function and get a warning message that I've used too few arguments for the function. When that happens check that you've included enough inputs for the function to work. Anything listed that isn't in brackets is required. So =RANDBETWEEN(bottom, top) requires that you enter values for both bottom and top but =CONCATENATE(text1, [text2],…) only requires one input.

If that's not the issue make sure that you have each of the inputs separated by commas and that your quotation marks, if there are any, are in the right places.

General Wonkiness

Sometimes everything seems fine but the formula just doesn't seem to be giving the right answer. If it's a complex formula, break it down into its components and make sure that each component works on a standalone basis.

You can also double-click on the cell for a formula and Excel will color code each of the separate components that are feeding the formula and also highlight those cells in your worksheet. Confirm that the highlighted cells are the ones you want.

For formulas you copied, verify that none of your cell ranges or cell references needed to be locked down but weren't. (I do this one often.) If you don't use $ to lock your cell references, they will adjust according to where you copied that formula. If that's what you wanted, great. If it isn't, fix it by going back to the first cell and using the $ signs to lock the cell references or by changing the cell references in the location you copied the formula to so that it works.

And, as we've seen here, sometimes there are choices you can make with a function that impact the outcome. So the value RANK will return depends on whether you tell Excel to look at your data in ascending or descending order. If you're working with a function you're not familiar with, open the Excel Help for the function and read through it. If that doesn't help, go to the website. If that doesn't help, do an Internet search to see if someone else has had the same issue.

CONCLUSION

So that's it for this guide. There are many more functions that I did not cover here. Excel is incredibly broad in what it can do, but also incredibly specialized at times.

If you can think of it, chances are there's a way to do it in Excel. So don't be afraid to go to Insert Function and poke around to see what's possible.

(And if there isn't a function for what you want, you can always learn how to write your own macros in Excel. Although be careful with those. And don't look to me for that one.)

There are some more advanced aspects to working with formulas and functions in Excel that I didn't cover here or brushed past. Things like named ranges and array formulas. If you want to learn about those, start with the Excel Help function and go from there.

I find that I take things past the basic level when I need to do something specific, so I go looking for that solution that I need. If you want to be more systematic about it, there are definitely exhaustive guides out there that will cover everything for you.

And if you have a specific issue or question, feel free to reach out to me. mlhumphreywriter@gmail.com. I'm happy to help. I don't check that daily, but I do check it often and will reply.

I hope this was helpful for you. Good luck with it! Remember, save your raw data in one place, work on it in another, take your time, check the individual components of complex formulas, check your threshold cases, and Ctrl + Z (Undo) is your friend.

APPENDIX A: CELL NOTATION

If you're going to work with functions in Excel, then you need to understand how Excel references cells.

Cells are referenced based upon their column and their row. So Cell A1 is the cell in Column A and Row 1. Cell B10 is the cell in Column B and Row 10. Cell BC25232 is the cell in Column BC and in Row 25232.

If you want to reference more than one cell or cell range in a function then you can do so in a couple of ways. To reference separate and discrete cells, you list each one and you separate them with a comma. So (A1, A2, A3) refers to Cells A1, A2, and A3.

When cells are touching you can instead reference them as a single range using the colon. So (A1:A3) also refers to Cells A1, A2, and A3. Think of the colon as a "through".

You don't have to limit this to a single row or column either. You can reference A1:B25. That refers to all of the cells between Cell A1 and Cell B25. That would be all cells in Column A from Cell A1 through Cell A25 as well as all cells in Column B from Cell B1 through Cell B25.

When you note a range the left-hand cell that you list (A1) is the top left-most cell of the range and the right-hand cell you list (B25) is the bottom right-most cell of the range.

You can also reference an entire column by just using the letter and leaving off any numbers. So C:C refers to all cells in Column C.

And you can do the same for a row by leaving off the letter. So 10:10 refers to all the cells in Row 10.

If you ever reference a cell in another worksheet or another workbook, this also needs to be addressed through cell notation.

For a cell in another worksheet, you put the sheet name as it appears on the worksheet tab followed by an exclamation point before the cell reference. So Sheet1!B1 is Cell B1 in the worksheet labeled Sheet 1.

For another workbook you put the name of the workbook in brackets before the worksheet name. So [Book1]Sheet2!$D$2 refers to Cell D2 in the worksheet labeled Sheet 2 in the workbook titled Book 1.

(I should note here that I think it's a bad idea to reference data in another workbook due to the odds that the formula/function will break as soon as that other workbook is renamed or moved to a new location and that I generally don't think it's worth doing.)

Now, before you start to panic and think you need to remember all of this and that you never will, take a deep breath. Because when you're writing a formula you can simply click on the cells you need when you need them and Excel will write the cell notation for you.

It's just useful to know how this works in case something doesn't work right. (And even then you can still use Excel to show you what each cell reference is referring to. Just double-click on the formula and Excel will color code the cell references in the formula and put a matching colored border around the cells in your worksheet.)

ALPHABETICAL LISTING OF FUNCTIONS

INDEX

CONTROL SHORTCUTS

For each of the control shortcuts, hold down Ctrl and the key listed to perform the command.

Command	Ctrl +
Select All	A
Bold	B
Copy	C
Find	F
Replace	H
Italicize	I
New Workbook	N
Print	P
Next Worksheet	Page Down
Prior Worksheet	Page Up
Save	S
Underline	U
Paste	V
Cut	X
Redo	Y
Undo	Z

ABOUT THE AUTHOR

M.L. Humphrey is a former stockbroker with a degree in Economics from Stanford and an MBA from Wharton who has spent close to twenty years as a regulator and consultant in the financial services industry.

You can reach M.L. at mlhumphreywriter@gmail.com or at mlhumphrey.com.

CPSIA information can be obtained
at www.ICGtesting.com
Printed in the USA
BVHW010214090522
636515BV00010B/185

9 781950 902040